Grief and Growth

R. Scott Sullender

Grief and Growth

Pastoral Resources for Emotional and Spiritual Growth

paulist press *new york/mahwah*

Library of Congress
Catalog Card Number: 84-61024

ISBN: 0-8091-2652-4

Published by Paulist Press
997 Macarthur Boulevard
Mahwah, New Jersey 07430

Printed and bound in the
United States of America

Contents

Acknowledgements

A book like this is the result of many people and many experiences other than just the author's. In this I appreciate the men and women of To Live Again, West Chester, Pennsylvania, and the hundreds of people before and since then, who have shared with me their sorrow. We have grieved together, grown together and learned together. I hope that this book embodies some of those learnings.

In addition my special thanks goes to Randy Riggs, who kept telling me, "You should write"; to Howard Clinebell, who inspired me to write; to Mary Kennedy, who kept typing even when I wasn't writing; and to my family, who relinquished some of our precious time together to allow me to write.

Preface

During my early years in the professional ministry, I was enrolled in a clinical pastoral education program as an intern chaplain in a large metropolitan hospital. I will never forget a woman, whom I will call Betty, who was dying of cancer. It was a privilege to come to know her during the last few weeks of her life. She and her husband had been married thirty-seven years and had raised three children. They had been high school sweethearts and never seemed to have lost that sparkle of romance. Even though John expected her eventual death, when it finally came, he went into an acute grief reaction. We were able to be together during those initial moments, sharing our common pain and our common tears. It was an agonizing wrenching experience, both for him, the grieving widower, and for me, the young chaplain who sought so hard to be of comfort in his time of need.

Some months later, I was surprised to find his name on the hospital rolls. He had been admitted to the hospital with a severe heart attack. I went to him, but he was very difficult to communicate with for both physical and emotional reasons. He seemed very depressed and withdrawn. He died five days later. One of the nurses commented, ''It was as if he had lost his will to live.'' My guess is that he literally died of ''a broken heart.'' I remember then being impressed with the potential **danger of grief**.

In recent years as a pastoral counselor, I have worked with many adolescents with various delinquent problems. In particular, I remember one young man, whom I will call Kevin, with a history of violent outbursts alternated by periods of withdrawn isolation. He had a pattern of drug abuse as well. Some years earlier, his father had ''walked out'' on the family, a move that caught Kevin by complete surprise. He rarely saw his father after that. My therapy with Kevin never got anywhere until I began to see his anger as a component of a prolonged grief reaction. He had idealized his father prior to his departure, and he was ''mad as hell''—at himself, at his father, and at life. In short, Kevin

1

was still grieving the loss of his father and their special relationship. I remember at that time being impressed with the **complexity of grief**. One significant loss is like a single pebble thrown into a pond. It sends out ripples and waves in all directions, down through the years following and spread out into the lives of others as well.

The church where my family currently attends is in a highly mobile community in southern California. Regularly, a good percentage of the membership moves out of the area, and, conversely, new families are constantly moving into the area. I recall talking with a young woman, whom I will call Janice, after worship one morning. She had recently moved here from the midwest. Janice sought me out a few days later complaining of mild depression, apathy and listlessness. As we explored her feelings, the themes of loss and grief kept surfacing. In the move to the west coast, she had lost a home, her friends, her favorite activities and routines. Furthermore, she no longer had her sisters and parents to regularly talk with. She had been robbed of her usual support system. Her husband, who now commuted thirty miles to Los Angeles, was increasingly less available. It was as if she had lost him too. Without a second car, her suburban home became like a prison. She was angry, depressed and lonely, but most of all grieving—grieving these compounded and interrelated losses. I remember at that time being impressed with the **subtleties of grief**. What would appear to some to be "an advancement," a promotion, something to be happy about, was in fact a cruel joke to her. Every life-change, no matter how seemingly positive, carries such elements of loss.

During my years in parish ministry, I had the opportunity to work with a group of widowed people who called their organization "T.L.A." (To Live Again). I remember one young woman from that organization whose husband was killed in an automobile accident, leaving her alone with two young children. After an initial brief period of shock, she emotionally threw herself into survival concerns. She took control of her life—learning to drive, getting a job, meeting the demands of parenthood. She seemed to be functioning well. Yet on the first anniversary of her husband's death, while worshiping in the same church where her husband's funeral was conducted, she emotionally collapsed. She began crying, weeping uncontrollably, to the point where she had to leave. This uncontrollable crying actually went on for several days. It was as if her grief had been delayed one full year, buried beneath the weight of her responsibilities. She never had time to grieve—at least not until now. On this occasion I remember being impressed with the tremendous **power of grief**. Her grief did not go away, as many of us had thought. Grief cannot be dismissed. Her grief demanded to be dealt with, and, sure enough, eventually she did deal with it, however late. Grief is indeed an emotion to be reckoned with one way or another.

This assortment of grief-related experiences from my personal life illustrate the stunning variety and power of the emotion we call grief. Grief is indeed a powerful emotion, a complex one, a subtle one and even a dangerous one. Even more importantly, however, it is also a universal and all-pervasive emotion—an emotion that many people, therefore, fail to recognize in themselves or in others. In one form or another, grief is almost universally and constantly present in us.

In the last two decades, there has been a new interest and appreciation of grief. This concern for grief grows out of the larger interest in death and dying issues. As a result of these trends, counselors and therapists are now more keenly aware of the importance of "grief work," researchers are exploring the many varieties and intensities of grief, struggling to formulate a concise definition of this once neglected emotion, and on the popular book shelves one can find many first-hand accounts of grief experiences that offer inspirational help and advice. Furthermore, today there are many more self-help groups, springing up across the nation, designed to assist the bereaved and divorced in adjusting to their loss.

Pastors and other health professionals who work with the bereaved are particularly interested in the interrelationship of grief and growth. There are some people for whom severe loss or separation events are "in the long run" growth-producing experiences. While never wishing for such experiences, such people can cite ways in which they have grown emotionally, spiritually, vocationally and interpersonally as a result of their loss. In contrast, there are other people who seemingly never recover from severe losses, but cling to the past with varying degrees of bitterness or nostalgia. Their grief remains unresolved or unfinished, sometimes with various "pathological" or abnormal expressions. They are indeed "stuck" in the past and usually need professional assistance to get their grief process moving again.

What are the factors that influence the difference between grief being a growing experience and being a crippling experience? Why are some individuals able to grieve fully and freely, while others seem unable to do so? Is there a normative style of grieving? What variables or situations block or facilitate a person's grief-growth process? In particular, does religion help people recover from their loss any easier or quicker than those without faith? These are some of the questions that researchers, counselors and authors like myself seek to address.

The purpose of this book is to review the modern understanding of grief and to assist pastors and other health professionals in their work with bereaved people.

In particular, this book will explore the role of four factors in contributing to a person's ability to fully grieve and grow. Those variables are: (1) community, (2) rituals, (3) beliefs and (4) faith. These four factors have been selected because they represent four of the traditional religious resources for dealing with grief. Today they still are four of the resources that pastors have most readily available. They are also four factors that have not been fully studied by modern psychological research into grief. We are interested in holding up these traditional pastoral approaches to grief in the light of modern psychology to determine if and how they are helpful in the healing of grief.

The clergy and religious institutions have always been involved with the bereaved. Along with funeral directors, the clergy are the other major profession that deals with the bereaved most often and most immediately upon the death of a loved one. This has been true historically and is still true today (although to a lesser extent in Western culture). Religious institutions and the clergy are also in the forefront of dealings with people bereaved due to non-death types of losses, like divorce, retirement, loss of possessions and developmental losses. Clergy deal with many more types of grief and many more occasions of grief than perhaps even they realize. This work is therefore aimed at the clergy. They are my primary audience, but I hope that anyone who is involved in a ministry with the bereaved will find this material useful.

For purposes of simplicity, I will use the general title "pastor" to cover all religious professionals, including ministers, priests and rabbis. Where the word church is used, please also read synagogue and/or temple. I write out of a Protestant Christian tradition, but it is my hope that pastors and professionals from other traditions might find these insights relevant. It has been my experience that the really crucial battles in today's world are not between us but between people of faith and the growing tide of secularism.

In this book I have also endeavored to eliminate sexist language forms as much as possible. The only exceptions are direct quotations, which were left intact.

I believe that this kind of study, as modest as it is, is important for several reasons. In recent decades, religion and its influence has been on the decline in Western culture. The triple impact of urbanization, secularization and value pluralism has eroded much of the traditional small town culture in which Christianity was rooted. Ritual and beliefs, for example, do not carry the same power that they once did in people's lives. Thus, in times of bereavement, these resources are less available, less meaningful and less helpful in comforting the bereaved. In addition, we see less death and grief today than older generations did. We are, therefore, less prepared for it, less comfortable in its presence and less knowledgeable of its dynamics. Yet, death and loss occur just as frequently as they ever did in human experience. The result of these twin factors is that there is a virtual epidemic of unresolved grief in our society. At any one time, there must be sixty to eighty percent of the population that is walking around carrying the pain of unhealed sorrow.

In these times, pastors face a difficult challenge. They are still the ones who are largely called upon to minister to the bereaved. The need is as critical as it has ever been. Yet, many of the traditional pastoral tools, such as ritual and beliefs, are no longer are helpful as they used to be. The changing culture has emptied the minister's black bag. The growth of psychology and counseling, of course, has partially filled this vacuum. Yet, the challenge to the church is still there: how to minister to grieving people in an age when traditional resources, structures and methods are changing. Therefore, this book is important because it attempts to look at traditional pastoral resources and to understand how and why they did work and how they might be strengthened, altered and enriched to become more effective. In short, my aim is to retool today's pastor.

I invite you to read this book, discuss it, digest it, and even argue over it. It is hoped that it will stimulate your imagination, your growth and your creativity. It seeks not to be the definitive word on this topic, but an important catalyst for your continuing learning. Most of all, my hope is that it will enrich and strengthen your pastoral care of the bereaved. May God bless your ministry.

1. The Variety and Universality of Loss

"Loss is an integral part of human existence, a fact which has profound consequences from birth to death."[1]
David Peretz

Grief is a universal emotion. It appears in the human psyche in countless hundreds of varieties and intensities. Its forms and expressions are as different as each individual on the face of the earth. Yet, grief is essentially the same in every person. As each of us loves, so each of us grieves. It seems to be inevitable—a basic part of our humanity.

Grief is much more frequent in human experience than most of us recognize. When we think of grief or mourning, we immediately think of death. This is the most obvious and, for most people, the most painful kind of bereavement. Yet, every loss, no matter how small or seemingly unimportant, involves grief. These seemingly "small" or less dramatic kinds of losses may be in fact more difficult for some people to adjust to—precisely because their grief is less noticed, less socially accepted and less ministered to by others. It is also true that how people resolve these "small" losses sets the pattern for how they will cope with the "large" losses. In this first chapter we want to review the wide variety of losses in life.

Loss of a Person

By Death

The loss of a loved one in death is undoubtedly the most profound and potentially severe type of loss possible. Consequently, the grief reaction is also potentially the most intense and painful reaction possible. The tragic and untimely death of one's spouse can disrupt one's whole life and thrust our emotions into the canyons of despair and anguish. The loss is devastating, complex and compounding. The grief is acute, immobilizing and long-lasting. It is one of life's most devastating crises—one that at least half of us will face. Yet, we are all so ill prepared.

The research of Holmes and Rahe has repeatedly demonstrated that our physical health is related to the degree of psychological stress and adjustment that we are currently experiencing.[2] This relationship is markedly true of conjugal bereavement. There are higher rates of death, suicide, office visits to physicians and use of psychological and clergy services for the bereaved during the first year of conjugal bereavement.[3] In the grief reaction to the sudden death of a spouse, we potentially see grief in its most dramatic and dangerous form.

We can also lose other very significant people through death. The loss of a child, for example, while not as common in the twentieth century Western nations as it was in antiquity, can nevertheless be what Geoffrey Gorer calls "the most distressing and long-lasting of all griefs." Perhaps the death of a child is experienced with greater repulsion and tragedy precisely because it is so uncommon in our times. There is something repulsive and "against the natural order of things" about the untimely death of a child. We say, "She died in the fullness of life," or "He was cut down with his whole life before him." The death of one's parents, while painful and at times tragic, is a more predictable life-cycle event. But the death of a child is horrifying, tragic and repulsive to the human spirit.

Grief reactions over the death of a loved one often begin long before the actual death. In cases where the deceased suffers many months or even years with a terminal illness, grief takes on an anticipatory character and often starts at the time of diagnosis. That terrifying word "cancer" can plunge many a family into an intense grief response. One of the first to systematically examine anticipatory grief in the dying patient was Dr. Elisabeth Kübler-Ross.[4] She identified five stages that marked the emotional journey of the terminally ill person. The fifth stage was labeled "preparatory grief." She characterized it as a type of depression. She considered such preparatory depression to be a necessary element "that the terminally ill patient has to undergo in order to prepare himself for final separation from this world."[5] What Kübler-

Ross also noted was that the patient's family went through a similar, parallel, grieving process. Grief can begin and sometimes even finishes long before the loved one is dead.

By Divorce

The permanent loss of "a significant other" may not be by death alone. Divorce is rapidly becoming one of the most frequent types of major loss. The statistics are staggering. By latest standards, anywhere from one-third to one-half of all marriages will end in divorce. There are over 300,000 divorces annually in the United States. Given that each divorce involves two parents and on an average two children, that adds up to 1,200,000 people who directly experience this form of loss annually! That is a lot of people dealing with a lot of losses!

Divorcing people can experience intense forms of grief. Marriage and divorce counselors have noted that the process of "psychological" divorce is not unlike the grief of a widowed spouse. "Divorce is indeed a death," writes Mel Krantzler in his popular book *Creative Divorce*,

> a death of a relationship; and just as the death of someone close to us brings on a period of mourning during which we come to terms with our loss, so too marital break-up is followed by a similar period of mourning.[6]

Many of the same elements, such as anger, guilt, depression, and loneliness, that are expressed in the widowed spouse are often present in the divorced spouse as well. Like the widowed spouse, the divorced spouse's mourning also involves several major life changes and secondary losses. Divorce may bring with it the loss of a home, the loss of an ideal, the loss/change of one's job, the loss of financial status, the loss/change of one's routine and the loss of friends. Besides these "griefs," the divorced person also must adjust simultaneously to the new demands, responsibilities, routines and problems of the single life. There is often too little time to grieve.

The loss of a spouse through divorce is different from the loss of a spouse through death in several ways. In general, divorce is a much more ambiguous event. For some people, divorce is unwelcomed, shocking and clearly a cause for grief. For others, who have fought bitterly with their spouse for years, and perhaps made considerable efforts to repair the relationship without success, the feelings are ambivalent.

They feel everything from relief, to anger, to guilt, to fear and, of course, to grief. My experience in working with divorced people has convinced me that even among those who wanted the divorce the most, there are still inevitable feelings of loss. No matter how much they say that they now hate each other, there usually have been some good occasions, some happy moments, some productive years, and some positive aspects to the marriage that can be cause for regret and sorrow. If nothing else, those married years are years spent, even years wasted, never to be relived again.

Another difference between the loss of a spouse through death and through divorce is that divorce always involves some element, however small, of personal choice and responsibility. The death of another is usually not chosen, but in divorce each partner has some element of responsibility for the dissolution. The issue of responsibility is a difficult and complex one. Many divorcing mates have great difficulty sorting out each spouse's relative responsibility for what happened. Others have great difficulty accepting the concept of a "no-fault divorce," wherein neither side is exclusively at fault. The responsibility issue impinges on the question of loss and grief. Generally, the more personal choice that one feels for the dissolution, the less one feels that that dissolution is a loss.

Another difference between the two types of losses is that, unlike death, divorce has no rituals or prescribed customs for its grief. There is no rite of passage that can help facilitate the passage of people from a marital state to a single status. Some clergy have advocated the development of such a ritual. In many circles, divorce still carries connotations of moral or personal failure. For others, it is an embarrassment, a sin or a tragedy. Society is still not entirely comfortable with divorce, and so no universal divorcing ritual has emerged. Without such a ritual, there is no easy way to communicate and to facilitate the changes in social role and status. Friends and relatives of the divorcing couple will continue to find social relationships with the two individuals awkward at best.

Another difference between divorce and death is that divorce is often not as final a loss as is death. When one's spouse dies, he or she is gone, completely—forever. The relationship is over—quickly, suddenly and totally. In contrast, for many divorcing spouses, it seems as though divorce never ends. Divorce can be a long, drawn-out legal and social process. In addition, divorced couples usually must continue to relate to each other as parents of their common children. I have heard many a divorced wife say, "I thought I got rid of him when the divorce was final. But now, my God, he's still around, interfering and disturbing our lives." Sometimes in divorce, the marital relationship does not so much die as it changes form.

It is important to note here that grief is not just a response to a lost love relationship. Relationships characterized by intense bitterness and anger can require as much grief work to successfully disengage from as the idealized love relationship. I have listened to many a bitter divorcee angrily trying to persuade me, "I could care less about that bum. He doesn't affect me anymore. I'm over him!" Such a person is not "over it" until both the anger *and* the sorrow have been dealt with fully. Grief, as will be discussed later, is a function of *attachment*, not love. Strong love and strong anger are both forms of attachment. Only the opposite—a relationship characterized by detachment or indifference—would exhibit the lowest amounts of grief upon dissolution.

Other Separations

Those of us who minister to adolescents have no doubt sat with a young girl (or boy), at one time or another, who is "crying her eyes out" because her boyfriend just dumped her for another. It is easy for us adults to discount such relationships as just "crushes" or only "puppy love." Often these relationships can be very intense, compounded by strong sexual needs and self-esteem issues. If so, "breaking up" can be an emotionally painful and socially awkward experience. After being "jilted" or "left for another," the abandoned partner can experience sorrow, loneliness, anger, weeping—many of the elements of grief. Here, the grief feelings are mixed up with feelings of rejection. One wonders whether such teenagers are crying for the lost love, or crying for themselves. In any case, this is a fairly common and frequent type of loss.

Pastors and parishes also can go through a grieving process upon the dissolution of a pastoral relationship. When a long-time trusted pastor leaves a parish, the whole congregation can experience feelings of grief, anger and rejection. One of the more common defense mechanisms against the pain of grief is the idealization of what is lost. We can see this phenomenon in congregations when a beloved pastor leaves for a new assignment. We pity the poor replacement cleric whose sermons are never as good as those of the fellow who left, and who receives in answer to all of his suggestions, "Reverend McThomas didn't do it that way." This kind of idealization needs to be understood as a symptom of a grief process, and church judicatories must find ways to help congregations grieve.

In recent years, I have had reason to do much more traveling than I might wish. I have relieved the boredom of waiting in airports by engaging in the wonderful pastime of "people watching." I've become quite a keen observer of humankind. Through this pastime, I have become convinced that one can learn a great deal about grief in airports. At every departing gate one can find embracing couples, crying children, and weeping parents. The pain of separation, however brief, is the pain of grief. Every goodbye, however temporary, is a prelude to the final goodbye. We fight off that pain with "promises to write," gestures of affection, gift exchanges, taking pictures "to remember her by" and so on. Yet all of these assorted rituals only point to the reality of the loss and the inevitability of grief feelings.

In the popular movie "E.T." a deep, empathetic bond is formed between Elliot and this creature from beyond. What one felt, the other felt. What one thought, the other thought. The bond was so complete that it almost caused Elliot's death, as E.T.'s vitality failed at one point in the plot. The moving conclusion of the film features E.T. saying goodbye to his beloved friend before departing in his returned spaceship. They embrace. They cry. They realize that they must part. Of the limited vocabulary that E.T. learned while on earth, one word alone captured the occasion: "Ouch"—so simple, so true and so deeply human. Parting hurts. Every separation from a loved one, however brief, is a "little death," an occasion for grief and a moment of pain. Ouch!

Loss of Some Aspect of Self

"Self" is defined as an overall sense of identity or self-image. We all tend to define ourselves by those ideas, roles, things and relationships to which we are emotionally attached. In a sense then all losses involve a loss of some aspect of the self. Yet, in this category, I want to focus in particular on those non-physical losses, such as the loss of status, an opportunity, an anticipated outcome or an ideal. These losses can be very powerful and subtle. They are normally given very little attention in the literature on bereavement. When we talk about the loss of an ideal, one's pride or status, the issue of perception becomes all-important. One's perception in part determines when and if something is a loss. "Loss is simultaneously a real event," David Peretz writes, "and a perception by which the individual endows the event with personal or symbolic meaning."[7] The same event may occur to two individuals, but it may only be a loss to one of them. How a person perceives an event determines whether or not it is experienced as a loss and correspondingly whether or not that person grieves.

An interesting kind of grief in this category is that grief expressed at the loss of a contest or an election. We are accustomed to seeing displays of grief involving weeping, anger or despair among people who have just lost a significant election or contest. Politicians cry before the cameras on election night. An athlete "hangs his head in sorrow" when defeated. What have such people lost in these situations? There is a loss of pride, a loss of an anticipated outcome, a loss of self-worth— all aspects of self. These losses are interesting because they are almost entirely anticipated losses rather than actual losses. These people never really possessed what they lost. Obviously, anticipation can be powerful enough to rival any actual loss.

Another common example of an anticipated loss of this kind occurs when a pregnant woman has a miscarriage. Many women (and men) can identify feelings of grief over the loss of their anticipated baby. Perhaps they had tried to have a child for many years. Perhaps, too, they had begun to fantasize what he or she would look like. Perhaps too, they had begun to redecorate that spare room into a nursery. Then suddenly—a miscarriage! They grieve. They grieve the child that might have been. The baby was not born yet, except in the hearts, hopes and dreams of the parents. Already the bonding between parents and child had started. Thus, feelings of loss and grief are felt.

The loss of an idea is a curious and powerful type of grief. When President Kennedy was shot in November of 1963, the entire country entered into a collective mourning process.[8] Jackie's grief was our grief. John-John's goodbye was our goodbye. We all felt the tragedy of a young visionary president being cut down in the prime of his life and career. More than that, we felt the loss of an ideal perhaps best described in the term "Camelot." John Kennedy was this nation's Camelot. He symbolized our collective confidence that we could do anything—even reach the moon—if we had vision, unity and a will to do it. In the years following Kennedy's death, the country was plunged into a period of social upheaval, unrest and conflict. This nation lost more than one man or even one president when Kennedy was killed; we lost a dream, an ideal and an identity of ourselves. We can all identify with King Arthur at the end of the movie, "Camelot." With his once noble knights now preparing for battle and with his idealistic Round Table shattered by the twin axes of jealousy and adultery, in the midst of the early dawn mist, he musically counsels a young boy:

> Don't let it be forgot
> that once there was a spot
> for one brief shining moment
> that was known as Camelot.[9]

The loss of a body part or a bodily function is increasingly frequent with the advent of modern surgical techniques. This type of loss is also a loss of self. Currently there are over 35,000 limb amputations annually in the United States, and the incidence of mastectomies and hysterectomies has risen in recent years with the rise of cancer. Dr. Bernard Schoenberg, a physician and thanatologist, argues that all bodily losses involve changes to the patient's body image. This body image has an integrity and intactness that when broken by surgery leads to emotional confusion and self-disfusion. He writes:

> Even in well adjusted persons . . . the almost universal reaction to such loss is that of grief, accompanied by depression and anxiety. On occasion, such emotions may be expressed only through somatic equivalents, but they are nevertheless invariably present in some form.[10]

Other kinds of bodily losses, such as the loss of a breast or uterus, involve even more complex changes in a woman's sense of identity, sexuality, worth, and relationships to her family. Schoenberg continues:

> The emotional impact of a mastectomy . . . has a significance to a woman that transcends functional or cosmetic factors, since a breast, like the uterus, is far more likely to symbolize a woman's

identity (femininity). Her reaction to losing a breast will therefore depend to a great extent on her feminine identity, which in turn is determined by her previous relationships with parents, other family members, and more currently her relationship with her husband.[11]

The loss of a body limb thrusts the patient into a grief process which parallels, on an emotional level, the same healing process in which the body is engaged.

Employment changes are so frequent in this mobile society that we seldom think about them as involving loss and grief. Yet, the loss or change of job inevitably involves a change in status, identity and self-worth. Such changes might result from a loss of employment, the loss of status in one's employment, or the loss of prestige or role definition in one's employment. Even if one is moving to a better job, the leaving of the old position is not without its element of grief. We must say "goodbye" to colleagues, friends, and the familiar environment. The grief feelings are ritualized with "an office party" or a "little going-away gift." In our culture, employment is a major source of our feelings of self-worth and identity. We define ourselves by what we do. We answer, "I'm a plumber" or "I'm a doctor." Consequently, then, employment-related changes involve feelings of identity confusion and shifts in our self-worth. These feelings mix thoroughly with the normal grief reactions, making for a complex set of emotions.

What I hope is becoming obvious is that many significant losses inevitably involve some change in self-definition. These "losses of self" may be more powerful and more difficult to deal with then the more obvious, external losses. Loss then is a function of the meaning that we assign to it—a very simple and yet profound observation.

Loss of External Objects

The loss of external objects can be losses of such things as money, pets, special mementos, home or even homeland. This latter type has been portrayed dramatically in such films as "The Sound of Music" and "Gone with the Wind." The amazing popularity of these movies is due in part to the fine expression that they give to our deep feelings of nostalgia and grief. In a country made up of emigrants, most of us can identify deep feelings of attachment and loss for the "Mother Country.'' The loss of one's homeland, even if by choice, is a complex phenomenon that also involves the loss of roots, identity, support and familiarity. Emigrants to this country know the anguish of this kind of loss, and the paradoxical emotional urges of "hanging on" to the old and "fitting in" to the new.[12]

The loss of one's home can also be by disaster, by changing homes or by leaving home. "Home" often involves more than just a building. It also includes one's family, security, childhood, familiarity, etc. Each summer when the children go off to camp there is often a very common form of this type of grief, termed "homesickness." A more powerful form of "homesickness" that too many of us underrate occurs when a family moves. Every year 40,000,000 Americans pull up roots and stake out on new ground. We are not nomadic by nature, but move we must in a mobile society. Alvin Toffler, in his book *Future Shock*, has called these frequent travelers "the mournful movers."[13] He suggested that increased mobility brings with it more occasions for grief and less of a commitment to place. Every move involves not just the loss of a home, but the loss of friends, schools, one's neighborhood, one's church. One can also lose the familiar—knowing where things are, the security of having established doctors, dentists, ministers and a needed support system. Repetitive and frequent relocations breeds rootlessness, apathy, and a lack of involvement with local issues, concerns and people.

Marc Fried has studied the emotional-social factors among people in Boston who were forcibly displaced from their homes by urban redevelopment. He writes:

> But for the majority it seems quite precise to speak of their reactions as expressions of *grief*. These are manifest in the feelings of painful loss, the continued longing, the general depressive tone, frequent symptoms of psychological or social or somatic distress, the active work required in adapting to the altered situation, the sense of helplessness, the occasional expressions of both direct and displaced anger, and tendencies to idealize the lost place.[14]

He speculates that the power of human grief over a lost place is related to the human need for spatial identity or "territory," which is, in turn, one component of a person's psycho-social identity.

I believe that moving is a much more complex and powerful type of loss than most people recognize. Moving is particularly difficult for children from ages five to fifteen. I am convinced that children need much longer to adjust than most parents realize. Many so-called behavior problems in children are really disguised forms of grief.

One of my friends and colleagues suffered an unusual and grievous loss when he and his family were moving across country. They had everything they owned in a U-Haul truck, except for a few items in the family car tailing behind. One night, while sleeping in a motel somewhere in the great midwest, the truck was stolen. They awoke the next morning to find it gone—completely gone, vanished! Everything they owned was gone. Later, the police located the truck—empty, of course. Everything that they had accumulated over years—the favorite easy chair, the family mementos, the children's toys, all of their clothes (other than the suitcase in the car), the family records—were all lost. At the moment of loss, they were involved already in a loss experience. A few days earlier they had said good-bye to their family home, friends, colleagues and jobs. Now their grief was compounded and intensified by the loss of all of their material possessions. Particularly painful to them was the loss of the family picture albums. "It seems cruel," they noted. "What would burglars do with such albums? They'd probably just throw them somewhere in a ditch." Suddenly their family history had vanished. "We lost more than the material things," they went on. "It was a loss of identity, history and our roots as a family."

My friend's experience, while unusual in the way it happened, is similar to that kind of loss associated with natural disasters. Natural disasters, such as fires, earthquakes, floods, etc., can be just as total in their scope. Often these disasters involve the loss of friends and family members as well as the wholesale loss of material possessions. This kind of grief, therefore, can be totally engulfing and all-consuming. Further, such losses often strike without warning—suddenly in the night. J.S. Tyhurst has studied the individual emotional reactions to various kinds of disasters.[15] He has isolated a three-stage process: impact, recoil and post-traumatic. He has labeled as "disaster syndrome" the elements of this process: guilt, recurring fears of catastrophic experience, emotional withdrawal, psychosomatic illness. The disaster syndrome is an example of a type of grief reaction, compounded by the unusual comprehensiveness and suddenness of the loss.

Developmental Losses

We humans are continuously changing on many different levels throughout our life cycle. We are continuously changing intellectually, physically, socially (role, status), spiritually and psychologically. Usually these changes are subtle and predictable. Occasionally, they are sudden and tragic. Only at certain transition points are we aware of how we have changed and the issues involved therein. With every developmental transition, a person loses the life-stage just completed, but gains access to the next emerging phase. With every transition or passage there is both loss and gain. Therefore, every transition involves a mixture of feelings—grief for that which is lost and anxiety for that which is gained. Developmental changes by their nature involve some degree of loss and, therefore to that extent, a degree of grief.

Loss in Second Half of Life

With advancing age in the second half of life, a person inevitably encounters losses that are probably quantitatively and qualitatively greater than any that he or she has previously experienced. For example, there is the increased frequency of the death of friends, colleagues, relatives, parents, and one's spouse. There is also the loss of one's job or career and with it the loss of status, money and independence. As one's body and health deteriorates, there are the losses of bodily functions, like eyesight, hearing, mobility, and to some extent sexuality. With retirement or the death of one's spouse, an individual frequently must give up his or her "home" and move (voluntarily or involuntarily) into a "home for the aged." The loss of one's home often includes the loss of a home town, some cherished possessions, a familiar routine, and, again, independence. Many senior citizens also speak of the loss of self-respect and the respect of peers as their wisdom and counsel are increasingly disregarded by younger members of society. All of these losses are not only significant in their own right, but the rapidity of their occurrence in the latter half of life compounds their effect upon the individual. It seems clear to me that loss and grief must therefore be regarded as integral components of later life.

One of the most clearly definable loss events in latter life, and therefore one of the easiest to research, is retirement. Robert C. Hatchley's study of retirement noted that one-third of his sample encountered difficulties in adjusting to retirement, the most difficult factor being the reduced income.[16] In twenty-two percent of the cases studied, individuals expressed strong feelings of "missing one's job." Apparently, these grief feelings involve not just the loss of money but the loss of status, peer group, friendships, routine and self-worth as well. Hatchley's study concluded that the impact of this loss depended upon a person's "hierarchy of personal goals." The higher the work or job was in an individual's personal hierarchy of goals, the more difficulty he or she experienced in adjusting to retirement.

The pioneering work of Daniel J. Levinson in the area of adult life stages has finally been published in a work entitled *The Seasons of a Man's Life*.[17] Levinson and his associates have been particularly helpful in identifying the dynamics and phases of a man's mid-life transition. The mid-life crisis is that period from forty to forty-five years of age, when a man passes from the relatively stable period of early adulthood to middle adulthood. The transition period is characterized by relative unstability—emotionally, socially and spiritually—as a man reflects on and re-evaluates his life course. One of the themes to emerge is that of loss and death. Levinson writes:

> A man at mid-life is suffering some loss of his youthful vitality and, often, some insult to his youthful narcissistic pride. Although he is not literally close to death or undergoing severe bodily decline, he typically experiences these changes as a fundamental threat. It is as though he were on the threshold of senility and even death . . . . Dealing with his mortality means that a man must engage in mourning for the dying self of youth, so that the self can be made more whole.[18]

The transition to middle adulthood requires the "letting go" of the ideas, images and dreams of youth. Grief is an integral part of this passage process. If a man is to be fully healthy as an adult, he must be able to grieve the passing of the old stage of life.

The sense of loss that accompanies growing older can perhaps be better described by the artist and the poet than by the research scientist. In the popular musical, "Fiddler on the Roof," Tevye and Golde pause during the marriage ceremony of their daughter to reflect musically on the passing of time. The lyrics of their moving and nostalgic song are:

> Is this the little girl I carried?
> Is this the little boy at play?

I don't remember growing older.
When did they?
When did she get to be a beauty?
When did he grow to be so tall?
Wasn't it yesterday when they were small?

Sunrise, Sunset, Sunrise, Sunset,
Swiftly flow the days.
Seedlings turn overnight to sunflowers,
Blossoming even as we gaze.

Sunrise, Sunset, Sunrise, Sunset,
Swiftly fly the years
One season following another,
Laden with happiness and tears.[19]

Most parents can identify with the grief feelings that accompany the rapid growth of children. Graduations, weddings, and confirmations become the developmental ''marker events'' not only for the children's lives, but also for the life cycle of the parents as well. Similarly, birthdays and anniversaries also mark the passing of time and dimly remind us that we are one year older. With each passing year, we not only lose the previous developmental stage, but time itself. In this latter sense, there is a pervasive almost existential loss that surrounds and permeates life itself.

Loss in the First Half of the Life Cycle

While change is continuous and sometimes traumatic in early life, most developmental changes are subjectively perceived as gains (or growth), and only secondarily as losses. Nevertheless, objectively speaking, every developmental transition involves a loss—the loss of the previous stage and the attachments associated with it.

Some writers perceive birth itself as a significant, perhaps the most significant, loss in the human life cycle. From the relative security of intrauterine life, a human infant is suddenly pushed into a life of stark brightness, extreme temperature changes and a new fearful ''separateness.'' The recent development of the Lamaze[20] and LeBoyer[21] methods of childbirth seek to minimize the traumatic effects of this basic and primal loss. The Lamaze and Le Boyer methods in varying degree recommend among other things the reduction of the lighting, the normalization of temperatures, the elimination of drugs whenever possible, and the keeping of the new infant next to his or her mother's body immediately after birth. All of these procedures and others are designed to minimize the trauma, ''separateness,'' and the loss associated with birth for the infant.

Psychoanalytic writers have focused on the loss of the mother's breast (or bottle) in weaning as the next significant loss event. Here, the infant loses not only the nourishment of the breast, but the warmth, security, and intimacy of this special relationship with mother. Psychoanalysts suggest that if this transitional event is handled poorly—too late, too suddenly, too early or too anxiously—a profound sense of loss can negatively affect all future emotional development of the individual. For this reason, the international organization of nursing mothers, the La Leche League, teaches that weaning should occur at the child's initiative, not at the mother's convenience or the culture's norms.[22] Only by waiting until then, when the child is ready, can the negative effects of this inevitable loss be minimized.

Childhood seems to be a time of repeated and inevitable losses. Many of these attachments and losses occur gradually and willingly. A young child will adopt a favorite doll, book, toy or friend, only to give up these ''objects'' a year later when new attachments appropriate to the older age take their place. The once favorite toy is now rejected with the declaration, ''That's for babies!'' At other times, a child will temporarily resist a significant loss and attempt to return to a time prior to the loss by means of a psychological mechanism known as regression. Robert A. Furman, who writes of children and death, describes a delightful and relatively mild example of this dynamic:

> A nursery schooler had just mastered tying her own shoe laces, something that had taken her weeks of diligent effort to achieve. She was duly proud of her new skill, and even untied her shoes before her grand-parents to be able to demonstrate this accomplishment. But one afternoon she suddenly balked at tying her laces. After several days of this behavior her mother was puzzled and pointed out how proud she had been of her grown-up skill. Her daughter was thoughtful, but then replied, ''Yes, but I do sometimes miss your doing it for me.''[23]

Many families encounter behavioral problems with the oldest child when a new baby brother or sister takes the cherished "center-stage" position in the family. The older child now senses the loss of attention, affection, and dependency upon the parents that he or she once exclusively enjoyed. Temporary behavioral problems or attempts to "regress" can be understood as a compressed and compounded attempt to "act out" grief feelings. Obviously, the more that parents can prepare the older children for this loss, by accepting their feelings and encouraging their participation in the birth event, the greater will be the likelihood that older children's grief feelings will be resolved in a gradual and natural process.

The modern educational process also provides the environment for many of our most significant attachments and losses. With each grade level and each school, a child makes emotional attachments to favorite teachers, coaches, friends, classes, activities, accomplishments and even "eras." Then with graduation, the individual leaves behind (voluntarily or involuntarily) those attachments for new ones. It is little wonder that most high school graduation ceremonies are characterized by nostalgia and weeping—two expressions of grief. Nevertheless, if an individual is emotionally "ready," the transition is smooth, however emotional; but if the individual is not ready, he or she will resist the loss and sometimes hang on to what is lost for years.

Like most members of the clergy, I have conducted many a wedding ceremony. In recent years, the form of those ceremonies has become more diverse. Always, however, I find it curious how and when crying occurs during the ceremony. Weddings can be emotional occasions for many people. Usually it is the immediate family, particularly the parents of the bride and groom that are most likely to shed a tear or two. On occasion even brides and grooms have recited their vows through a veil of tears. I have seen many guests come up to the wedding party after the ceremony with tears streaming down their faces saying, "I'm so happy for you." I have often wondered about those "tears of joy." There is some joy in it, I'm sure. I believe that there is also some sadness as well. The wedding ceremony marks a transition from one life stage to another. There is both loss and gain; therefore, there are feelings of both sadness and fear. For the bride and groom, there is the loss of the single life with all of its attachments, freedoms, friends, routines and self-images. In our culture we ritualize this loss in the form of the groom's "Bachelor Party" and the bride's "Wedding Shower."[24]

Weddings are also the marker events for the transition of the bride and groom's parents, who are passing from one life stage to another. Well-meaning friends reassure them, saying, "You're not 'losing' a son (or daughter) but gaining a daughter (or son)." Even in such "happy occasions," there is a hidden loss or two.

The advent of parenthood is another seemingly happy event that does not appear at first glance to involve loss and grief. After childbirth, however, a new mother is said to feel "post-partum blues."[25] Peretz writes that a new mother.

> . . . loses a part of herself in giving birth to her baby and in addition may lose whatever special feeling, attention or importance was attached to pregnancy.[26]

The new father can also experience a sense of loss associated with the redirecting of his wife's energies and attention to the new infant. Suddenly, he is "ignored" where once he was his wife's prime object of affection. Thus, the arrival of a new baby involves a life cycle transition in the lives of the parents, as well as the new child itself. In fact, from birth on, every transitional event in the life of the child will also initiate a change (loss and gain) in the life cycle of the parents.

Loss is inevitably present in all of the life cycle, from birth to death. To the extent that loss is present, then grief is present too as the human psyche seeks to adjust to the "rupture" of emotional attachments. To be psychologically healthy from a developmental perspective requires that we be regularly, if not constantly, grieving. Dr. Carr writes:

> If mourning is accepted as an understandable normal response to loss or separation, it suggests that to some degree we are always in mourning, although not necessarily clinically depressed. Losses, specific and non-specific, are constantly presenting themselves and must be dealt with, if only on the periphery of our awareness. Because we are constantly experiencing losses, we are routinely struggling with the task of integrating them. Mourning is thus a relative and continuous process associated with all events which entail some type of loss, separation or withdrawal of emotional investment . . . . Loss then is a continual experience; bereavement, as a matter of degree, is an unceasing state.[27]

Loss is universal and inevitable in the human life cycle. One cannot grow without losing. Thus we are constantly dealing with grief in one form or another, in one degree of intensity or another. Therefore, there seems to be one obvious conclusion: if we wish to maintain psychological health and to grow developmentally, we must become "experts" in grief. More personally and precisely, we must become expert grievers. Future chapters will explore how we can accomplish both of these tasks.

2. What Is Grief?

"Bereavement is a universal and integral part of the experience of love. . . ."[1]

C.S. Lewis

Given the tremendous universality of loss experiences, we might
think a precise definition of grief would be an easy task. On the contrary, the task of defining grief is not an easy one. First, grief itself is a
process and, therefore, it is always changing and becoming. Grief is
never a fixed commodity. Grief is itself different at different stages in
its process. Second, grief varies with the type of loss involved. The
grief that we might experience over the death of a parent is not exactly
the same as the grief we might experience over the loss of a job or a
prized possession. The type of loss colors the type of grief. Third, grief
reactions vary widely with the unique individuals involved. Variables
such as age, sex, religious beliefs, personality structure and length and
intensity of the relationship with the lost object will make each person's loss uniquely his or her own. Finally, expressions of grief will
vary with different cultural contexts. Even within one culture, various
subcultures and family systems will mold the social expressions of
grief. How a British gentleman expresses his grief would be worlds
apart from how a similar Iranian man would express his grief. In part,
our culture determines how we grieve.

Our search for the answer to the question "What is grief?" can
begin with the last chapter's overwhelming observation. Grief is the
human emotional response to loss. Loss comes in an infinite variety of
forms. We can lose people, places, objects, relationships and even
ideas. In addition, grief may be triggered in response to an anticipated
or perceived loss, as well as to actual losses.

Still, questions remain regarding what exactly is this feeling called grief. What does it feel like? What are its dynamics? What is its essential purpose in the economy of the human psyche? Is it a single uniform emotion or a mixture of assorted human reactions? In order to answer some of these questions, this chapter will review three of the current theoretical approaches to an understanding of grief. By necessity then, this chapter will be more theoretically oriented than other chapters. Nevertheless, I believe that this is the best way for us to get a clear view of this amazing phenomenon we call grief.

GRIEF IS SEPARATION ANXIETY

One major approach to understanding grief is to conceive of grief as "separation anxiety." Otto Rank, one of Freud's earliest followers, is probably the father of this point of view. Yet, unlike some psychoanalytic writers, Rank posited that the origin of separation anxiety lies not in the fear of abandonment or starvation, but in the birth event itself.[2] After all, a person's first experience of life is birth. The birth event is the primal and original separation experience. A birthing process that is easy and natural contributes to the child's later psychological health as an adult. Conversely, a birthing process that is anxiety-ridden or difficult influences the child's later development in a negative direction. Furthermore, Rank argued that all of life is characterized by a continual series of such separation experienced, each one linked back to the primal anxiety. How one experienced the original primal separation colors how one will handle these later separations. At the point of each separation event, there is a "pull back to the womb" and a "push toward self-dependence."[3] This latter push toward autonomy is a function of the will. Each person's will can be mobilized to push the person in the direction of growth. Neurosis, according to Rank, was the result of a fixation of this process or a "stuckness" of the normal flexible flow between separation and union impulses. Psychotherapy, therefore, involved an inevitable reliving of the birth trauma (or in our terms a "regrieving"), freeing up the will to renew its drive toward self-dependence. Rank has built a whole system of psychology based on the importance of separation experiences, beginning, of course, with the first separation experience, birth.

In recent years, the most articulate presentation of grief as separation anxiety has been written by pastoral theologian David Switzer who strengthens the psychoanalytic traditions with the work of Harry Stack Sullivan. Building upon Sullivan's interpersonal theory of psychology and some fascinating work on the function and purpose of language formation, Switzer argues for the essential interpersonal character of the Self. He writes:

> The foundation of the Self is comprised of the internalized response of the significant other. The individual self is interpersonal at its core, arising out of and continuing to be dependent upon the other.[4]

The self develops gradually as a growing child interrelates with his or her family and environment. The mechanism of that interaction is language. Through speech one learns not only to interact with others, but to identify, clarify and understand who he or she is. Language and selfhood develop together, mutually reinforcing and strengthening each other.

Understanding the self as an interpersonal unity opens up the way to view anxiety in an interpersonal perspective as well. A loss or separation from another person triggers anxiety. The self perceives any sever or threat of sever of a significant relationship as a danger, "as a threat to the loss of its unified existence." When a significant relationship is actually destroyed, a part of the self is experienced as lost. Indeed, many widowed or bereaved people will describe their loss by saying, "A part of me has died." In a very real sense, according to this view, this remark is accurate. A part of the self does die with each loss or separation.

Switzer notes that an acute grief reaction is remarkably similar to a classic anxiety attack. The symptoms—restlessness, increased heart and pulse rate, inability to eat, insomnia, "nerves," perspiration, shortness of breath, sighing—are similar. Anxiety is painful and acute anxiety can be overwhelming. In the face of such threats, the self utilizes various defense mechanisms. These "protective devices" are psychological mechanisms to avoid or to diminish the severity of pain and anxiety. The typical defense mechanisms associated with grief are: denial, repression, regression, idealization, identification. As with any other type of anxiety, the grieving person's psyche employs these defenses in varying degrees, in order to prevent itself from being overwhelmed by pain that is ''too strong to bear.'' In a sense then, these defenses are necessary. Yet, too severe a defense or a defense employed too rigidly or for too long a time can actually block the healing process.

The popular Christian writer C.S. Lewis begins his personal story of bereavement with this entry:

> No one ever told me that grief felt so like fear. I am not afraid, but
> the sensation is like being afraid. The fluttering in the stomach, the
> same restlessness, the yawning. I keep on swallowing.[5]

Indeed, anxiety is often loosely defined as generalized fear. If grief is a type of anxiety, then fear can also be a descriptive term for grief. Yet, what is it that the griever fears? For Switzer, what one fears is the loss of the self through separation. Grief, especially acute grief, ''feels'' like fear and looks ''behaviorally'' like anxiety. Therefore Switzer concludes that grief is a form of anxiety, namely, ''separation anxiety.'' He writes:

> . . . the conclusion seems inescapable that at the very center of
> grief is separation anxiety. Grief is one among many of a lifetime
> of separation experiences, each stimulating reactions of anxiety,
> differing in intensity because of factors, yet all being of basically
> the same order.[6]

Grief is best understood as separation anxiety, an acute fear in the self over the loss or threat to lose a segment of the self associated with the lost object.

The centrality and importance of separation anxiety in grief is now widely accepted by scholars and writers. Listen to how Lily Pincus in her book on grief and the family describes it:

> . . . the loss of a loved one reactivates everybody's most painful
> nightmares, the most primary infantile fears and panic, the anguish
> of abandonment and the terror of being left alone, having lost love
> . . . . The baby experiences the loss of his mother as a threat to his
> existence, and it is this primordial fear that is reactivated in the loss
> of the closest person. Every significant death may bring in some
> sense of repetition of this anxiety.[7]

Even those scholars who have proposed new theoretical models of grief have done so, building upon the central premise and experiental data of grief as separation anxiety. Parkes, for example, writes: "I think it fair to say that the pining or yearning that constitutes separation anxiety is the characteristic feature of the pang of grief."[8] Bowlby, who has also rejected the psychoanalytic model in favor of an ethological one, agrees that separation anxiety in the human infant is the "prototype of all adult grief."[9] Separation anxiety is the irreducible element in grief. The grief of the adult finds its origins in the anxiety of the infant.

Some Implications

There are several interesting implications of this theoretical understanding of grief. First, if grief is basically separation anxiety, then all mourning is essentially regressive behavior. All grieving, even in adult life, is a partial reliving of our primal childhood fear of abandonment. To the extent that this is true, we would expect to see various degrees of regressive or "childish" behaviors in grieving people. Sure enough, what do the acutely bereaved do most? They weep. We say, "She cried like a baby." Some widowed people report strong dependency needs in bereavement. They want to be held, to be taken care of, to be nurtured. These are all regressive images.

Second, if grief is essentially separation anxiety, we would expect that one of the initial strong impulses of a person in acute grief would be to "hold on." The opposite of separating is bonding or holding on. Sure enough, what do people do most in airports and bus depots? They hug . . . they touch . . . they squeeze tightly. They are holding on to that which is being lost. The more anxious one feels, the tighter one holds on.

One of the most common dynamics that I see in families illustrates this very tendency, to hold on tighter as one becomes more anxious regarding separation. Consider John, for example, age forty-four, married eighteen years, who feels that he "is losing his wife." Nothing has been overtly said or decided, but they have been silently drifting apart for years. Three years ago Susan got a full-time job which took her out of the home. Last year she started spending one evening a week out with her girl friends. Now she is talking about going back to school and "making something of her life." As Susan becomes more independent, John feels increasingly anxious. His first urge is "to hold on tighter." So he wants sexual relations more often. He wants to know where she is all the time. He wants her to talk to him more. He wants her to stay home more, and when she does, he wants her to sit next to him on the couch and watch TV together the way "they used to." He anxiously tries to please her in hundreds of ways. Unfortunately, this behavior is exactly the worst response he could have. Susan experiences his sudden over-attention as a "prison." She feels increasingly trapped, watched and smothered. So she actually seeks to distance herself even more. The cycle feeds upon itself—the more she distances, the more he tries to hold on, the more she distances, and so on. This is a fairly common dynamic. I sometimes see it in mothers of teenage children, as those children become increasingly independent. When we begin to feel separation anxiety, our first instinct is to hold on even tighter.

Viewing grief as separation anxiety offers some suggestions regarding the treatment of the bereaved. If grief is essentially a form of anxiety, then grief can be treated as an anxiety attack. The usual tools and techniques for the treatment of anxiety could be applicable to acute grief reactions. Indeed, the prescription of tranquilizers for the bereaved is a very common practice in some circles. In other circles, the practice is controversial.

Another suggestion is that grief is mitigated by any and all efforts toward human bonding and closeness. The best antidote to separation anxiety is people. A supportive, close community of friends and family members goes a long way toward mitigating the pain of separation. So it is that sometimes the best cure for a loss is a new love relationship. This perspective also suggests why verbalization is so therapeutic for the bereaved. Talking is a way of symbolically and conceptually "staying close" to the lost loved one. By keeping a mental image of the deceased, the griever is "holding on to her," much in the same way that he held her physically close when she was alive. "Talking it out" is still one of the best ways to mitigate separation anxiety.

GRIEF IS A FUNCTION OF ATTACHMENT INSTINCTS

A second major theoretical approach for understanding grief is to conceive of grief as a function of attachment instincts. This view of grief began with Freud, who understood mourning in terms of his concept of libido or psycho-sexual energy. The libido is that energy that attaches itself to all sorts of "loved objects." When one of those objects no longer exists, the ego demands that the libido be withdrawn. This withdrawal can be extraordinarily painful, but it is a necessary process if that libido is to be "displaced" onto a new object. Therefore, grief's purpose in the economics of the psyche seems clear. Grief's task is to withdraw the libido from the lost object, thus freeing it for new attachments.

The bereaved have long comforted one another with the advice that "where grief is, love was." While a simplification, there is some truth to this adage that this model of grief highlights. Alexander Bain, an early British psychologist, once put it this way: "Sorrow is in proportion to the power of the attachment."[10] Grief is experienced in response to the loss of any object to which one is emotionally attached. This is why people with unhappy relationships to a lost person will often grieve just as intensely as those who have had happy relationships. Grief is related to attachment, not to love. Attachment feelings can be, and usually are, ambivalent.

Understanding grief as a function of attachment has received some insightful attention in the pastoral care community. Edgar N. Jackson, building upon Freud's model, describes grief as a "reclaiming of emotional capital."[11] He writes that grief is that emotion "whereby a person seeks to disengage himself from the demanding relationship that existed and to reinvest his emotional capital in new and productive directions for the health and welfare of his future and society."[12] The emphasis here is on the necessity of grief. Unless the "grief work" is completed, a person's emotional life remains trapped by the past, and he or she is unable to invest himself or herself in anything or anyone.

William Rogers, an early writer in the pastoral care movement, takes this view of grief as well. He suggested that people build "emotional constellations" with their environment and other people. "People and objects become extensions of ourselves. Feeling tone develops around these persons and objects according to their importance in the individual's attempt to meet his emotional needs."[13] He then makes a keen insight:

> The important point to remember, however, is that grief is *not* the result of what happens to the loved one. It is rather the result of what happens to the bereaved.[14]

Grief is caused not by the loss of a loved one, but by the valuing process of the griever. Grief exists because the griever valued and gave meaning to that which is now lost. In short, grief is a function of attachment.

John Bowlby and Colin Murray Parkes are probably the two leading scholars in the field of bereavement in the world today. Bowlby has pioneered the development of the ethological model for studying grief.[15] Ethologists study species-specific behavior patterns, asking the question, "What is the purpose or function of such behavior in the evolutionary development of that species?" Charles Darwin was one of the most famous ethologists and actually had much to say about mourning and weeping in humans and animals.[16] Konrad Lorenz is another well-known ethologist who has studied instinct behaviors of young goslings.[17] In contrast to psychoanalytic and learning theorists, both of whom reject the concept of instinct, Bowlby argued for the presence and importance of certain human "species-specific" behaviors or instincts. Included in his list of human instincts is crying, smiling, sucking and attachment. The latter instinct is the tendency in children from about six months onward to emotionally attach themselves to the familiar mother-figure.

In particular, Bowlby has focused his lifelong research on the disruptions of this bonding in children between the ages of six months and six years. The importance of this work cannot be understated. He notes that there is a mounting evidence pointing "to causal relationship between loss of maternal care in the early years and disturbed personality development."[18] Bowlby's studies were of children who were otherwise healthy and well adjusted, but who were separated from their mothers for various lengths of time due to the mother's hospitalization. Children so separated showed a predictable sequence of behaviors—protest, despair and detachment—which he posited "is characteristic of all forms of mourning."[19] Adults, like children, go through these simple phases and, in fact, must go through them in order to be restored to health.

In this model, anger, in the form of "protest," is a very necessary and integral part of the grieving process. "Following an unexpected loss," writes Bowlby, "there seems always to be a phase of protest during which the bereaved person is striving, either in actuality or in thought and feeling, to recover the lost person and is reproaching him for desertion."[20] The function of this anger appears to be to add punch to the strenuous efforts to both recover the lost person and to dissuade him or her from deserting again. The view that the presence of anger in mourning is a sign that the grief is pathological is soundly rejected by Bowlby. On the contrary, the inability to express angry feelings in grief is a sign of concern and possible pathological development. This insight has tremendous implications for pastors. For, all too often, religion has been used to persuade the bereaved to repress their anger, lest they appear unbelieving or disrespectful to the deceased. In reality, religion could serve the cause of sound mental health by encouraging ways to release this natural anger.

Once a child has entered the third phase of detachment, Bowlby noted that he or she seems no longer to be preoccupied with the mother. When the mother does return, instead of greeting her enthusiastically, the child seems hardly to notice her and remains remote and unresponsive. Most returning mothers find this response incomprehensible. If the separation has not been too long, this condition soon reverses itself. In fact, the detached behavior is eventually replaced by attachment of "a greatly heightened intensity." Data suggests that the affectional ties have not been forgotten, but only repressed, remaining latent and ready to become active again at a high intensity level if the mother returns. If the mother does not return, as in the case of her death, the unconscious material remains repressed and becomes the impetus for pathological personality development. Bowlby suggests that the two abnormal results—permanent emotional detachment or heightened attachment—are both the result of significant separations at this crucial period in a child's life. They are both types of "scar tissue," distorting the child's later psychological development. It appears that there is a crucial developmental period for the "learning" of attachment, just as there is a crucial period in which a child needs to learn to speak or to walk. If a child fails to learn this developmental task at the appropriate time, his or her learning of that task at a later time is exceedingly difficult, if not impossible. The crucial time for "learning" to make and maintain affectional bonds is from six months to six years, when the natural instinct for such emerges.

According to this ethological model, Bowlby argues that grieving developed in the human species because it served an evolutionary purpose. Grieving, including crying and protesting, is a type of alarm system that functioned to keep the child's family in close proximity and to prevent them from "losing" her or him. In the case of death, weeping served to engage the sympathy and assistance of other members of the species and to rebond the mourner to a new support system. One can easily see that grief, as so understood, served as an evolutionary advantage for those humans who grieved well. The bereaved person, who was unable to cry, would have a greater probability of perishing through isolation, starvation or destruction. The very survival of a griever depended upon how overtly he or she grieved, because such displays of anguish worked to bring others to his or her aid and helped form new bonds in the human community. Even in this day, Bowlby suggests, grief still serves to promote attachment not only by its end-product—the detaching of a person's emotional energy from the lost object—but also by the very act of weeping itself which lures others to the mourner's side. In this sense, grief is by definition and by intention a social activity. The instinct to cry when in need, for whatever reason, and the instinct to respond to weeping with assistance, is a part of the psychological heritage of human beings, imbedded deeply in our collective unconsciousness by eons of evolutionary development.

Some Implications

This theoretical view of grief suggests that grieving is not just a function of a loss, but a function of the attachment of the bereaved to that which is lost. Obviously, if we lose someone who means very little to us we grieve very little, even though the loss might seem to be a major one to outsiders. Conversely, the loss of an object of seemingly minor significance may be, in fact, a major loss to someone, because that person had great emotional investment in that object.

Let me recount one personal illustration of this point. As a young parish minister, I remember calling one day on an elderly lady who lived alone. It was the first time that I had visited her in her home, although I had talked with her after worship on occasion. Earlier in that month one of her friends, Jack, a man in his eighties, had died. The funeral was the last time that we had seen her in church for several weeks. The senior minister and I were anticipating that she was grieving some and felt that this would be a valuable time to call upon her. Sure enough, as I visited with her in her living room, it was clear to me that she was not her usual self. She was low-key, despairing, and at one point in the middle of an unrelated conversation, she began to cry. I let her cry for a while and then launched into a comforting homily about God's care for those who are deceased. She seemed to be listening through her tears, so I continued. Then to make matters worse, I recounted some of the positive qualities of her late friend, Jack. At that point she held up her hand and gently but firmly, as only a woman who was three times my age could do, she stopped me. She then clarified that she was not crying because of Jack. "It's Sandy, pastor," she went on—"my cat. She's been missing now for three days. I am worried sick about her. I'm just sure that she's been hit by a car and is lying somewhere in a ditch." After I took the egg off my face, we went on to have a very pastoral and even delightful conversation about fear, grief and general foolishness. I had learned a valuable lesson. Sandy was far more central to this woman's emotional life than any human friend could be. Sandy was her companion who shared the lonely nights. Her attachment to this cat was great. So her grief, even only due to the *possible* loss of her, was far greater than the grief over her friend's death.

Loving and Grieving

If grief is a function of attachment as Bowlby suggests, then as soon as we begin to emotionally attach ourselves to anyone or anything, we become vulnerable to loss. The more we attach ourselves in quantity or quality, the more potential we have for loss and grief. Furthermore, the instinct to attach oneself is a universal human tendency. This propensity of human beings "to make and maintain affectional bonds" is not limited to children. Every normal adult inevitably, almost automatically and unconsciously, forms emotional attachments. Each of us lives within a network of emotional attachments—to people, places, objects, activities, roles, beliefs and so on. Like a spider in the center of its web, we have emotional ties in all directions and at many levels of intensity. If any one of those ties breaks, we grieve. Grief is, therefore, an inevitable part of life. If we choose to love (emotionally attach ourselves), then we inevitably choose to grieve.

Religion has traditionally encouraged people to care, to get involved and "to love your neighbor." By so doing, pastors are implicitly asking people to grieve as well. We should be clear about that. Grief is an inevitable part of love. The more we ask parishioners "to care," the more we are asking them to be willing to grieve. One cannot truly care without being hurt. I remember the young woman who told me how she took up her priest's challenge to get involved in a nearby nursing home for the aged. She did involve herself and very intensely so. She "gave it her all," to use her words. Sometime later one of the patients, of whom she had grown very fond, died. Our helping friend was devastated. She went back to her priest at that point, angrily demanding, "O.K., Father, you got me into this! Now tell me, what am I supposed to do with my emotions?" She never told me what her priest's answer was, but it struck me that her question was a deeply theological one as well as a psychological one. I would have liked to have heard the priest's answer. If we wish people to be "lovers" and caregivers, then we, as pastors, must help them learn how to grieve. Grief is a part of love. If our style of pastoral ministry tends to deny, avoid or repress grief feelings, then we will inevitably repress love as well. We will teach our congregation how to love, when we can teach them how to grieve.

Grief, Values and Identity

As we think about the connection of identity, values and grief, let me suggest an exercise. Imagine that you are in the center of a series of concentric circles, each one, like the ripples in a pond, a little larger around you. In the innermost circle or "bull's eye" place those people or objects to whom you are most intensely attached. This circle might include such items as your immediate family, a home that you have lived in for many years, a very special friend, several "ideas" or beliefs that you hold dear. In each progressively larger circle place those people or objects that are progressively less emotionally important to you. In the last outer circle would be those things in which you have the least emotional investment. Now step aside and look at this configuration. Such a configuration would be a "map" of your attachments— from the most to the least important. It could also be said that this may represent your value hierarchy. The inner circle is filled with those things you value most in life, the outer circle with those things that you value least, and all of the progressive degrees of valuation in between. Valuing is another way of talking about attaching. We value those "things" that we are emotionally attached to, and we become emotionally attached to those things we value most.

In a sense, this map is also a statement of your identity. Your identity is made up of your closest emotional attachments. Switzer has argued that the Self is essentially interpersonal in nature, made up of a summary of our closest relationships. Similarly, identity is made up of the collection of those items in the innermost circles.[21] We define ourselves by our closest attachments. In response to the question "Who are you?" you might answer, "I am a minister" . . . "I am a Texan" . . . "I am a father of three children" . . . "I am a Christian" . . . "I am a homeowner" and so on. Attachment is also another way of describing your identity and a way of representing your values.

Now imagine that we can flip over this configuration so that we are looking at its back side. The items are the same, but now we are talking about loss. The back side represents the grief potential for each item in your map. The innermost circle is filled with those people and things whose loss would be most devastating. The outer circle includes those things whose loss would have only marginal or no effect on your life. Such a map is an assessment tool, a way of evaluating the relative intensity of a person's loss. Each loss or life-change involves a reshuffling of this map. Every loss involves changes in our identity, particularly if we define ourselves by that which was lost. Every loss is also a possible change in our values, particularly if we valued that which is lost or that which is lost represented a cherished value. Loss events trigger changes in our identity and in our values, but always in proportion to the relative position of the lost object in our map of attachments.

Grief Is a Process of Realization

The understanding of grief as a process of realization does not have any single spokesperson and cannot be found in any particular textbook. Freud, the father of modern psychology, touched on this theme when he described grief this way:

> Reality testing has shown that the loved object no longer exists, and it (ego) proceeds to demand that all libido shall be withdrawn from its attachment to that object. This demand arouses understandable opposition . . . . This opposition can be so intense that a turning away from reality takes place . . . but normally, respect for reality gains the day.[22]

In the Freudian scheme, the ego is that segment of the psyche that reg-
ulates and negotiates the demands of the Id with the demands of reality.
This conflict between the demands of reality and the desire of the libido
to remain attached to the loved object creates great psychic conflict and
pain. The process of gradually withdrawing libido is therefore "piece-
meal" and "extraordinarily painful." Eventually, when one completes
his or her grief work, the psyche accepts the new reality. Grief's task is
to adjust the psyche to reality.

In the case of bereavement, the demand of the Id is to "hang on
to" that which is lost and the demand of reality is to accept the painful
truth that the loved object is lost. Translating these terms, many grievers experience a split between their inner emotions and their cognitive
knowledge of reality. For instance, a widower may say, "Yes, I know
Betty is dead, but I cannot accept it. My head and my heart are worlds
apart. Every night my heart cries out for her." It is as if the mourner's
emotions need time to "catch up" with reality. Grieving can be understood as that process of catching up our emotions with reality. Grief is
a process of emotionally accepting a new reality.

The simplest and most obvious fact that can be said about loss and
grief is that "it hurts." When all else is said and done, grief is painful.
Losses rupture the bonds of attachment and love that binds us one to another and to other love objects. If our attachment is intense, the resulting pain is intense. In such situations, the psyche's first response is to
recoil, to deny the reality of the pain. The pain is too great, too threatening to face. Gradually, in the process of grieving, the pain becomes
more bearable, more acceptable, more eased, and, eventually, healed.
One gradually adjusts to the new reality and makes the necessary
changes. "Grief is a process," writes Colin Parkes, "of realization, of
'making real' the fact of the loss."[23] When that process is complete, the
new reality no longer hurts. One is again fully "in touch with" reality.

The psyche cannot face grief's pain, particularly if it is severe,
constantly or indefinitely—just as we cannot look directly into the sun
indefinitely. Periodically, we must "look away." Similarly, grief is a
process of facing the painful reality of the loss, alternated by periods of
"looking away." Parkes has called these periods of looking away
"mitigations." One of the chief forms of mitigation is defense mechanisms. Defense mechanisms can be defined simply as psychological
devices whereby the psyche defends itself from pain. A grieving person can and usually does employ various defense mechanisms as a part

of his or her grieving process. The defense mechanisms, more commonly associated with grief, are:

A. **Denial/Repression**: Denial is a defense mechanism that is employed when something is so painful that it threatens the very life of the psyche. The intensity of that pain or threat is beyond the scope of the person's ability to cope with it, so the psyche denies the reality associated with the pain.

B. **Identification/Idealization**: Identification and idealization are two common defense mechanisms associated with grief. They are often found in tandem. Identification is a psychological process whereby the griever seeks to identify with that which is lost. Identification is a way of "staying close" to that which is lost. Idealization is a mechanism whereby the mourner idealizes that which is lost. The normal negative thoughts associated with all human attachments are glossed over in favor of an idealized view.

C. **Regression**: Regression is a defense mechanism whereby the psyche regresses or "goes back" to a period prior to the painful loss. Regression can take many forms and intensities. Regressive behavior is usually characterized by childish, dependent, "needy" features.

Many people who have been exposed to modern psychology have been schooled to view defense mechanisms as negative things, as blocks to full health. We mistakenly believe that all defense mechanisms must be broken down, to allow the person to face the inner pain and feelings. In the case of bereavement, just the opposite view of defense mechanisms prevails. Defense mechanisms are necessary pauses amid the waves of pain. One must be able to rest periodically—lest the pain would be too much to bear. When we pastors come upon a bereaved person who is obviously denying the full realization of his or her loss or idealizing the loss object, it is not helpful for us, armed with our amateur psychology, to try "to break down his or her defenses." On the contrary, we must respect defenses. Defenses only become blocks to healing when they become rigid and permanent. As long as the defenses are alternating with periods of painful realization, the grief process is probably proceeding well. We can conclude then, at least in a generalized way, that the best kind of pastoral care is one which both confronts and comforts. A pastor who is all confronting or all comforting will not be as helpful as the person who can do both. It is admittedly a delicate balance.

Viewing grief as a process of realization also touches on the dynamics of remembering and forgetting. In some ways, grief is a process of remembering and forgetting. At first, the reality of a loss is too painful to think about. We cannot remember. We have forgotten (denial). Gradually, as we grieve, we remember more and more. We reminisce over the history of our relationship to what was lost. As grieving continues further, we remember better and better. There is an increase in clarity. There are less distortions due to idealization or undue bitterness. As each painful segment is remembered, it is released to be forgotten, but, this time, permanently and peacefully forgotten. This can be a confusing experience, especially for a child. Eda LeShan, writing to children about grief, touches on this dynamic:

> But after a while a very scary thing happens; you can't remember, no matter how hard you try. Sometimes this happens in a few months, sometimes not for a year or longer. But sooner or later it happens to most people, and when it does it may make you feel more sad and lonely than ever. Losing these memories seems to happen at about the same time you begin really to accept the death.[24]

Grieving is a curious process of forgetting, remembering and forgetting again. The ultimate goal of grief work is to be able to remember without pain, but such a remembering only releases those memories to be truly forgotten. One of the most helpful things that a pastor can do for a bereaved person is to help him or her remember, clearly and fully, and then let him or her forget.

Grief is a process of realization, but this process is not a smooth flow. It is made up of two alternating tendencies—one to avoid pain and the other to face reality, one to remember and the other to forget. The two tendencies oscillate, so that a period of intense mourning will alternate with periods of conscious or unconscious avoidance of pain. Defense mechanisms alternate with and co-exist with periods of painful realization. Forgetting alternates with periods of remembering. Yet, the general and eventual thrust of all grieving is toward a full realization of the loss.

Conclusions

This chapter has surveyed three main theoretical approaches to grief, noting along the way a few implications of each for pastoral care. At this point it may seem as though grief is an incredibly complex emotion. It is. Each theoretical approach offers a slightly different perspective on grief's nature. Each has its insights to offer. Each raises still more questions to answer. Nevertheless, let us see if we can summarize our conclusions.

We can begin where this chapter began, by noting again that grief is the human emotional response to loss. Losses may be real, perceived or anticipated. That which is lost may be anything of value—a person, an object, a relationship or even an idea. Then we learned that the irreducible element in all grief, particularly in its early stages and in its anticipatory form, is separation anxiety. The pain of loss is the pain of separation. Every grief echoes and to some extent relives our infantile fear of abandonment.

Next, we learned that an individual's grief reaction is always in proportion to the degree of that person's attachment to what is lost. The more that we value something or are emotionally attached to it, the more grief we will experience when we lose or are separated from that valued object. Forming attachments is an inevitable part of the human experience.

Three simple observations seem obvious. First, *grief is painful*. Grief is a psychological wound that comes when someone or something dear to us is taken from us. Grief is seldom welcomed. We initially resist it, and only gradually, as healing takes its course, do we come to accept its painful truth. Therefore, grieving takes hard work. Second, *grief is necessary*. The completion of this grieving process is necessary before a person can be restored to health. Before people can love again, they must complete their grief work. If the process is not completed, the bereaved person remains in a perpetual state of sorrow. Third, *grief is good*. Grief's purpose is to restore a person to health. The grief process is therefore essentially good by nature. It is part of God's good creation. We can trust it. Grief is on our side. We can look upon grief not as an enemy to be shunned, but as a friend to be welcomed. If allowed to do its work, uncontaminated by pathology or a repressive environment, grief will flow of its own accord—naturally and automatically—toward its goal of fully restored health.

3. The Dynamics of Grief

"Separation anxiety, grief and mourning, and defenses are phases of a single process."[1]

John Bowlby

Suppose one day a parishioner comes into your office, a woman in her early fifties, always a strong church supporter. She is mildly depressed, listless, nostalgic and has a recurring sense of sadness that she can't quite put her finger on. She is confused, bewildered, and says, "Why do I feel this way? What is wrong with me? Am I going through the change of life again?" There are no obvious losses in her life. Nobody died. Nobody divorced. It was only last month that you married her youngest daughter to a fine Christian man. It was a grand occasion! Everyone was happy . . .

Like the above fictitious case, many people in our congregations are in a state of bereavement and do not know it. They have suffered one or more losses, but these events are too small to worry about or are not normally thought of as losses, so they do not recognize what they have been through. They cannot figure out why they seem more vulnerable to stress, more easily hurt, or more irritable with their family than usual. Other bereaved people may appear to be stressed, or to be "drinking more than usual," or to be more compulsive about their work. Grief is often camouflaged.

Grief can take a variety of forms, shapes and expressions. Grief has many faces. By helping parishioners to recognize their losses, we help them to begin to recognize their grief feelings as well. What a relief it is for many people to discover that they are "only grieving." Then by helping parishioners "talk out" these feelings in an atmosphere of understanding and acceptance, we facilitate their healing.

Obviously it is important that we learn to recognize grief's symptoms, its processes and the conditions that make for its healing.

THE MANY FACES OF GRIEF

The variety of losses is endless. So, too, the variety of individuals—their ages, life situations, personal histories and personalities—is endless. These "varieties" combine to make the many different faces of grief. Following are the major expressions of grief.

Tears and Sorrow

The most obvious and, in a sense, the easiest sign of grief's presence is sadness and sorrow. Grief is a function of pain. Pain hurts. What do people do when they are hurt? They cry. As the painful loss is realized, the human psyche recoils with a volatile release of energy. We weep. We wail. We lament. Tears are as associated with grief as laughter is with joy. The best medicine is to let them flow.

In our modern rational culture, crying is difficult for many people. We perceive crying to be a "weakness," "an embarrassment," or "an imposition on other people." Especially the open display of weeping in public is frowned upon. When we observe such weeping, it makes us feel uncomfortable. We find ourselves staring or avoiding such "displays." Sometimes this attitude is reinforced by a misuse of Scripture. Well-meaning Christians advise the bereaved, "Be strong in the Lord," or "Don't let yourself give in to pity." The assumption is made that grieving is a sign of a lack of faith. "If your faith was really strong enough," so the argument goes, "you would be so confident that your loved one is in heaven and happy with the Lord that you would not need to grieve. You would have nothing to be sad about." Such an assumption denies the reality of human pain, separated love and broken attachments. Jesus himself wept openly and publicly when he heard the news of the death of his friend Lazarus. The shortest verse in all Scripture comes in this passage which reads, "He wept" (Jn 8:14). This little verse, however, captures so pointedly the depth and sensitivity of Jesus' humanity. Curiously, too, Jesus also wept in the garden of Gethsemane as he anticipated his own betrayal, suffering and death. For

Jesus, faith was not the absence of sorrow, but the courage to be obedient unto the Father even in the face of death.

This culture has molded most men to resist crying. "Tears are a sign of weakness," so the masculine message goes, "and men are not supposed to be weak." I too tend to resist tears. Like most men—and maybe like most people—I experience a build-up of tears. Little sorrows or little hurts are stored up in what I call "my storehouse of tears." I carry this storehouse around daily. When it gets filled, I find myself much more sensitive than usual and much more vulnerable to crying. Little things will touch me deeply and start the tears flowing. It is as if I "needed a good cry," needed to empty my storehouse. Some people experience the same dynamic with laughter and say, after an extended belly-laugh, "I think I needed a good laugh."

Most people that I have talked to have a similar kind of storehouse and periodically they need to empty their load of tears. Because we don't release it often enough in this culture, we almost have to structure situations in which it is acceptable to cry. Sometimes I advise people who need help crying to go to a sentimental movie ("a real tearjerker") or listen to sad music. Invite yourself to empty your storehouse.

Stress

In recent years there has been a wealth of material written on stress.[2] Simply, stress is a physiological response to a perceived danger or threat. In such situations, our body automatically (autonomic nervous system) mobilizes us for action. This reaction includes several changes in body functions: adrenaline is pumped into the blood system; muscular tension increases as blood is transferred from other organs to the muscles and the limbs; blood pressure goes up; the heart rate increases; breathing becomes shallow and more rapid; there is an increase of sweating and an improvement in vision; and excess energy is mobilized as glycogen and is converted to sugar. This reaction, in total, has been labeled the "fight or flight" reaction, because all of these changes prepare the body to fight or to flee. In either case, we are prepared for action.

This fight or flight syndrome has served humans well, particularly in earlier eons, when our survival depended on our ability to quickly mobilize our physical resources. The dangers of modern technological civilization usually do not require such strenuous physical activity. Yet, many varied situations—such as job insecurity and marital discord—can be causes for stress. The body mobilizes for action, but there is no action to do. So it is that prolonged threatening situations create a state of perpetual stress. We cannot remain in a state of readiness without "wearing out" the body's resources and organs. The connection between various physical ailments and chronic stress is well documented.

A major loss or even the threat of a loss is also occasion for alarm. The more vital the attachment, the more threatening the loss and the more stressful the response. "A woman who loses her husband," writes Parkes, "has good cause for alarm. Not only has she lost a source of protection, but she is likely to be exposed to novel situations in her new role as a widow, for which she may be quite unprepared . . . . It will hardly surprise us to find her showing signs of alarm."[3] Extensive empirical research by Parkes and others have documented this connection between grief and stress. During the first few months of conjugal bereavement, widows show signs of increased restlessness, muscle tension, a high state of arousal, loss of appetite and insomnia. It is little wonder that there is a general increased frequency of illness in all forms during these mourning periods.

Symptoms are even more overt in situations where grief is anticipatory in nature. A woman, for example, who is on the verge of losing her job for a full year is in a chronic state of alarm. She anticipates this loss and is perpetually preparing for it. Similarly, the family who watches their loved one die a slow death is also in a prolonged state of stress. There is much in the stress research that is applicable to bereavement. Stress is a good sign that one is either grieving or anticipating a loss.

The close connection between loss events, bereavement and physical health have been studied by many scholars.[4] Reed and Lutkinds found that during the first year of bereavement, the death rate among widowed people was 12.2 percent versus only 1.2 percent in the controlled group of the same age, sex and stress factors.[5] In another study of 4,486 widowers over the age of fifty-four, Michael Young and his colleagues discovered that during the first six months of bereavement, the death rate of these men was almost forty percent higher than that of married men the same age.[6] After a review of several of these studies, Parkes concludes:

> I accept the evidence that bereavement can affect physical health, and that complaints of somatic anxiety symptoms, headaches, digestive upsets and rheumatism are likely, particularly in widows and widowers of middle age. Finally there are certain potentially fatal conditions such as coronary thrombosis, blood cancers and cancer of the neck of the womb, which seem in some cases to be precipitated or aggravated by major losses.[7]

The connection link between bereavement and physical ailments is stress. Bereavement, like all kinds of major losses, is stressful. Grief and stress are closely related.

If nothing else, this link underscores the importance of a pastor's work with the bereaved. In a very real sense, pastoral care of the bereaved is preventive medicine. We are the physician's ally. Our ability to recognize stress symptoms in bereavement and to mitigate these symptoms through effective pastoral care will greatly influence our congregation's physical as well as mental health.

Anger

The presence of anger or hostility in the normal grief process has been documented by nearly every researcher in the field of bereavement. Rather than being understood as a sign of abnormal grief, anger seems to be a normal part of the grieving process. Dr. Elisabeth Kübler-Ross observed in her work with terminally ill patients that anger was so prevalent that she characterized it as one of "the stages" in the grief process.[8] She called it the "Why me?" stage. Whenever we have been deprived, we feel angry. This anger can be expressed as self-recrimination, guilt, general irritability, revenge, over-aggressiveness, depression and even rage. Anger can also be sprayed—shotgun style—at everyone and everything in sight.

Unlike many emotions, anger has the ability to be displaced. All anger has a target or targets. We are always angry *at* someone or something. Yet, we often get our targets confused and displace our angry feelings onto objects at which we are not really mad. Most of us are familiar with this dynamic. We have a bad day at work and come home to yell at our children or to pick on our spouse. This displacement dynamic is complicated in bereavememt. Whom do you get mad at when your mother has just died of cancer? Whom do you get angry with when a fire has destroyed your home of eighteen years? Many people blame the doctors who failed to save mother, or the firemen who didn't come soon enough, or the in-laws who "never liked me anyhow," or the insurance company that is too slow in processing our claim, or the funeral director who charges too much, or the pastor who didn't show enough respect to mother, or, yes, they can even be angry at themselves.

Health care professionals and attorneys who work with people in loss situations are well aware of the anger that the next of kin can mistakenly displace onto them. Many a malpractice lawsuit has been filed and fueled by the anger of a grieving family. Many an act of revenge can best be understood as an expression of grief feelings. Many a custody fight in divorce court has been fought not so much on the basis of "what is best for the children" as on the basis of "how I can get even with my spouse." Angry feelings are a part of grief.

There are two targets for anger in grief that are especially difficult to deal with for most people. First, there is anger at the deceased. If your husband divorced you, it is relatively easy to get mad at him for leaving you or for his various assorted offenses. If your husband has died, however, he is more difficult to be angry with. After all, "it wasn't his fault . . . ." After all, "you are supposed to be sorrowful . . . ." After all, "at least you are alive." Yet many widows, in fact, do feel some anger at their deceased spouse—for drinking himself to death . . . for not watching when crossing the busy street . . . or for not spending any time with the children. These kinds of thoughts are normal. At any given moment in our lives, we have various little resentments that "bug us" about each family member. After the loss of that person, these angers and others can surface in our grief. Pastors can do widowed people a service by helping them to articulate their anger and by reassuring them that angry feelings are acceptable.

The other target that is hard to be angry with is God. Whom do you get angry at for a fire that destroys your house? Or for cancer that robs your teenager of a full life? Or for a flood that levels your church? Are not these events called "acts of God"? Yet it is difficult to be angry with God. We unconsciously or consciously fear that God will punish us further if we blame the Divine. Do we feel we are hurting God's feelings or that anger is not a part of faith? Job, of course, loved God deeply, but he lashed out bitterly at his Lord for the ills and tragedies of his life. For him, anger was a part of faith and his on-going living relationship with his Redeemer. Again, pastors can do their parishioners a valuable service by helping them to find the right target for their anger. If they are indeed angry at God, so be it. Why not join them in lifting up that anger in prayer?

The intensity of a person's anger in bereavement will vary according to the type of loss, the personality of the griever, and so on. Certain kinds of losses tend to magnify the anger component of the grief process. Anger is magnified in losses that are tragic, like a child who is cut down in the prime of life. Anger can be severe following divorces where the loss is compounded by years of bitterness, destructiveness and betrayal. Anger can also be intense in any loss situation that appears "unfair." "That's not fair Mommy," protests a child at age five. From our earliest years, we assume that life is fair. So when life does not seem fair, we protest.

Anger is hard for pastors and other care givers of the bereaved to deal with. When people are filled with anger and rage, they are unpleasant to be around. It is easy for us to take it personally. It is easy to get caught in their web. It's almost as if they are looking for something to fight with . . . and we are it. Yet it is important for clergy to hear their people's anger. We need not rush in to defend God or the church or even the deceased. Angry feelings do not necessarily mean a lack of faith. The most healing thing that we can do is to just listen to our people's feelings.

Depression

Since the time of Freud, psychiatrists and psychologists have debated the causes and treatment of depression. Aaron Beck summarized this discussion in a helpful way in his book, *Depression: Clinical, Experimental and Theoretical Aspects.* He notes that one way of understanding depression is by classifying depression according to its etiology or "its degree of reactivity to external events."[9] Exogenous or reactive depression is depression caused primarily by some external event. Endogenous or autonomous depression is thought to have its origins "inside" the person in chemical, physiological or psychiatric dysfunctions. On a theory level the distinction is a debatable one, but on a practical level it is often a helpful one for lay people in psychology, including pastors, to understand. What is clear is that there is a certain type of depression that is reactive in nature, associated with and linked to loss events. By implication, reactive depression is thought of as temporary in nature. Theoretically, when the triggering loss event is adjusted to, the depression will pass. If, however, depression does not pass in a reasonable period of time, the depression may be of the endogenous variety. Some people have a history of depression that predates a major loss. Such people are likely to experience an intensifying of depression in bereavement: the normal incident of depression plus their usual weakness for it. It seems clear that loss events can trigger periods of depression—to some extent in all of us and to a greater extent in people who have a tendency toward depression to start with. Depression is a normal part of the grief-growth process.

What exactly is depression? The standard clinical definition of depression which dates back to Freud's work is that depression is best understood as internalized anger. Depressed people almost universally don't like themselves. Self-reproach and self-hatred are common themes. Even when anger should be realistically expressed at some external object, the depressed person blames himself or herself. They turn their anger inward. A good rule of thumb in counseling depressed people then is to ask them, sometimes repeatedly so, "What are you angry about?" or "Who are you angry at?" Helping people acknowledge their anger, appropriately express their anger and clarify the right target for their anger usually goes a long way to relieve depression.

Another helpful distinction that is sometimes made is between depression and despair. These terms are often used interchangeably, but I for one, based on my own clinical experience, believe that they are distinctive emotions. Depression, as noted, is usually defined and experienced as "internalized anger." Despair, on the other hand, can be defined as hopelessness. They are indeed similar emotions in mood and appearance. They are both reactive in nature, but despair is future oriented, whereas depression is past oriented. In despair, the future seems dark, pointless and without meaning. In depression, the past is unfinished, still coloring the present.

Glenn Davidson in his book *Living With Dying* calls despair "the abandonment of hope."[10] The despairing person gives up on life. He or she is apathetic, listless, and without direction or energy. Despair is closely associated with a loss of faith and a sense of being abandoned by God. Despair is therefore more overtly a spiritual problem or, if you will, a spiritual disease. The absence of hope is a key element in despair. Hope is essentially a religious quality, closely linked to a person's ability to have faith. I agree then with Roy Fairchild that the primary purpose of pastoral care with despairing people is "the recovery of hope." He writes:

> The kind of hope needed by the depressed person (he confuses the terms) enables him to say 'Yes' to life, to believe that it is always possible to imagine another way to go. Such hope sees reality as open ended and having resources as yet undiscovered and untapped. Certainty may be lacking, but he has the courage to act 'as if it existed.'[11]

This is hope and the kind of hope that the despairing person has lost.

Both depression and despair are direct contributors to suicide. Some people take their own life as an ultimate expression of self-hatred and self-rejection (depressive feelings). Others commit suicide because they have lost all hope (despairing feelings). Either way, the connection between depression/despair and suicide is strong. This link between bereavement and suicide has been well documented. The suicide rates for widowed people during the first year of bereavement are dramatically higher than for non-bereaved people of the same age and status.[12] Suicide is the third ranking cause of death in widowed men.[13] Among divorced people, Durkheim reported that the suicide rate is four times that of married people.[14] In another study of seriously suicidal patients, it was found that ninety-five percent of them had suffered the death or loss of an individual closely related to them under dramatic circumstances.[15] These studies have all isolated the more obvious types of losses: death and divorce. I suspect, as many of my colleagues do, that the cumulative effect of many little losses is also a major contributing factor in some suicides. Maurice Farber in his *Theory of Suicide* has called suicide "a disease of hope" and listed hopelessness as the key element in suicide's etiology.[16] He goes on to say that hope is a function of both situation and competence. A person's suicide potential is related both to the situation (loss event) and to the person's capacity to deal effectively with that situation. Yet for many people that necessary ego strength is also diminished during periods of bereavement. Thus the bereaved, particularly those with strong components of depression/despair, are greater potential suicide candidates than their non-bereaved peers.

Guilt

Another significant emotion that is almost universally present in the grief process is guilt. After any major loss, the bereaved comb the events leading to that loss, looking to reassure themselves that all was done that could have been done to prevent the loss. Questions like, "What if . . . ?" and "If only I had . . . " can haunt them. These questions are normal and inevitable. Most people who study bereavement report that such tendencies to feel guilty are common. The intensity of guilt varies depending on the person and the circumstances of the loss. Guilt feelings can take many forms and expressions. We may recognize guilt by such behaviors as self-punishment, self-justifying behavior, ritualized obsessions, depression, over-compensation, ostentatious funerals or undue hostility. There are countless examples of each of these expressions.

In a sense, anger and guilt are companion emotions in grieving. Anger is the reverse side of guilt. Grieving people can flip back and forth between the two feelings, depending on whom they determine to be responsible for their loss. Anger blames some other person or events for the loss—"They are responsible!" Conversely, in guilt the grieving person blames himself or herself—"I am responsible!" In reality, there is a continuum of responsibility between the two extremes: the survivor being one hundred percent responsible and the survivor having no responsibility for the loss.[17]

Generally, normal guilt is guilt feelings that arise when we have done something or neglected to do something for which we feel we were responsible. Neurotic guilt is feeling guilt for events or things for which we have no responsibility. Guilt assumes responsibility. The neurotic feels responsible for the loss. Neurotic guilt is also feeling guilty way out of proportion to the degree of responsibility. Neurotic guilt has its roots in a life script or type of personality wherein the person "needs to feel guilty." Both types of guilt can be activated by and present in any major loss.

Most major losses involve a mixture of responsibility and, therefore, a mixture of guilt feelings. Consider the marriage that dissolved after eighteen years. Sure, he may have been the one who actually filed for the divorce, or she may have been the one who actually moved out first, but how can anyone say "It's his fault" or "She's to blame." No doubt there were hundreds if not thousands of occasions over those eighteen years of marriage where the eventual fate of the relationship was determined. What judge can say who is the guilty party or who is the innocent party? Responsibility is more complex and subtle than that judgment could indicate. Both are "at fault" because both had responsibility for what happened.

In most major losses, like the dissolution of a marriage, it is a very difficult task to sort out the normal from the neurotic guilt. Amid the intense pain of a loss, it is easy to get the facts distorted. It is easy to blame others too much or not enough. It is easy to blame oneself too much or not enough. Doctors, friends and other eye-witnesses to the loss can be very helpful at this point. The bereaved seek out such people in order to "check out" their perceptions and memories. Such friends do their grieving friends a disservice by giving them platitudes and soft-pedaled information, reinforcing their tendency to blame or dismiss their responsibility. Grieving people have an honest need to sort out the facts and thereby understand their relative responsibility.

How can pastors be helpful? First, we can help the bereaved sort out their relative responsibility and, therefore, help them sort out what are normal guilt feelings and what are neurotic guilt feelings. This is an important task—to clarify, classify, listen to the bereaved's perceptions of the loss event. Second, we can mitigate forgiveness. All losses carry some element of real responsibility and, therefore, some element of real guilt. It may be big sins, such as having cheated on one's spouse—leading to the loss of the marriage—or "little" sins, such as sloppy workmanship—leading to the loss of one's job. The pastoral response to real guilt should be to encourage and assist people to openly confess their sins to God and to accept God's forgiveness. They need also to confess their sins, seek forgiveness and make restitution to others. Third, those people who are neurotically guilty should be encouraged to identify the underlying issues that give rise to such a need to feel guilty. Make sure that bad theology does not play a role in that pathology, such as in the case of the man who believes that God has punished him for his sins through the death of his wife. Repetitive or intense neurotic guilt should be referred to a mental health professional for treatment.

THE PROCESS OF GRIEF

In spite of the wide variety of grief symptoms, scholars in the area of bereavement are almost universally agreed on one fact: grief is a process. Like any process, grief has a starting point (the loss/separation), a series of successive "stages," and an ending point (restoration/recovery). In this way, grief is different from most other mental or physical illness which have one set of symptoms that rise and fall in intensity and basically remain the same set of symptoms throughout the course of the disease. In contrast, grief is not a single state that is clearly recognizable from moment to moment, but a dynamic, changing process, more varied and complex in its many forms than any single emotion could ever be. While it is frustrating to scholars who attempt to study this ever-changing pattern, the process character of grief can offer hope to the griever. Toward the end of his personal diary of grief, C.S. Lewis poetically captures the process nature of his inner journey with these words:

> I thought I could describe a state; make a map of sorrow. Sorrow, however, turns out to be not a state, but a process. It needs not a map but a history . . . .There is something new to be chronicled every day. Grief is like a long valley, a winding valley where any bend may reveal a totally new landscape.[18]

Even in grief, which is often such a painful and agonizing emotion, there is a sense of a hidden growth potential. While grieving, one feels as though he or she is on a journey—hopefully, a journey toward wholeness.

Most professionals who study bereavement also agree that the grief process varies widely according to a number of factors. Those factors include: the manner of loss, the intensity of attachment feelings to that which is lost, the griever's social and cultural milieu, the resources available to the griever, the mourner's typical grieving pattern in the past, and the length of and opportunity for anticipatory grief. Each of these factors will influence the duration of the grief process, its dominant expressions, the presence and type of defense mechanisms employed and the relative intensity of various "stages." For example, a death by suicide tends to increase the intensity of guilt in the grieving survivors. The bereaved loved ones of such a person inevitably wonder, "What did I do wrong?" "Could I have prevented it?" or "Why did he or she hate us so?" A sudden, unexpected death of a vital family member tends to increase the elements of shock and anger in contrast to the gradual expected death of an older member of the same family. These two kinds of death experiences are totally different, and so their grief processes also can be so different. Every loss and every individual mourner is unique. So everyone's grief process is different in intensity, character and flow.

When Does Grief Start?

If grief is a process, then it must have a starting point. Simply stated, grief begins at the first awareness of loss. For people who suffer sudden loss, that starting point is obvious. Sudden losses can be so unexpected that the person's first reaction is shock. In the face of extreme pain, the psyche recoils. One is temporarily anesthetized, stunned, dazed. It has been described as being in a trance or even mildly drunk. "The necessity for shock in early grief," says Bernadine Kries, "can be compared to someone in pain who 'passed out.' It is nature's way of protecting him from unbearable pain."[19]

One's first awareness of loss also can pre-date the actual loss. In such cases, grieving begins in anticipation of the loss. This is a relatively common phenomenon. In a sense, we are always anticipating one loss or another in our lives. Anticipatory grief can be quite intense, as in the case of a loved one who dies a slow, lingering death. The next of kin begin their grief work at the first realization that their loved one will die. Anticipatory grief also can be quite prolonged and subtle, as in the case of a family who begins anticipating a major relocation six months prior to the actual move. In any event, the principle seems valid: grief begins with the first awareness of loss.

The Stages of Grief

Because grief is a process, it has been very tempting and at times very logical to view grief as a series of stages. Kübler-Ross in her famous book *On Death and Dying* probably popularized the concept of stages. She counted five stages: denial, anger, bargaining, depression and acceptance.[20] Other writers, including many in the pastoral care field, have followed with differing lists of the stages that the "average" griever goes through in the course of bereavement. Granger Westburg in his little book *Good Grief* listed ten steps: shock, expression of emotion, depression, physical symptoms of distress, panic, guilt, anger, immobilization, hope and affirmation of reality.[21] In an early work, Wayne Oates poetically described six stages: "the shocking blow of grief," "the numbing effect of the shock," "the struggle between fantasy and reality," "the break-through of a flood of grief," "selective memory and stabbing pain," and "the acceptance of loss and affirmation of life."[22] In a more contemporary book, entitled *Facing Death*, ex-priest/psychologist Robert Kavanaugh listed these stages: shock, disorganization, volatile emotions, guilt, loss and loneliness, relief and reestablishment.[23]

The trouble with all of these longer lists of stages is that they are often like mixing apples and oranges. Many of these so-called stages occur simultaneously and out of order. Most people who have lived through intense grief can confirm that the grief process is not so simple, sequential or as easily identifiable. Everything is all mixed up. One often "takes two steps forward, and one back," or as Wayne Oates later put it, "Feelings are not respectors of categories."[24] Many of the above-mentioned writers have since repented of their structured stages.

Researchers who have worked with the empirical studies of grief and bereavement, especially in more recent years, tend to favor a three or four stage pattern of the grief process. John Bowlby suggests that there are three stages: (1) urge to recover lost object (weeping and anger), (2) despair (later called disorganization) and (3) "reorganization directed towards a new object."[25] Colin Murray Parkes' stages are: (1) numbness, (2) yearning, (3) disorganization and despair and (4) reorganization.[26] His scheme closely parallels Bowlby's as the two men share a common theoretical model. These shorter lists of stages are more general and, therefore, more accurate and also, therefore, less usable.

What is useful about these attempts to list grief's stages is that the lists have served as "markers" and guidelines for many grieving people. When bereaved persons begin to feel intensely angry and physically distressed, they can reassure themselves with the knowledge that this was a part of the process. "This was stage six," one might say. "This is a sign that I am normal. I shall not worry." In this sense, stage lists can be very pastoral.

The Wave Dynamic

All of the discussion about the stages of grief has functioned to obscure one of the more obvious features of grief, that is, grief comes in waves. The subtleties of this dynamic were brought to light initially by Erich Lindemann in his study of the survivors of the Coconut Grove fire. Lindemann described grief's process as a series of "waves lasting from twenty minutes to an hour at a time . . . ."[27] Most grieving people, particularly those who have suffered through an acute grief reaction, will liken their pain to the rise and fall of waves hitting against the shore. A wave of pain overwhelms them with anguish and uncontrollable weeping, only to recede again. "Then sometime later," grievers will say, "a friend will say something, or something else will happen that reminds me of my loss, and suddenly all the pain comes flooding back again."

The griever's suffering is never constant. The waves of pain are alternated by lulls of momentary rest. Initially, of course, in acute grief situations the waves are intense and frequent. Gradually, as one is healed the waves are less intense, less prolonged and less frequent. One can almost imagine the wave patterns charted on a graph, like radio waves. Each peak represents a mountain of pain, each valley a restful lull. Initially, the peaks are high and long, the valleys are narrow and short, and the frequency is high. Slowly, the peaks mellow, the valleys lengthen and the frequency decreases. Gradually, ever so gradually, the storm quiets. Yet months and years later an isolated wave can still come crashing ashore. On sentimental holidays, for example, the memories of lost loved ones are often raw. "Every Christmas," says a widowed, middle-aged woman, "after all the busyness is over, I sit down and have a good cry." Periodically, an isolated wave of grief washes against the shore of one's soul.

Atypical Grief

The terms "abnormal grief" or "pathological grief" are problematic at best. During the renewed interest in death and bereavement in the last twenty years, there have been many attempts to distinguish between abnormal and normal grief or between healthy and pathological grief reactions. Each attempt has been less than satisfying. There are so many cultural and individual variations to grief that it is difficult to say what is normal and what is not. In recent years, the focus has shifted from "pathological grief" to "abnormal grief" and then to "atypical grief." The whole issue of what is healthy grief and what is not is an ambiguous one to grasp. Yet, the issue remains an extremely practical one because front-line care-givers, like pastors, need some criteria to assist them to be able to identify when a person is not grieving well.

The concept of grief as a process is helpful in providing criteria between normal and abnormal grief. Normal grief can be understood as a movement through the grief process. Conversely, abnormal grief can be defined as "getting stuck" or "fixated" at one particular phase of the grief process. The key distinction between the two is *process*. If bereaved persons are moving through their grief process, no matter how bizarre the various components might be, then they are probably "normal." On the other hand, if bereaved persons are not moving through the process and appear stuck indefinitely at one phase, then they are probably in need of professional or medical intervention.

One of the key variables then is timing. Denial would be normal within the first days of a severe bereavement, but if a person was still denying the reality of his or her loss several months later, then his or her grief could be termed "pathological." Anger is a normal and inevitable component of most people's grief process, but if a bereaved person was stuck in his or her anger months—even years—later, then his or her grief is abnormal. Similarly, identification behavior would be normal within the first few months following a significant loss, but in time identification, like other defense mechanisms, should gradually loosen and give way to a more full acceptance of reality. The key criterion of grief's normalcy is *process*. As long as a person is moving through the process, then he or she is in the process of healing. The key determination is the moving picture, not the still picture.

One way to understand the role of a care-giver is as a facilitator of the bereaved person's process. You or I are there to make sure that "they keep moving." In a sense, we are the sheepdog that roams around the herd, braking, pushing, leading, catching strays—in short, keeping the herd moving in its appointed direction. As long as bereaved parishioners are moving, then their grief process is probably within normal limits. When they become fixated, then the healing process is arrested. They are stuck. They could remain stuck for years (as some people do). At that point professional or medical assistance is warranted. Most mental health clinics, accredited pastoral counseling centers or psychiatrists can be of assistance in this regard.

How Long Does Grief Take?

The answer to this question, of course, is that there is no average length. Grief has no prescribed timetable. There are people with seemingly minor losses that go on grieving for years. Their attachment to that which they lost was very intense and/or there are "other issues" that have contaminated and delayed their grief process. There are also people with seemingly major losses who recover rapidly. In such situations their attachment to that which was lost was relatively minor and/or they had an opportunity to do some anticipatory grieving that gave them a "head start" on their eventual adjustment.

In general, most people that I have cared for and worked with underestimate the length and severity of their bereavement. Most people expect to be over their grief "by now." This expectation seems to be a part of the general cultural impatience with suffering and pain. We want an instant cure. I can recount story after story of bereaved people who have come to me within a few weeks after their loss saying, "There must be something I can do to get over this, Doctor. Can you give me a shot, some pills? Do something, will you?" My response to this type of demand, of course, is that there is nothing I can do. Grieving takes time. Grieving is painful. Each person's grief has its own schedule. The only way to shorten the process is actually to thrust oneself further into the process, into the pain and agony. The more one "gets into it," the easier and quicker the process will be completed.

Many religious traditions, like the Jewish mourning period of one full year, recognize that mourning is not over until the first year anniversary of the loved one's death. Dr. Herman Feifel, an early writer in the area of death and bereavement, has frequently supported the idea of one full year for the mourning of the death of a significant other.[28] In our culture, which tends to short-change and deny the importance of grief, such statements are a helpful counterbalance. People need to grieve a lot longer than our culture normally would expect. I am frequently advising divorced and widowed adults not to rush into any new intimate relationships for at least one full year. This advice is very hard for people who are lonely, dependent and grieving to hear. The temptation is to "grab the first man (or the first woman) that comes along." This is often a fatal mistake, resulting in future marital unhappiness and a possible sequential divorce. As a general rule of thumb, the loss of a significant loved one requires a full year of grieving before one can be said to be fully "recovered."

When Is Grief Finished?

Grievers are finished with their griefwork when they can remember clearly that which is lost without pain. The tendency to idealize the deceased fades away. Similarly, a tendency to be overly bitter and angry fades too. They can now remember both the good and the bad of what is lost and accept "what was as what had to be." They are at peace with the past. Their emotional capital has been freed from its attachment to that which is lost. As this freeing gradually occurs, that energy becomes available for new attachments. Gradually, grievers are able to invest themselves again into new relationships, new identities, new roles, new jobs, new dreams and new commitments. The ability to "love again" is one sign that the bereaved are nearing full recovery. As people heal, they begin to be more future oriented. The future which had looked so dim now looks hopeful again. Instead of resisting the future, they begin to embrace the future. This embracing of the future is made possible by a "letting go" of the past.

THE HEALING ENVIRONMENT

Every mourner has heard the traditional saying that "Time heals all wounds." There is some truth to this adage, but any serious study of grief indicates that there is also mistruth. The simple passage of time alone does not heal wounds—either physical wounds or emotional wounds. There is a natural grieving process that seeks to heal the person's emotional wounds, but this process needs a healthy environment in which to do its work. The process can be blocked, contaminated or delayed—temporarily or even permanently. Time alone will not heal, but what one does with time can.

What is a healthy grief environment like? Research scholarship over the past thirty years has supported the conclusion that the single most important factor is the individual's free and full expression of his or her grief feelings. "Successful management," writes researchers Caroff and Dobrof, "appears to be associated initially with the ability . . . to experience emotionally the reality of the loss and to find some means of expressing the feelings engendered."[29] In contrast the more we deny, avoid, delay or repress our grief, the more blocked, drawn out and eventually painful the grief work will be.

Switzer, who is very familiar with the extensive research on this topic, draws this conclusion in his book on *The Minister as Crisis Counselor*:

> It is difficult to avoid the conclusion that early full grieving, the overt exhibiting of emotional behavior, produces a reduction in later symptoms of disturbance, while the repression or covering up of initial affects leads to a greater severity of those feelings when they finally do emerge.[30]

If grief feelings are not allowed to be expressed in typical overt ways, grief will seek covert expressions as physical ailments, depression, nervousness or insomnia. Our choice is not whether to grieve or not to grieve. Our only choice is how we wish to grieve. Do we want our pain quick and intense or long and lingering?

The classic works of Lindemann and Kübler-Ross have also supported this conclusion. The latter author especially has emphasized the dangers of permanent or chronic denial. Grief cannot begin until the death/loss is fully emotionally realized. Permanent or chronic denial of the reality of death only inhibits that process and thereby blocks growth. There are many willing or unwilling accessories to this atmosphere of denial. Modern American civilization goes to great lengths to deny the reality of death and pain. Specifically, the funeral industry has received bitter attacks over the years for its tendency to cover up the reality of death in the name of "protecting our loved ones." The medical professions have also received criticism for the common practice of immediately administering sedatives or tranquilizers to the bereaved upon first receiving the news of the death of a loved one.[31] The assumption that by protecting people from pain we are doing them a service is false and the truth may be even to the contrary. Kübler-Ross proposes that instead of sedatives, hospitals provide a "screaming room," where the bereaved could go immediately upon hearing the news of their loss to give free license to their natural emotions.[32] Such a procedure is based upon a different assumption: that by facing one's pain and giving expression to one's grief, the grief process is facilitated and growth maximized.

Another false assumption that is often made is that feelings are bad and in particular that negative feelings are bad. We should avoid, delay, suppress and certainly not admit that we have negative feelings. In bereavement the opposite assumption is made: that grief feelings are natural, inevitable and morally neutral. As noted earlier in this chapter, there is a full range of feelings associated with bereavement. Every one of them is fully natural and normal in its context. The healthiest attitude to have is one of acceptance toward all human feelings whatever they are. Such an attitude of acceptance will facilitate healing, no matter how tragic or terrible a loss might have been. In the introduction of her book on bereavement in children, Eda LeShan summarizes her extensive experience with this observation:

> What we have found is that families who try to run away from their feelings suffer longer and often never recover from their grief. Families who face their loss and all the feelings that go with it, who learn to accept all of the normal stages of grief human beings seem to need to go through, become stronger and are able to begin to go on growing and living full and satisfying lives.[33]

Successful grieving is based on an assumption that feelings are best accepted and appropriately expressed. By doing so, negative feelings are released and we are freed from the destructive power of negative feelings to control, infect and disturb our lives.

Facing one's grief and the pain therein is not always an easy task. Most humans initially recoil from pain, especially the severe pain of a sudden and tragic loss of a loved one. Grief, however, is one of those situations in which "the only way out is through." Yet, going through often takes great courage and faith. Roy and Jane Nichols, funeral directors, believe that in grief "our choice is only to permit pain to be experienced fast and hard or to be experienced slow and hard; that's our only choice.''[34] They tell the story of the young parents of a one-year-old Mongoloid child, Keith, who after painfully adjusting to their son's condition, and learning to love him, suddenly lost him to a ''swift invasion of pneumonia.'' They chose to take their grief ''hard and fast,'' because with a second baby on the way, they had about six weeks to resolve their grief and get ready to love a new child. The key was active participation in the funeral process. They spent hours with Keith's body prior to the funeral, held the casket during the service and carried ''little Keith'' to the grave site. The story continues:

> Rob and Sue on their knees at the grave slowly, spontaneously, without prior intent, placed Keith's body and casket into the grave, and carefully began to pull dirt into the grave. The astute minister said only, 'I think the kids need some help.' Forty friends passed along the dirt, handful by handful, with no shovels, until the grave was filled.[35]

These young parents chose to thrust themselves totally into their pain and grief. By doing so, they accelerated their grief work and maximized their growth.

The key criterion for a healing environment is attitude—an attitude of acceptance and openness to human feelings and human pain. People who are comfortable with their feelings are natural grievers and natural grief facilitators. People who are uncomfortable with their own feelings will grieve only with great anguish, pain and resistance. If we are to be effective pastoral care givers and agents of God's healing, we must be people who are comfortable with all sorts of human emotions. To be so comfortable with the emotions of others, we must first be comfortable with our own emotions. We must acknowledge, accept and freely share our own sorrow.

Grief emotions are typically strong emotions. Expressions of crying, anger, depression and guilt can be very powerful and even frightening if one is not used to them. If we are uncomfortable around strong emotions, our very presence is going to inhibit the griever's free and full release of those emotions. Ministering to the bereaved is hard work. It is painful, emotionally exhausting and time-consuming. Not everyone or even every pastor is able to do it well. It requires that we be comfortable with the strong emotions—those of others and those of ourselves.

The general attitude of this culture is that of the denial of death and the avoidance of pain. Suffering is un-American and un-Christian in some congregations. This generalized attitude combines with individual attitudes, preferences and personal histories to make many bereaved people reluctant, fearful and resistive to openly expressing their pain. Yet, clearly their health and healing would be maximized if they could. We pastors must be able to give these people "permission" to grieve. We must invite them, encourage them and even lure them to share their sorrow.

This permission-giving must be more than just words. Sometimes people say, "Come on, grieve," but by their attitude, non-verbal communication and mood, they say, "Don't you dare break down in my presence! I can't handle it." We often communicate a subtle message to the bereaved, that it is not appropriate to grieve. Such "communications" block the bereaved from grieving. Instead we must communicate an openness to feelings and to grief feelings in particular. Openness is crucial. Only with it can we establish a healing environment in which grief and growth are both possible.

Conclusion

Many bereaved people that I have known personally over the years have likened bereavement to a journey through a long, dark tunnel. Their analogy in an apt summary and conclusion to this chapter. The darkness of the tunnel is grief's pain and anguish. The light at the end of the tunnel is their new life. They were fond of exhorting each other, "The only way out is through." This means that the only way to get over grief is to enter into it. The pain must be faced directly. One cannot avoid the tunnel; neither can it be delayed indefinitely. The only way out *is* through.

The most healthful approach to grief is to fully enter into it, into the tunnel. The painful, raw emotions must be processed, and as we do so, we pass through the tunnel. One must keep moving. Don't get stuck anywhere along the way. The temptation is always to go back or to cling to the walls and remain in the darkness indefinitely. Keep moving. Keep processing. In the darkness there will be a few signposts to mark the way; we call these lights "stages." In addition, there will be fellow travelers with whom we will share our pain and sorrow and so speed each other along our way.

In time, the light at the end of the tunnel grows larger and larger; the darkness of pain recedes ever so gradually. Finally there comes a time when we can say, "I think I am through it." Now, in the light of a new day, we can look back at our journey and agree, yes, the only way out *was* through.

4. Grief and Growth

"Two of the best kept secrets of the twentieth century are that everyone suffers and that suffering can be used for growth . . . ."[1]

Lawrence LeShan

At first glance, grief and growth appear to be unrelated, opposite experiences. Grief is associated with loss and loss by definition is a negative event. No one likes to lose a loved one, a job or a valued possession. Few of us would ever seek out a loss. No one wants to cry. In contrast, growth is ordinarily conceived of in positive terms. Especially when growth is put in terms of "personal growth," it is something desirable. We like to grow. Growth is something that many people do seek after. Yet, when we put the two words together—loss and growth—somehow they do not seem related. Seldom do we consider that loss can trigger growth or that growth implies loss.

Bereavement can be a time of tremendous growth and creativity. Some of the finest works of art and literary endeavors have been born out of suffering. Many of the greatest music compositions by Bach, Mozart, Schubert and others were born out of personal loss and focused on themes of loss/death. Some of the great philosophical systems of all times have been born out of or built around loss, such as those of Montaigne, Schopenhauer and Kierkegaard. Viktor Frankl and Alfred Alder both built psychological systems around the central importance of loss, termination and death in human existence. One needs only read the collected poems of any great poet to find the recurring themes of loss, grief and death. Myths, fairy tales, stories and fables have been created partially as a means of making sense out of loss and suffering. Artistic expression can be a channel through which the author can "work out" his or her grief.

65

The dynamics of this connection between bereavement and creativity has to do with the interplay between structure and chaos. On the behavioral level, people form habits, routines, accustomed ways of doing things. Similarly on a mental-emotional level, people form mental structures. Losses are events that rupture these mental structures. Suddenly all of the old structures, old attachments, old ideas and routines are disrupted. Structure is replaced by chaos. The essence of grief is a striving to restructure life. In bereavement, people endeavor to put life "back together." George J. Seidel of Notre Dame University says that "creativity and growth are a reordering of restructuring of chaos."[2] Creativity is the act of putting the raw experience together in a different way. Chaos is necessary for creativity. The cycle is: structure—loss—chaos—restructuring.

Loss events activate imagination and imagination is the source of creativity. The activation of imagination triggers creativity. Therefore, Gregory Rochlin suggests, "Creativity does not depend upon peace and quiet, or affluence and optimism. Nor is it a restricted function exclusive to the gifted. It is basically part of the psychology of discontent and the striving to overcome it."[3] Loss triggers the unconscious striving to restore loss, which in turn opens up the floodgates of creativity and growth. It has been said: "Necessity is the mother of invention." We might reword this cliché to read, "Bereavement is the mother of growth."

DEFINING GROWTH

Growth is a generalized term. Like the words "life" or "love," the word "growth" is used to cover a multitude of experiences. When people say, "I have grown," they may mean, "I am a year older," or "I have gained weight," or "I am a better person," or "I am experiencing the world differently," or "I have changed," or, even, "I have not changed for once." The term growth is employed in some confusing and even contradictory ways. We must begin our discussion of grief and growth with some definitions for "growth."

Growth Is Change

For purposes of our discussion, growth is change. One cannot grow without changing. If one says, "I have grown," something must be different. Like those advertisements for weight loss, there must be a clear contrast between the "before and after" pictures. When people suffer a severe loss, they are psychologically wounded. Grief is the process of healing that wound. When the grief process is completed, people say of the bereaved that they have "recovered," "been restored," or healed. These words imply that they have returned to being the same people that they were before the loss. Indeed others might say, "Gee, Susan is her old self again." Yet, many grievers will tell us that they are not just recovered or healed in the sense of being the way they were prior to the loss. On the contrary, they have grown in the process of being healed. There are unmistakable new elements in their life—new skills, new attitudes, new relationships and new insights. They are "new" people, different from the way they were prior to the loss. To the extent that they are different, we can say that they have grown. Growth means change.

Growth Is Change in a Health-Oriented Direction

The terrible, but obvious, fact that must be acknowledged is that not everyone grows as a result of a loss. Some people do not grow. They seem never to get over the loss, never to recover. They remain psychologically crippled for years, consumed by bitterness, nostalgia or deep sorrow. In a sense, such people have also changed as a result of their loss, but the change is not necessarily a better one. They have regressed or gone backward. From our perspective, they have changed in an unhealthy direction. In contrast, growth must be defined as a change in a health-oriented direction.

Immediately, one may ask the question, "Well then, what is health?" This is not an easy question and a full answer would be beyond the scope of this book. There are many varied definitions of psychological health. Let me quickly suggest six features that seem to summarize the common features of these definitions:

1. Healthy people perceive reality accurately. They see life, others and themselves as they really are. They see reality as it really is, no matter how painful that reality might be. They reject defense mechanisms, illusions and other means of self-deception.
2. Healthy people are fully aware of themselves, their feelings, body sensations and cognitive processes.

3. Healthy people fully accept themselves. They have an accurate assessment of their strengths and weaknesses. They have a stable, positive self-esteem that enables them to accept themselves, forgive themselves and even like themselves.
4. Healthy people are wholistic. The various components of their psychic, social and spirtual lives are integrated. They are congruent throughout.
5. Healthy people have a capacity for love. They are able to form close interpersonal relationships, characterized by warmth, caring, intimacy and honesty.
6. Healthy people are competent people. Such people have skills, knowledge and confidence to seek out and be successful in their chosen vocation.

One might now ask, "Does anyone meet all of these criteria? Is anyone really healthy?" Of course not. No one is completely healthy. Yet, hopefully we are all striving toward it. Each of us is on a particular stage along that journey. So when we talk about growth in the context of loss, growth must be defined not in an absolute sense, but in a relative one. Growth is change in a health-oriented direction, in a direction that increases a person's accurate perception of reality, full awareness, self-acceptance, wholeness, competency and capacity for love. This is growth.

Growth Is Interrelated

Growth is multi-dimensional. People can grow physically, intellectually, socially, psychologically, vocationally and spiritually. These various avenues of growth are interrelated. Growth in one area triggers growth in another and vice versa. One might even say that people cannot grow in one area of life unless or until some growth has occurred in another one or more dimensions. In a sense then, growth can be likened to a linked chain—each dimension of life is linked to every other dimension in the "chain of life." Growth in one dimension is linked to growth in all of the other areas.

All dimensions of life are potential growth areas. All growth is interrelated. Suppose I "grow" physically, for example, by losing weight and improving my health. Now I look better and feel better. Hopefully, I no longer think of myself as a fat person with all of the emotional-social implications of that image. My view of myself has changed. Therefore, it is not just my body that has grown, but my self-image has also grown. I see myself differently. I am a different person emotionally and perhaps spiritually.

Perhaps now I will be more attractive to the opposite sex. Perhaps my employer will view me as more self-confident and competent. If I were to see myself still as a fat person, I may be uncomfortable with my new social popularity. I may return to overeating in order to relieve the tension between my self-image and the person that others think me to be. I can also use this growth in my physical health, and the corresponding reaction of others, as an opportunity for growth in the social dimension. Perhaps I will now learn new social skills, a new confidence with the opposite sex, and so on. Growth in one dimension can and does trigger growth opportunities in the other dimensions.

Growth Is Ageless

Growth in all dimensions of life can continue throughout a person's whole life span. "Growth" tends to be associated with the first twenty years of life when humans make the most rapid growth, especially in the physical and mental dimensions. This growth in the first third of life is natural and almost inevitable. It occurs automatically. Yet it is now also abundantly clear from research that adults can continue to grow throughout their entire adult lives as well. Each stage of adult life can be an opportunity for new growth. Growth in the adult years is by choice, not by nature. In some measure adults must always choose to grow. The two most prominent areas of adult growth are in the intellectual and spiritual areas. It is possible, however, for adults also to grow socially, vocationally and even physically (in the sense of learning new skills and improving health). Each and every occasion in a person's life can be an opportunity for growth.

What is growth then? Growth is change in a healthy direction. Growth is a process encompassing the whole person and something that potentially occurs throughout the entire life-cycle.

How Do People Grow?

A person can grow gradually and quietly or suddenly and dramatically. Probably most of our growth is of the gradual, subtle variety. Only after a period of time do we have occasion to look back on a period of gradual growth and realize, "I have grown." Those are pleasant and thankful occasions. On other occasions, we may resist growth, particularly in a certain area, for years upon years. Eventually, some dramatic event forces us to face the necessity of change. That event can be most anything from an illness to a divorce, but chief among those type of events are loss events. Loss events have a way of initiating periods of rapid growth.

Precisely, how do people grow? What are the dynamics of the growth process? Sidney M. Jourard was one of the leading humanistic and growth-oriented psychologists before his untimely death. He proposed the image of a voyage as a paradigm of personal growth.[4] A voyage involves three phases: (1) a leaving home, (2) a traveling to new places, and (3) a returning home with an enlarged self.

The first phase is that of leaving home. "Growing entails 'leaving home'," writes Jourard, "a letting go of one's clutch upon one's present way of being involved with other people and with one's projects."[5] People's "projects," as Jourard called them, consist of their commitments to the way they view the world, others and themselves. Such commitments impose structure upon the way they experience the world. People define themselves, and all of life, by their commitments. Once they believe that they know who they are, they are inattentive to all other perceptions, memories and data, save the ones that fit with their identity. When they are forced to "let go" of a secure identity or cherished beliefs, they begin to see the world anew. "The suspension of our normal ways of being involved in the world," says Jourard, "is akin to opening a door to a hidden room or to a new world." "Letting go" releases all modes of experiencing from repression.

The means of letting go, of suspending one's present ways of doing things, are numerous. Meditative disciplines, such as Zen, Yoga or prayer, function as a means of disengaging the person from the usual ways of experiencing reality. Religious ceremonies and rites are also ways of letting go. Fasting, chanting, praying, dancing and even solitude in the desert were employed by believers in former centuries to disengage them from the usual worldly consciousness. Once they were cleansed of the worldly thoughts, God could reveal to them something new, something totally new that they could not have seen amid the old identities. Disengagement is a prelude to revelation, in the same way that leaving home is a prelude to growth.

In a more gradual way, education does the same function. True education disengages people from their present world view by exposing them to an increasingly larger perspective than their own. Higher education, at its best, is supposed to facilitate growth in this way. Take the young man from a small provincial town that "leaves home" and enrolls in a major cosmopolitan university. During the first year, he experiences a type of cultural shock: he meets people from different ethnic and cultural backgrounds; he studies subjects that transform his earlier learnings; he meets people from different political and theological persuasions; he encounters students with differing moral principles and many with no morality at all. Initially, his neat, well-defined world view does not work anymore. Not only has he left home literally, but now he must leave home philosophically and emotionally. He is temporarily disengaged from the old, while he expands his world view. Disengagement is a prelude to the development of a larger world view.

Another way of "leaving home" is to literally leave home. Sometimes it takes a vast amount of energy and courage to put oneself on an airplane or a train and go elsewhere. The growth potential of such a leaving is most noticeable with adolescents. Recently I was talking to a young man who grew up in a close-knit family. Following high school, he got his first job at his father's shop, and he attended a commuter college, while continuing to live at home. During this time he had decided to enter the seminary and study for the ordained ministry. This pleased his family greatly. Yet he began to feel that this was a decision and a task that he had to do on his own. So he chose a seminary some three thousand miles away, realizing that he needed "the space" in order to grow. Getting on that airplane was "the hardest thing I ever did," he told me, and the first year was "very lonely." Yet, a year later, he reported that "leaving" forced him to build more self-reliance and responsibility. It gave him space to develop his own theology and professional identity. It gave him the freedom to question and to grow, without the subtle pressure of family expectations. For him, as for many adolescents, leaving home was a prelude to growth.

The middle phase of the growth paradigm is being in a strange country. This is a limbo-state, when the old patterns and maps do not make sense out of the new experiences, but one has not yet developed any new structures. One is left structureless, identity-less and roleless. In this "strange country," there is the insecure feeling of being without roots, foundations and guidelines. Depending on the type and severity of the transition, one may experience panic, confusion and pain. It is tempting at this point to want to return home, to cling to the old certainties, to run home to "the womb." (And many do.) It takes a certain courage to grow when one cannot see the other side of the transition. Yet one must keep moving forward in "leaps of faith." In this way, growth always involves a risk. The growing person is therefore a person of courage and faith.

Finally, growth according to the present metaphor entails a return to the place one had left as a new self. The growth cycle is never complete until the person integrates the new knowledge and experiences into the old identity. Growth is never a complete displacing of the new for old, never "a throwing out of the baby with the bath water." Growing is always the integrating of the new with the old, thus creating a new synthesis. Some people, of course, simply adopt the new and discard the old, and some cling to the old and never consider anything new, but genuine growth comes from the integration of the new and old. In this way each growth experience is an enlarging of the self.

GROWTH MOTIVATION

Abraham H. Maslow is considered to be the father of Humanistic Psychology. Maslow's unique contribution lies in that he was the first to focus psychology's attention not on the sick psyche, but on the healthy one. He studied the healthiest people, the top one percent of the population. This "growing tip" group he termed "self-actualized people." He wanted to know what made these people so healthy. One of the chief features of these self-actualizers was their motivation for growth.[6] They seem to be motivated by something different than the rest of us ordinary people. He termed this special kind of motivation "growth motivation" or Being motivation (B-motivation) which stood in contrast to Deficiency motivation (D-motivation). Growth motivators were people who had satisfied all of their basic needs for safety, self-esteem, love and status and were now motivated by B-values. They were now motivated by such Values of Being as truth, beauty, justice, charity and so on. However, most of all, they were motivated primarily by a desire to grow, to fulfill their inherent potential, to self-actualize. In contrast to this attitude D-motivators were people who were still primarily motivated by a desire to fulfill what they lacked. They were motivated by their deficiency.

Deficiency motivation is based on a tension-reduction model of human personality. Its basic principle is that the organism seeks to maintain equilibrium by reducing tension. When a need emerges, such as hunger, tension is created in the physiological system. The equilibrium is disturbed. Tension mounts. The person is now motivated to seek food. When the person's hunger is satisfied, then tension dissipates. This is the primary model of behaviorist psychology. Humans are motivated by a desire to reduce tension.

In this system we can easily substitute the word "pain" for the word "tension" without changing the essential dynamics of the model. When I have a pain in my stomach, I am motivated to look for food. When there is a pain in my psychological life, e.g. low status, rejection, loss, I am motivated to fix it. This model suggests that humans are not motivated apart from pain. It further suggests that humans do only what they have to do to reduce the tension/pain.

Growth motivation is based on a biological model of growth. Each organism has a potential, a blueprint within its core which describes what its best self is supposed to be. Each organism will grow toward that potential, if unencumbered. Growth is fueled by its own energy. This is a tension-increase model. Tension will be momentarily increased when these people grow. Yet they will voluntarily encounter tension and move through it to a new enlarged equilibrium. The desire to grow and to fulfill their potential is stronger than the momentary discomfort of pain and tension. In Maslow's terms, the desire to self-actualize is stronger than pain. For such growth-motivated people Maslow says, "Growth is, in itself, a rewarding and exciting process . . . ."[7] For these people, growth transcends pain.

In recent years the term "wellness" has been introduced into the medical community. Wellness refers to that optimum state of physical health, the fulfillment of one's growth potential. Imagine a health continuum in which normalcy is given an arbitrary numerical value of zero. When we are diseased or ill, our functioning falls below zero into the negative numbers all the way down to a maximum negative score of minus 100 which we shall call death. The scale also goes into the plus numbers, rising above zero or "normal," all the way to a maximum score of plus 100 which we shall call "wellness."

The traditional medical understanding of health and disease focuses on the negative half of this continuum. Health is defined as the "absence of disease." When people are without disease, they are normal or "healthy." On the wellness continuum, they are hovering around zero. A disease, depending on its severity, could knock them down into the negative numbers. A case of flu would push them down to a -10. Cancer could push them down to a -30. Their physician's job is to restore them to health by returning their health score to zero.

Wellness is concerned with the positive side of this continuum. Wellness is taking the relatively normal person and increasing his or her wellness. Wellness people seek to move their patients (they would not use this term) into the positive numbers—"to get ahead a little." As people build up wellness, they are better prepared to respond to illness. An illness will not knock them down so far, because they began with a positive score. Or a disease may pass them by entirely, because their health has been so maximized that their bodies resist the infection.

The wellness model of physical health is a growth model. The goal is to increase, to maximize people's growth toward their potential. The accent is on what used to be called preventive health, instead of just curing disease. The motivation for increasing wellness is growth motivation. The emphasis is on initiating changes, and not just on reacting to changes. Deficiency motivation works only when people become ill, or "lack health," whereas growth motivation pushes people to reach toward wellness, fueled by their own inner desire to self-actualize.

It is safe to say that each human being has elements of both motivational systems in varying degrees. The distinction between the two motivational systems is not as sequential as Maslow's Hierarchy of Needs sometimes suggests. An individual can be empowered by both sets of motivation. A middle-aged woman may enroll in a college degree program because she wants to prove to her boss that she is not as stupid as she has been labeled to be (D-motivation) *and* she may want to improve her mind just for her own satisfaction (B-motivation). The motivation for the practice of medicine may be a desire for money (D-motivation) *and* a quest to find new ways to relieve suffering (B-motivation). A male carpenter may do a job just for a paycheck (D-motivation) *and* because he wants "to build it right" (B-motivation).

Spouses resist marital infidelity because their partner will leave them (D-motivation) *and* because they are committed to a principle (B-motivation). People attend church regularly because they are afraid of hell (D-motivation) *and* to fulfill a deep longing to nurture their souls (B-motivation). People can be motivated both by a desire to gratify needs and avoid pain *and* by a desire to fulfill their potential—"to be true to one's self." Even though both motivational systems exist in all of us, according to Maslow, the more we are in tune with growing motivation, the healthier we are likely to be and to remain.

One of the basic principles of growth psychology is that there is no growth without pain. People must be willing to endure pain in order to grow. That is why so many people, motivated by a deficiency attitude, do not grow. They do not like pain and seek to avoid it at all costs, even at the cost of their own growth. Growth-motivated people are willing, at least within reason, to encounter pain. They know that only through pain can one grow.

Deficiency-motivated people want the pain to go away. They do not want to face it. They will avoid, deny, or delay their pain as long as possible. They will not talk about it. They will employ various defense mechanisms to make the loss seem less painful. Even as the reality of a loss inevitably becomes more clear, they still resist. If they grieve at all, they will enter into it "kicking and screaming all the way." They will face the pain only when they have to and only to the extent necessary. They desire "to get it over with as soon as possible," and to get back to normal. They do not wish to "leave home."

Growth motivators do not like pain either. They hurt just as much as others do, but their attitude is that the pain is something that must be gone through if they are to benefit from this experience. They will enter into the pain with courage and with the faith that they will find new life at the end of their journey. They look at their loss, as tragic as it might be, with the attitude, "What can I learn from this experience?" and "How can I bring some good out of this suffering?" The growth motivator's attitude toward pain is to move through it, rather than to avoid it.

Growth motivation and deficiency motivation offer us two contrasting approaches to the pain of bereavement. In a sense, all of us when we are bereaved begin with deficiency motivation. After all, loss is by definition a deprivation. We "lack" something. In particular when those losses strike at our basic needs for physical comfort, self-esteem, love, and safety, we must focus on these needs first. During this period of bereavement, we are partially incapacitated. Gradually, as we complete the restructuring of our life at these lower levels, we return to our "old self."

Yet growth will also occur to the extent that we transcend our deficiency motivation with a growth attitude. Once the lower needs are again satisfied, the focus can shift to "How can I grow from this experience?" and "How can I transform this loss into a permanent gain?" With such an attitude, we who are bereaved may do more than just return to normalcy. We will "grow." We will become "better" people than we were before the loss. We will actually use our losses to make significant gains in our lives.

FREEDOM, RESPONSIBILITY AND CHOICES

When a severe loss enters our life, suddenly and without welcome, we feel helpless. We feel powerless to control it. We may feel that we are a victim of the forces of fate, bad luck or an evil god. This is a normal reaction to a sudden and unexpected loss. All losses, particularly those that are unexpected, include some element of loss of control. To the extent that people feel this way, they will not feel free or that they have too many choices. It will seem as though most of their choices have been made for them.

Growth psychology has suggested that people grow to the extent that they perceive of themselves as having freedom, responsibility and choices. Most people in fact have more choices in crisis situations than they realize. In the midst of the emotionality and stress of the moment, they lose sight of their choices. It is easy to feel helpless. Normally, none of us can choose not to lose. The loss has occurred. Bereavement is a fact. Yet we can choose to grieve or not to grieve. We can choose how we shall grieve, with whom and when we shall grieve. In short, we can choose our response to the loss. Growth begins to occur when we recognize our choices and assume responsibility for our lives. We are deciding in those moments not to let fate control us. Rather, we shall control fate. We shall take charge of our lives and make something good out of whatever tragedy has befallen us.

In recent years, research in the field of psychology has tried to study how and why some people feel helpless amid crises. Martin E.P.

Seligman coined the term "learned helplessness" to describe persons who consistently perceived themselves to be victims of external forces.[8] Seligman first developed his work in the laboratory where animals were subjected to random, uncontrollable shocks. The animals were frustrated by the uncontrollability of the aversive stimuli. Soon they developed an avoidance syndrome that he labeled "Learned helplessness." This syndrome featured three deficiencies: motivational, cognitive and emotion. First, the subjects showed a "retarded initiation of voluntary responses." In other words they saw all of their efforts as futile and gave up trying to control their destiny. In addition, they showed greater difficulty in learning—even when the pattern was changed and they could control the shocks. Third, they showed a marked depressed mood. Later, through human research, a fourth category—self-esteem—was added. Learned helplessness positively correlates with lower self-esteem.

Seligman's work has been repeated with humans who have suffered repeated uncontrollable crises or losses. Examples of such people might be those with sequential deaths of loved ones, one or more disasters, repetitive illnesses or prisoners of concentration camps. The "learned helplessness" syndrome appears in humans as well. The key issue again appears to be the controllability of the crisis. If people were able to exercise some control over the crisis, however small that control, they did not learn the helplessness of the victim state. In contrast, people who perceived that they had no control over the crises learned to be helpless and suffered from reduced emotional, cognitive and motivational functioning.

The interesting point about this research is that the ability to have some measure of control over one's life seems to be a key variable in assisting people to recover and grow from loss experiences. People who perceive that they have no control, no choices and no power to influence the course of their life tend to develop this learned helplessness. People who perceive, and are able to exercise, some measure of control over tragic events recover better.

These concepts are not too dissimilar from Maslow's concept of growth motivation. Growth motivated people are not just a victim of circumstances however tragic. They are able to do more than just react. They are able to initiate some measure of novel response. They can initiate changes, actions and creativity. In short, growth motivators feel that they have some measure of control over their lives.

It should be noted again that most grief-stricken people begin bereavement in a helpless state. Losses that strike us "out of the blue" do make us feel helpless. That is reality! Yet even the most disastrous of life's tragedies have some room for personal response and choice. We can choose how to grieve. We can choose our companions in grief. We can choose and design our rituals of grief. We can choose not to be alone. We can choose when and how to express our pain. We can choose how to interpret the events of our lives. Recognizing choices and exercising choices is one key to maximizing growth amid bereavement. I believe that this is why the hospice movement has advocated the maintenance of dignity for the terminally ill. A part of the "dying with dignity" philosophy is allowing the patient to maintain as many choices as possible as long as possible. When patients feel that they no longer have any choices, they become victims and "give up" on life.

It is curious that in our American society where we have more personal freedom than any other nation on earth, people tend to view life as offering only limited choices. Most people feel trapped by their emotions and their personal histories. This tragic state of mind is nowhere more prevalent than in loss situations. When death comes, people act like prisoners of their own emotions. They feel locked into behaviors that they do not understand and helpless to say what they really feel inside. People say, "I can't help being depressed," or "Men aren't supposed to cry," or "We have to do it this way." Richard C. Nelson in an article on choice awareness and bereavement suggests that one of the most growth-facilitating functions that a care-giver can do for the bereaved is to assist them to recognize their choices. "Living is choosing," he writes:

> We need to learn—and help others to learn—to make the kinds of choices that leave us with less guilt, less regret, more joy, and a greater sense of meaning when death faces our loved ones or us.[9]

We have choices, hundreds of choices, every day of our lives. Yes, life deals us some pretty cruel blows, but even amid these "blows," we have choices. Even in the face of death itself, we have a choice in how we shall respond. Shall we meet it as a helpless victim of fate or as a free, responsible person of faith? Therein lies one key to bringing growth out of loss—*recognizing our choices.*

Recently, I was watching the New York City Marathon on television in which some sixteen thousand men and women ran twenty-six miles through the streets of New York. The last runner to finish that grueling race was a crippled woman with multiple sclerosis, who was running on crutches. Long after everyone else was finished, she was still "running"—five, six, eight hours later. She was still in the race as the sun went down and the national television coverage went off the air. Obviously she was not going to win, but it did not matter. She was running for something else—pride, self-respect, growth. She was a winner already, a winner in the race against her disease. She had transcended her handicap. In those moments, she was more of a whole person than most of us normal people.

Such people amaze me. There are millions of handicapped people of all sorts and varieties in this country. Their handicap may range from blindness to that of a quadriplegic. In recent years we have enjoyed the resurgence of interest in and support for the handicapped. Yet I know that the struggle by which this woman, and many like her, have overcome their limitation is enormous. I do not know this particular woman, but I can imagine that when she first suffered her affliction, she was emotionally devastated. Multiple sclerosis can be arrested, but never cured. She faced a life of increasing amounts of crippledness and suffering. She probably felt sadness, anger, anxiety, helplessness and incredible frustration. She probably experienced a period of bereavement in which she mourned for her lost capacity, her lost health and a future that will never be. She probably had periods of deep sorrow, self-pity and depression. She could have spent the rest of her life as a cripple, a helpless and dependent person, resigned to her condition. No one could have blamed her. Yet something deep within her soul cried out for life, for life in all its fullness. At some point she decided that she wanted to live. She wanted to grow. She wanted to fulfill her potential. She set for herself a new set of goals—to be a runner. She began to train, to work out, to discipline herself, to voluntarily endure even more pain. Why? To grow!

The key to her transformation was attitude. At some point or maybe at many points, she moved away from a position of helplessness to a position of control. She recognized that she still had some control over her life. She still had choices. She chose to live. She chose to take the control of her life back from the disease. She would determine her future life style, not the disease. I venture to guess that she has grown a great deal since her handicap. We might even say that she is a better person today because of her suffering. While never wishing for such a disease, it did trigger in her a period of intense growth, accomplishment and integration. Suffering was the soil out of which growth emerged. Loss became transformed into gain. The key to this transformation is that she was a growth motivator, someone who recognized her choices even amid hardship and took control of her life.

GRIEVING, THEN GROWING

Grief and growth are intricately related. Their interdependence might be likened to a continuum where the poles progressively blend into each other. At the grieving pole there is always some growing however small. At the growing pole there is always some grieving however small. The middle phases represent various mixtures of grieving and growing. Grief work inevitably involves both healing and growing. It seems to be impossible to experience one without at least some elements of the other.

While grieving and growing are two overlapping processes, there appears to be a sequential priority of grieving over growing. Grieving is largely past-oriented. Grieving helps the psyche to "let go" of the past emotional attachments that are now lost. Growth is largely future-oriented. Growing helps people move into new directions, make new commitments and enter new stages of development. There is a sequence to this process in which people must first grieve and then grow. Grieving sets the stage for growth. The past must be finished with before the future can be welcomed. People must first recover their emotional energy from the past before that same energy can be reinvested into the future. Growing is largely impossible until one has grieved. People cannot go forward until they have let go of the past. Therefore, I conclude, that grieving is a prerequisite for growth.

For the moment, consider again the image of the voyage, used by Sidney Jourard to describe the growth process. Jourard noted that the growth process begins when one "leaves home." Leaving home is disengaging ourselves emotionally from our old attachments and identities. Disengagement is the first step in the growing process. Loss events are one of the more frequent and common means of initiating a "leaving home." Sometimes people want and are ready to leave home. Sometimes they choose to leave home just because it is "something that has to be done," like growing up. At other times they do not choose to leave home at all. Home is taken from them, or, to put it differently, they are driven from home. Loss forces people to "leave home."

Whether by choice or by tragedy, we must at times leave home. What is grief, then, if not simply the process of emotionally leaving home. Each time we "leave home," we grieve. Grieving is saying "goodbye" to old attachments. Only when our grieving is complete and we are fully disengaged can the growing process proceed. Grieving is necessary for growth. Grieving is a prerequisite for growing.

The dynamics of this process are never as clear-cut as have been just described. In reality, people do not first grieve and then grow. Most bereaved people grieve a little and grow a little; and grieve a little and grow a little; and so on. This is so because each major loss is a complex set of many losses—the loss of a role, the loss of self-esteem, the loss of money, the change of environment and so on. Every loss involves a multitude of changes and smaller losses. The bigger the loss is, the more numerous are the possible sub-losses. So the bereaved must not grieve just one loss, but many times. A widowed person must grieve the loss of a spouse, a parenting partner, a sex partner, a best friend, a breadwinner, an ideal image, and so on. Certain aspects of this loss may be easier to grieve than others. So in bereavement more often than not one grieves some and grows some and grieves some more. Yet the general thrust of the relationship between grief and growth is that one must grieve as a prelude to growth. If one does not grieve, one never grows.

GRIEF AND DEVELOPMENTAL GROWTH

The priority and necessity of grief over growth is nowhere more clearly illustrated than in the case of developmental growth. At an appropriate time, a young male infant must lose his mother's breasts in order to grow developmentally into greater autonomy. If this infant is not allowed to "lose" in this way, he would have his emotional and developmental growth blocked. He must lose in order to grow. Similarly, a young female adolescent must lose her teenage attachments in order to grow into the roles and responsibilities of adulthood. If she reached the age of thirty still acting like a teenager, she would be classified as emotionally immature or even retarded. In order to grow developmentally, she must let go of adolescence. She must grieve in order to grow.

The successful completion of the grief process is a necessary condition to further developmental growth. "Life begins with one separation after another," writes Arthur Freese; "there is no developmental growth without separation, loss . . . where parents prevent separation pathology develops."[10] In the second half of life a middle-aged couple must grieve the "loss" of their children when those children leave home in order to grow into a new and richer relationship with each other and their children. If they do not successfully grieve this loss, their developmental health is blocked. They live in the past, still locked into their old roles as "mother" and as "father." Such roles not only limit their growth, but prevent them from discovering a new richer relationship to their adult children. Grief is necessary for developmental growth. People must grieve these losses before they can fully move into a new life-stage.

Many psychologists have noted that one feature of a healthy personality is the ability to be emotionally in the present, to "live in the here and now." A healthy person's emotional life should always correspond to the current life-stage reality. Evertt L. Shostrom, for example, has described the results of his "Personal Orientation Inventory" which measures the dominant time frame of people.[11] On the basis of his study, he proposed that "the healthy individual is one who lives primarily in the present," as opposed to the "pathologically past-oriented" or the "pathologically future-oriented" individual. He is worth quoting:

> The self-actualizing person appears to live more fully in the here-and-now. He is able to tie the past and the future to the present in meaningful continuity. He appears to be less burdened by guilts, regrets, and resentments from the past . . . and his aspirations are tied meaningfully to the present working goals . . . .The pathologically past-oriented individual is characterized by guilt, regret and the undigested memories of the past. He is the depressive who keeps remembering past hurts.[12]

Shostrom's definition of health fits well into this discussion of grief and growth. The healthy person is the person whose emotional life is fully in the here-and-now, engaged in and corresponding to the person's current life-stage.

The difficulty in being psychologically healthy in this way, that is, keeping one's emotional life fully in the present, is that the present reality is always changing. Change is continuously and pervasively occurring throughout our entire life. Included in that change are continuous and sometimes traumatic losses. In order for us to be healthy, we must continuously, or at least periodically, adjust our emotional life to a new reality. The emotional mechanism for this periodical adjustment is grief. Periodically, we grieve what has been lost by recent changes. "It is as though," writes Sidney Levin, "that one had used a form of deficit financing for many years and was suddenly asked to make up the accumulated debt."[13] Actually, from a purely health point of view, it would be preferable if there was as little accumulated debt as possible, in order for the grief process to be as continuous as possible. Most of us, however, are only dimly aware of developmental losses until they are focused in some symbolic transition event or loss. To repeat then, in order to grow developmentally and to be healthy, one must at least periodically bring one's emotional life "up to date" by grieving what has been lost in recent life-cycle changes.

In the counseling office, I once worked with a young family with two children, ages seven and five. The presenting problem was that the mother, a twenty-five year old woman, was very bored with family life and wanted to "run away." After only a brief period of counseling, she did in fact leave her family. I had great difficulty understanding how this person could abandon her children and family to flee to another state under the banner of "to find herself." I began to do some study and reading into this subject. I found that this pattern is common enough that researchers have put a label on it, calling it the "Lost Adolescence Syndrome." A couple caught in this syndrome can come for counseling for a variety of complaints, writes Anthony and Julie Jurich, but there is one underlying factor:

> . . . an overidealization of the 'single carefree life' which has shaken the satisfaction with married life of one or both spouses. This overidealization is caused by the failure of the complaining spouse to experience what he defines as a 'typical adolescence.' . . . In essence, the spouse is complaining that he has lost his adolescence and is trying to recapture it by abandoning his present marriage.[14]

Most often couples in this situation were married at an early age before they were developmentally ready. One or more children followed quickly and soon the marriage was overburdened with the responsibilities of adulthood. Typically, the couple buckles down and struggles through the initial five to seven years. There is not much time to do anything else. Later, when the children reach school age, and the parents "come up for a breather," one or both begin to feel a nagging sense of loss.

Robert J. Havighurst and Erik H. Erikson have both delineated the major developmental tasks of adolescence.[15] Particularly for the latter author, the major task of adolescence is the establishment of a strong personal identity. The typical adolescent fulfills this need through peer interaction, through experimenting with several different identities, and through the development of independence. An early marriage or an exclusive love-relationship isolates teenagers from their peers, limits their social experimentation and restricts their independence. The individual adolescent shifts his or her dependence from his or her parents to his or her spouse. He or she moves from the "role of child to the role of spouse and parent without the opportunity to define his or her identity independent of these two powerful roles." Adolescence has been short-circuited.

The early years of a Lost Adolescence Syndrome marriage are typically happy and generate little marital stress. Later, one or both spouses begin to feel trapped, over-burdened and unhappy. The routine of family life becomes boring. They look back longingly to the freedom of adolescence. The single life is idealized to be everything that is currently missing from their family life. They want to be free, to live an exciting, carefree life. They claim that they never got a chance to "sow their wild oats" or to "get it out of their systems." Such spouses are, of course, very vulnerable to extramarital affairs. Some marriages adjust by trying to give the complaining spouse more freedom within the limits of the marital responsibilities. Other marriages end up in divorce or with one spouse just "running away."

The dynamics of this syndrome illustrates clearly the tremendous power of uncompleted developmental tasks and unfinished grief. When those developmental needs are not met, people may feel that they are missing something, that they have lost something. Idealization of what is lost is a classic type of defense mechanism that enables bereaved people to "cling to the past." This longing can be terribly intense, compounded as it is by unmet needs for independence and identity formation. An alternative to running away is to deal more openly with the pain and grief of the lost adolescence. To complete one's grief work over the lost adolescence would release energy for growth in the current life-stage.

Needless to say, the initial response of the non-complaining spouse is often acute anxiety and hostility. It is not easy to get the non-complaining spouse over his or her feelings of hurt, anxiety and jealousy. Yet, whatever success I have enjoyed with these couples has come when they both were able to recognize their common pain and loss, and then to talk about that pain, and then to grieve together. This is the only reasonable alternative to running away: dealing openly with the feelings of sorrow, loss and grief. The real key to unlocking this destructive syndrome is to facilitate the bereaved spouse's grief. If this woman had completed her grief work over her lost adolescence, she would have been released to deal creatively with her current life-style. Growth would have become possible only after she grieved the past.

IMPLICATIONS FOR PASTORAL CARE

Pastors must keep in mind the importance of timing as they approach a person or a family in bereavement. Repeatedly, we have seen that there is a sequential priority of grief over growth. We must grieve before we can grow. The early stages of bereavement are not usually the time to introduce growth questions. Questions such as "How are you going to grow from this loss?" will appear too academic and insensitive to the weeping family. Such questions would function to block, deny, repress the necessary grieving that must occur. Rather, in the initial stages of an acute grief situation, the pastor's first concern needs to be focused on facilitating the grief process, ventilating feelings and giving the mourners permission to weep. Then, as the grief work is gradually completed in the weeks and months following, the concern for growth issues will surface. Obviously, grief and growth are not an "either/or" issue. Grief and growth blend into each other, the former giving way to the latter as healing proceeds. Normally, grief-stricken persons will set their own pace for this process, and the sequence of their needs will be clear to us if we listen closely.

As pastors deal with people in crisis, one way to help them mobilize their growth potential is through helping them to become aware of their choices. As noted, even in the most severe of tragedies, we have some choices. We are not just victims, not just helpless creatures in a world ruled by the irrational whims of angry gods. On the contrary, God has given us the capacity to choose, to be responsible for our lives and for those we love. When I talk with people in loss situations, one of the questions that I keep near the tip of my tongue is, ''What choices do you have now?'' Humans have a tendency not to see their choices amid crises. That lack of foresight contributes to a learned helplessness, which in turn increases the incidents of depression, futility and even suicide. The more we can help people to recognize their choices and through those choices to exercise some measure of control over their lives, the more they will be able to bring growth out of loss.

Remember that grief is an essential ingredient in the maintenance of health. The ability to successfully grieve is a key element in a sound mental health. Pastors must regularly teach their flock how to grieve and how to grow. Teaching people to bring growth out of periods of loss and crisis is critical. Hopefully, clergy will not speak of these issues just in times of crisis. Rather, all of our sermons, prayers, teaching and general pastoral care can help prepare our people for the inevitable periods of loss.

In theological language this topic is essentially the problem of suffering put in a practical context. How a person of faith deals with suffering is the acid test of his or her beliefs. Most people have some difficulty understanding why God allows suffering and how they can respond best to bring goodness out of evil. This is a crucial issue, and the task of teaching people how to grow in times of loss is a formidable one. We might say that our task is to teach people how to suffer—how to suffer in a way that brings forth spiritual growth. This subject—the connection between loss and spiritual growth—is one to which we now turn.

5. Spiritual Growth in Times of Loss

"In death and grief we do not need as much protection from painful experiences as we need the boldness to face them. We do not need as much tranquilization from pain as we need the strength to conquer it. If we choose to love, we must also have the courage to grieve."[1]

Roy Nichols

Suffering can spark renewed spirituality. This is especially true in the case of bereavement. Many people report that their spiritual life has been deepened, renewed or altered as a result of their loss. In contrast other people will report that they "lost their faith" or "dropped out of church" as a result of their tragedy. How can suffering stimulate spiritual renewal instead of spiritual degeneration? At what point does suffering cease to be facilitative and start to be destructive to a person's soul? How do people grow spiritually? These are some of the questions on which this chapter will focus.[2]

There needs to be a clearer definition of spiritual growth. The term is ambiguous. It is used in such a great variety of ways. Parishioners may say, "My faith grew as a result of Marge's death," or "I am closer to the Lord now," or "I now understand what real love is," or "God used my tragedy to show me my sins," or "I have much more compassion toward others since the loss of my own job." Each of these phrases suggests that the speaker has grown spiritually, but each of these phrases describes a different aspect of spiritual growth. A precise definition of spiritual growth is difficult.

For purposes of clarification and simplicity, I have chosen to take a fairly limited focus in this chapter by looking at St. Paul's understanding of spiritual growth. Obviously, there are other spiritual giants in the history of Christianity that have much to contribute on this topic. Yet, within the limited space that is available to us in this book, we have time only to study one individual. St. Paul is one of the theological founding fathers of the Christian faith. Pauline theology can be a good starting place for a discussion of spiritual growth and its role in bereavement.

SANCTIFICATION: SPIRITUAL GROWTH

The noun "sanctification" or the verb "to sanctify" finds its roots in the Hebrew term meaning "separateness" or "to set apart" as sacred from ordinary use. In New Testament times, the terms "to sanctify" and "sanctification" are scarcely found outside of biblical Greek, and the noun "sanctification" occurs exclusively in the Epistles of Paul and other Gentile Christians. While the RSV translates ἁγιαζω as "to sanctify" or "to consecrate," Bultmann suggests the more simple "to make holy," "holiness," and "the holy ones."[3] Since the noun sanctification evolved in New Testament writings from the verb "to sanctify," Procksch suggests that a more fitting translation is "sanctifying" (instead of sanctification), which suggests the process-character of this concept.[4]

Paul's concept of sanctification is overshadowed by his dominant interest in justification. Justification refers to the initial gracious act of God in the death and resurrection of Jesus Christ, which "makes right" or righteous a person's relationship with God. When a person responds in faith to God's grace, he or she completes this initial stage of salvation, which is usually reflected in that person's baptism and incorporation into the Christian community. Sanctification, then, refers to the subsequential process of literally "being made holy" or being "transformed into the likeness of Christ" (2 Cor 3:12–18). In short, sanctification refers to a process, as opposed to an initial decision, event or act of grace. Sanctification is, however, a special kind of process. It is a spiritual growth process, of being transformed into the likeness of Christ or into what God intended for humanity in creation.

Perhaps the clearest descriptive passage of sanctification occurs in 2 Corinthians 3:12–18. Here, Paul is addressing again the question of the Jews' unbelief, this time, borrowing an analogy from the Old Testament. Paul interprets the story of Moses' veil (Ex 34:29–35) as an effort to hide from the Hebrews how temporary the old covenant was. Like Moses standing before God with an unveiled face, Paul and his fellow Christians ("we") now see God face to face in Jesus Christ, or, as Paul says, "beholding the glory of the Lord." Through this living relationship with the Lord, Christians are "being transformed into his likeness, from one degree of glory to another."

This verse suggests several insights. First, the sanctifying process is clearly gradual and progressive ("from one degree of glory to another"). Second, the goal or telos of this process is to become "like Christ." The same goal is described in Galatians 4:19 ("until Christ be formed in you") and Romans 8:29 ("to be conformed to the image of his Son"). The Greek term "likeness" suggests the similar Hebrew term, in the Genesis story of creation (Gen 1:26). For Paul, the goal of sanctification is to be transformed into this same likeness: the likeness of Christ, which, in turn, is the likeness of God, which is also the same "image" given to humanity initially in creation. Theologically, the sanctification process completes a circle from creation, to Jesus, to the Christians, to the parousia, and finally to re-creation. In this sense, sanctification is a part of God's overall salvation plan.

Third, to be transformed into the likeness of Christ suggests that sanctification is a multi-dimensional process. It is certainly more than a mere physical likeness (2 Cor 4:16). It must include a likeness to Christ in the mind (Phil 2:5; Rom 12:2), a likeness to Christ in attitudes (Phil 4:8f; Rom 12:9–21; 6:11) and a likeness to Christ in behavior (Rom 12:12–14).

Fourth, it is clear from this passage that this sanctifying process comes from the risen Lord, who is the Spirit. The Holy Spirit is the author and sustainer of this growth process (Rom 15:16b). In fact, the close connection between the Holy Spirit and holiness or sanctification has led Procksch to suggest that the descriptive term "holy" in reference to the Spirit suggests both its character and its operation.[5] Besides being holy, the Spirit also functions to "make holy."

For Paul, this sanctifying-growing process is closely tied to the church and the unity of the church. Paul freely refers to Christians collectively as "the saints." This suggests both a status already present—they are made holy in their conversion out of the world—and a process to evolute—Christians are in the process of being made holy. In 1 Corinthians 1:2, Paul refers to the Corinthians as "those [already] sanctified" which reflects the first use, and in 1 Corinthians 1:18 Paul refers

to the Corinthian Christians as "those who are being saved" which reflects the second use. Again, the term "holy" suggests both a description and a function. The church is both holy and functions to maintain
and sustain holiness or sanctification. Outside of the church, sanctification or the maintenance of the sanctifying process is nearly impossible.

One additional verse needs special attention.[6] In Philippians 2:12–
13, Paul advises his readers to "work out your salvation with fear and
trembling, for God is at work in you . . . ." Again, this verse suggests
a growth-process understanding of salvation. It also reflects a polarity
between human effort and divine grace. Growth involves human effort,
struggle and pain.

Yet, growth is also a product of the activity of God. Like the experience of justification itself, sanctification is also an experience of
the free, unmerited grace of God. Bultmann describes this polarity as
between the indicative and imperative.[7] In one sense Christians are already "the holy ones," and in another sense they must work to become
holy. Growth is both a free gift and hard work.

ESCHATOLOGY: JUDGMENT AND LOSS

Like his Jewish forebears, Paul understands history as a chrono-
logical progression. History or time which began in creation will end at
the parousia. Both events, the creation and the parousia, will be au-
thored by and ruled over by God. To the basic two-aeon framework,
Paul adds the conviction that the parousia has already begun in the advent, death and resurrection of Jesus Christ. The eschatological hope of
the Hebrew prophets has been fulfilled in Jesus (Rom 1:1–6). The
Christ-event marked the dawning of the new age. Thus the church has
become the new people of God, the remnant of Israel awaiting the consummation of the Lord. Being so convinced that the last times foretold
by the prophets has begun, Paul believed that the parousia or the "day
of the Lord" was imminent (Rom 13:11–14; Phil 4:5), and that on that
day Christ would return to earth to usher in the Kingdom of God.

Paul understood his particular time as being a very unique period.
It was the "in-between time." Christ had come. The former age was
passing away. The new age had "already begun," but was "not yet"

fulfilled. Full salvation would not be completed until the parousia (Rom 5:10; 8:23). This "already-not yet" polarity gave the present age its unique character. "This present age" was still an evil age dominated by sin and death (1 Cor 15:56). Only in the age to come would sin and death be ultimately defeated, although they were initially defeated in Christ's resurrection.

While the new age is yet to be fully consummated, Paul understands that the new aeon has also already arrived. The decisive eschatological event for all history—the death and resurrection of Christ—has already taken place. The Spirit, which essentially belongs to the new age, is already present and available to Christians. The power of the resurrection is now available and operative in the present age. Furthermore, as each person makes a decision for faith, he or she is delivered from the old evil age to the new age (Gal 1:4). The eschatological-occurrence is in the present act of faith. Bultmann writes:

> The salvation-occurrence is the eschatological occurrence which puts to an end the old aeon. Though Paul still expects the end of the old world to come as a cosmic drama that will unfold . . . that can only be the completion and confirmation of the eschatological occurrence that has now already begun.[8]

The faithful already belong to the new age to come. The new creation, promised in its fullness at the end of time, has already come in Christ and to each Christian as he or she becomes "one with Christ." Therefore, for Paul the "day of salvation" is *now* as well as *then* (2 Cor 6:2). Writing of Paul's eschatology Hans Conzelmann says, " . . . the essential point is the bracketing of the future with the present, the indication that the future can be experienced now."[9]

When the parousia does come, there will be three events: the second coming of Christ, the resurrection of the faithful and the last judgment. Concerning the judgment, Paul understands that the God who created the world will at the end of time be the world's judge. He believes that all people will be judged: Christians and non-Christians alike (Rom 14:10). God's judgment will be based on what each person did in this life (2 Cor 5:10). Everyone will be judged according to "his works" (Rom 2:17–27; 2:6). At this last judgment, those who have been "one with Christ" in this life can be confident. For them there will be no condemnation. For the unfaithful and non-believing, there will be condemnation and the wrath of God, although Paul does not describe the exact character of that punishment.

Given the present age's unique polarity, judgment is not only to come at the parousia, but is also already present. Judgment is possible now because God's righteousness is rooted in the moral order of the world. The ungodly and the wicked experience God's wrath now as do the sexually immoral (Rom 1:18–27). In 1 Corinthians 11:27–33, Paul argues that Christians bring judgment and even punishment on themselves by their divisive behavior. In 1 Thessalonians 2:16, Paul speaks of the wrath of God already punishing the Jews in this life. Judgment seems to be built into the very nature of immoral and evil acts. "People reap what they sow." All people judge themselves by their behavior and decisions. In this sense, the last judgment is actually perfunctory, simply confirming what people have already "earned" for themselves in this life. The real arena for judgment is this present age.

It has been argued from Paul's writings that eschatology inevitably involves an experience of judgment. There is judgment in the age to come and there is also judgment built into the daily eschatological occurrences of this life. An experience of judgment can lead to repentance or to condemnation. People might come to see the errors of their ways (self-judgment) and choose a new life based on faith and righteousness. Or they might ignore the judgment dynamics and simply continue in the same destructive line of behavior, thus leading to condemnation. As long as judgment occurs in this life, this side of the last judgment, it is "pen-ultimate." Judgment in this life leaves open the possibility of repentance. There is always time to start over again. Only the last judgment at the end of time is "ultimate" and permanent in the sense of being without the possibility of repentance.

One way to describe the experience of judgment that is built into the eschatological occurrences of this life is in terms of the dynamics of loss. When a person experiences loss, there is an element of judgment in it. Any severe loss usually motivates people to evaluate the meaning of that which is lost and the meaning of their life without that which is lost. Often people make significant changes in their life-styles following a severe loss experience, precisely because the loss experience forced them to evaluate or judge themselves and their life up to that point. The loss of a loved one, the loss of one's own life, the loss of one's possession, status, health, etc., are all potential "eschatological occurrences'' in the sense that they remind the participants of the shortness of time and hence initiate a period of judgment. Loss can also be anticipated. Paul frequently warns his readers of the coming parousia (1 Thess 4:6) in the hope that the anticipated loss of life would initiate self-judgment and in turn repentance. [10] The dynamics of loss offer a helpful perspective on Paul's eschatology and the role of judgment therein.

How Does Loss Facilitate Spiritual Growth?

Life is full of all kinds of sufferings, death and hardships. The general descriptive word for all of these hardships in Paul's writings is "affliction." All afflictions, whether death, suffering, persecutions or other hardships, carry a common element of loss. Loss is inevitable and unavoidable in this life. For Paul, this is so because this eschatological age is still ruled by the power of Sin and Death. Only in the Messianic age to come will all loss and sorrow be vanquished.

The Dynamics of Judgment. Because affliction and loss were so common in Paul's life, his theology reflects a deep concern for the role of loss in spiritual growth. As noted earlier, all loss experiences initiate a period of self-judgment in which the participants evaluate the meaning of that which is lost and their life without that which is lost. This is so theologically, because loss experiences are essentially eschatological occurrences, vividly reminding the participants of the shortness of time. Such periods of self-judgment often result in repentance and self-correction.

Judgment can be an effective spiritual growth tool. This is true in terms of God's judgment as well as the use of judgment by the church. Theologically, God's judgment is a function of God's love. God desires to punish or eternally damn no one. God desires to see all people saved and in proper relationship with God. The purpose of God's judgment, at least this side of the Last Judgment, is to bring about self-judgment and repentance. In 1 Corinthians 11:32, Paul suggests that when Christians are judged by the Lord, they are "instructed" or disciplined" in order that they may not be "condemned." The purpose of God's judgment, at least to the extent that it is built into this present age, is instruction or discipline. In short, God's purpose in judgment is repentance. Judgment is not the same as punishment. This is a very important point psychologically as well as theologically. All Christians and even the Apostles will be judged by God, but not necessarily punished or condemned (Rom 8:1). Judgment is meant to test or evaluate each person's work and character, just as fire tests the strength and worth of metals. Judgment's purpose is to reveal the truth, and thereby evaluate, *so that* self-correction and repentance can be initiated while there is still time.

A similar positive understanding of judgment as a tool of spiritual growth is implied in the church's use of judgment. Upon hearing of the immorality of a Corinthian Christian, Paul freely pronounces judgment "in the name of the Lord Jesus" (1 Cor 5:4) and advises the Corinthian church to do likewise and also punish this individual by driving him out of the church. Paul suggests several arguments for why judgment is necessary in this case (1 Cor 5:6–13), in contrast to his usual advice which is to avoid judgment (Rom 14:13). He suggests that it is permissible for the church to judge those inside the church, while leaving those outside the church to God's judgment. The implication here is that judgment can be an effective tool for spiritual growth for those inside the church. Judgment can be used to assist Christians to periodically evaluate their lives and faith, in hopes that this self-judgment will lead to greater spiritual growth. Judgment, whether initiated by the church, by the nature of the misdeeds themselves, or by a loss/death experience, leads to self-judgment in the individuals and the possibility of self-corrective action.[11]

Theologically, the purpose of judgment then is not punishment (as commonly thought), but spiritual growth. Judgment is designed to motivate people to be self-evaluative and self-corrective. Only by doing so can people continue to grow spiritually. Loss therefore, since it embodies judgment dynamics, can be an important catalyst of spiritual growth. Faced with the pain of a severe loss or death of a loved one, grievers are reminded that life is short. They are thrown into a "crisis of meaning" in which they must reevaluate their life in light of their loss. That reevaluation process can lead to many significant changes in beliefs, values, and life-style, as well as personal and interpersonal relationships.

Pauline Images of Spiritual Growth. Paul uses three images to describe the process of spiritually growing through loss. First, he likens the experience of growth to Christ's death and resurrection (Gal 2:20). Paul sees his sufferings as "a dying with Christ" (Rom 6:6; 2 Cor

4:11), and his deliverance from death as a resurrection experience (2 Cor 1:8–11; Phil 3:10–11). Second, Paul uses the images of "loss and gain" to describe the same process. He personally had to lose all of his Jewish credentials in order to gain Christ (Phil 3:5–8). One must lose in order to gain, just as one must die in order to rise to new life. Third, Paul uses the imagery of weakness and strength. Paul understands that by being weak he is strong (2 Cor 12:10). For Paul, weakness refers to bodily vulnerability (2 Cor 4:7), the lack of eloquent speech (1 Cor 12:10), human vulnerability to hardship, disease and calamities (2 Cor 12:10), and an anti-boastful attitude (2 Cor 12:1–10). The polarities are self-sufficiency and dependency. By being weak, it is clear that the Gospel's acceptance and advancement is not due to Paul, but to God's power (2 Cor 4:7ff). This power to bring strength out of weakness is the same resurrection power of God that brings new life out of death and gain out of loss. It seems clear that all three images refer to the same dynamic, a growth process that involves loss. This is Paul's proof of the existence of God, based not on the abstractions of logic but on the experiences of a life lived in faith.

Paul uses this dying-rising pattern (or loss-gain, strength-weakness) as a description of spiritual growth (Gal 5:24; Rom 6:6). The central point of this principle is that spiritual growth comes from a periodical "letting go" or losing. Conversely, spiritual growth is *not* fostered by an intentional reliance on one's own efforts. For Paul, spiritual growth is a cyclic process. New advances only follow periods of dying (losing, or weakening). One almost gets the impression that, for Paul, dying or losing are necessary *in order* to rise or to gain.

In terms of spiritual growth, Paul would suggest that we do not "lose" *in order* to gain. We cannot worship growth. We must worship the Father and respond in simple obedience and trust. God then responds to that, our act of trustful obedience, by "rising" out of loss events new spiritual growth. In this way, spiritual growth is essentially a gift of God's grace and not exclusively a product of one's own efforts.

Paul has described the overall experience of spiritual growth as a cyclic process of dying and rising (losing/gaining and weakness/strength). Obviously Paul has many kinds of losses in mind. There are accidental losses that seem traumatic and hopeless, but out of which God brings goodness and new life. There are also those intentional losses in which one purposely "gives up" an old sin, behavior or pride.

Through such an act of self-surrender, God responds to bring strength out of weakness and new life out of death. Loss, in whatever form, is an essential and even necessary part of spiritual growth.

In summary, all losses, no matter how distant, are eschatological occurrences in the sense that they remind us of the shortness of time. All eschatology involves an element of judgment. There is the last judgment at the end of time and "little judgments" embodied in every loss event of life. Losses are catalysts, forcing us to reflect on the value of life, on the value of what is lost, and on ourselves. This self-evaluation process can lead to what Paul calls repentance. There may be a deepening of spiritual commitments, a change in spiritual values or belief, a new sensitivity or compassion for others. In all of these ways, the original loss has been a catalyst to spiritual growth via the dynamic of self-judgment.

AVENUES OF SPIRITUAL GROWTH

Sanctification or spiritual growth has already been defined as a "growing into the likeness of Christ." Earlier it was noted that this definition suggests a multi-dimensional process, including at the least cognitive, emotional and ethical dimensions. Becoming like Christ means becoming like him in one's thoughts, one's attitudes, one's emotions, one's values and so on. Spiritual growth, as so defined, is a very multi-dimensional process. Here are five avenues or dimensions along which people grow spiritually in the midst of loss.

Loss Strengthens Faith

Loss and similar afflictions can build faith. Paul's own personal experience is that afflictions/losses have strengthened his trust and faith in God. Loss is given to him so that the power of God might be more evident (see 2 Cor 4:7). With every loss, affliction or hardship, Paul must rely on God's resurrection power and not on his own efforts. Loss continually reminds Paul that he is not self-sufficient. He must continually surrender his self-sufficiency to God's grace. In this way, repeated losses give Paul repeated opportunities to strengthen his trust and dependency on God. Loss experiences continually "bring him to his knees." His trust and dependency on God increases. His boastful attitude decreases. Many bereaved people can identify with this experience of total reliance on God. Most loss situations are beyond control. When people feel most helpless, they are forced to rely most on God.

Related to the increase of faith and trust in God is the increase of hope. In the face of suffering, death and loss, one must all the more hope in the future based solely on faith in God. If the situation is to be redeemed at all, God alone must do it. There is nothing left to do but to hope. Paul suggests, especially in 2 Corinthians 4:17ff, that suffering increases one's hope and anticipation of the life to come. By sorrowing now, believers appreciate all the more the joy that is to come. True hope which is a hope in things unseen (2 Cor 4:18; Rom 8:24–25) is actually strengthened in suffering. Loss experiences increase our reliance on hope.

Faith and hope have the common theme of total reliance on God. Loss can increase our trust in the Divine. The increasing of faith is one avenue for being "like Christ," for spiritual growth in times of loss. So confident is Paul of the growth-producing qualities of afflictions/losses that he can claim, as he often does, to "rejoice in our sufferings" (Rom 5:4).

Loss Builds Maturity

Loss also builds "character" qualities, like patience, endurance, humility, long-suffering, gratitude, and self-control. For Paul, loss can be a catalyst that enables people to strengthen their patient endurance, character and hope (Rom 5:3–4). So it is that Paul advises Christians who are amid crises: "Be patient" (Rom 8:25) or "Be steadfast, immovable" (1 Cor 15:58) or "Do not lose heart" (2 Cor 5:6; 4:1). Paul wants his readers to look upon afflictions as an opportunity to increase their patience and to learn along with him, "to be content in whatever state I am" (Phil 4:11).

Psychologically, we would call the building up of such qualities as patience and self-control an increase in "maturity." Children are notoriously immature, wanting immediate gratification of their needs. As children grow into adults, however, they learn to be more patient, more self-controlled and more reasonable. They learn to balance their needs with the needs of others. In this way, they become less narcissistic and more loving and humble. We say that people who are patient, self-controlled and grateful are psychologically mature.

Suffering tends to build maturity. Suffering can teach people that they cannot have everything they want, whenever they want it. Suffering teaches them to be patient and to be more grateful with what they do have. Suffering teaches them to be more compassionate with others who suffer. Again, not everyone will learn such qualities through suffering. Some people remain "childish" until their dying day. Many others, however, will develop maturity and character. Loss events can be catalysts for spiritual growth; spiritual growth defined as an increase of maturity. Patience, gratitude, self-control and love—these are the fruits of the Spirit (Gal 5:22) and the signs of spiritual maturity.

Loss Changes or Strengthens Beliefs

Amid suffering, hardships or severe loss experiences, people inevitably ask why: Why has this happened to me? What is the meaning or purpose of this experience? Theologically, these questions focus on the issues of evil, suffering and the nature of God. Hopefully, these crises of meaning will initiate new insights concerning the nature of suffering and the nature of God, insights that will strengthen one's belief system.

The Purpose of Suffering. In 2 Corinthians 12:1–10, Paul recounts the story of his own personal struggles with his handicap, which he refers to as a "thorn in the flesh." Apparently, he struggled with his handicap for some time, asking the Lord to remove it on three separate occasions. Eventually Paul came to understand that the purpose of his "thorn" was to maintain his weakness, so that God's power would be all the more evident in him and his work. Later, this personal experience translated into a general theological principle of the interrelationship of God and suffering (2 Cor 4:7).

Similarly in Philippians 1:12ff, Paul struggles with the meaning of his recent imprisonment. He concludes that what has happened to him has served to advance the Gospel, in particular to the Praetorian Guard, and has also served to make other Christian preachers even more confident in their preaching of the Gospel. Behind each of these passages,

Paul, like all humans, asked the theological question, "Why?" While in the midst of suffering, it is often difficult to see any purpose. Perhaps, too, one's previous "beliefs about suffering"—e.g., it is a punishment for sin—no longer make any sense. Grievers struggle to find meaning in their suffering. Every severe loss experience initiates a new search for meaning, including a struggle with the theological issue of suffering. Each time one's belief system is inevitably changed or strengthened, however slightly.

Nature of God. Crises of meaning brought on by severe loss or affliction experiences also raise theological questions concerning the nature of God. Paul is not primarily a speculative theologian. He has surprisingly little to say about the nature of God per se. Paul's understanding of God grew out of his lived experience, including his experiences of loss and affliction. For example, in Romans 8:23, Paul makes an amazing and bold statement: "We know that for those who love God, everything works for good . . . ." This statement suggests an understanding of God that is unique. God is not the judge who authors afflictions and losses, but the ever-present spirit who actively works for good, even amid tragedy. I believe that this understanding of God, which is so different from portions of Paul's Jewish heritage, grew out of Paul's experiences of loss, affliction and tragedy. Note, for example, the plural pronoun ("we"), implying that this conviction grew out of their common experience together. Paul's proof is not the kerygma, the Scriptures or the Lord, but their own personal knowledge ("we know"). The entire passage in which this verse occurs is devoted to a discussion of sufferings and losses (Rom 8:18). I believe that the view of God embodied in this verse was born out of the anguish of Paul's experiences of loss and affliction. His loss experience transformed his vision of God.

Another Pauline understanding of God is found in 2 Corinthians 1:3–11, which is also a passage concerned with the nature of suffering. Here Paul refers to God as a "God of all comforts" and writes deeply of how he experienced God's comfort during his recent times of affliction. Through these affliction experiences, he has obtained a clear vision of God as one who comforts. God is not "above it all" dispassionately observing Paul's plight, but involved in the pain, anguish, and sorrow of Paul's life. It is not possible to say if this vision of God is new to Paul. It is certainly different from certain portions of the Old

Testament and Greek philosophical traditions. At the very least, it could be suggested that Paul's experience of affliction and loss make this vision of God clearer, if not totally new.

Loss experiences, suffering and tragedies inevitably lead people to ask questions about the nature of God. If God is all-loving and all-powerful, how is it that God allows such things? One's former beliefs about God may no longer make any sense. In the process of grieving, however, many people discover a new image of God—an image of God as one who is working for good in all things, and an image of God as one who comforts them, even in their worst sorrow. Loss, then, can lead to a strengthening and sometimes to a transforming of one's beliefs about God and about the purpose of suffering.

Loss Builds Love and Community

When people suffer a loss or similar affliction, they understand the deep pain and sorrow that such tragedies can bring. Such a full empathetic understanding of their own pain often makes those people thereafter more sympathetic to the needs of others who are going through similar experiences. Thus, the bonds of friendship and love can grow stronger in times of crises, hardship and loss. People who have been through similar circumstances reach out to others in compassion, sympathy and concern. Suffering experiences can help create in people attitudes of love and compassion, both during the time of those tragedies and often continuing afterward as well. Strengthening one's attitude of love and compassion for the less fortunate is also an avenue of spiritual growth. The more loving and compassionate people are, the more they are becoming "like Christ."

This theme is found in many scattered places in Paul's writings. Throughout Paul's letters, he continually advises his readers to love one another, to be compassionate and to do this especially in times of crisis and affliction. In times of grief and sorrow, for example, he advises the Thessalonians to "comfort one another" (1 Thess 4:18) and the Romans to "weep with those who weep" (Rom 12:15b). Increasing one's love, compassion and sympathy for others is certainly another avenue of spiritual growth, another avenue of becoming "like Christ." Experiences of loss and tragedy actually seem to stimulate and strengthen the bonds and gestures of love and compassion, especially between fellow sufferers.

Loss Transforms Values

Eschatology transforms the "normal" values and priorities into a value system which is reversed from the usual "order of the day." Christians who live on a permanent basis by this new order live always "as if" the Kingdom of God is about to break into history. Every loss experience in life is an "eschatological occurrence," a moment in which one is aware of the shortness of time and a moment, therefore, full of judgment. Thus, loss and affliction experiences have a tendency to transform values and priorities.

When the time is short, either cosmically or personally, one's normal values and priorities are dwarfed by the urgency of new "ultimate concerns." The values and pursuits that previously seemed so important mean little in the face of death. Many bereaved people can identify with this experience. The values of materialism, success and power can seem so meaningless in the face of death. In such circumstances, many will ask themselves: "Why did I waste my time on those things?" Thus, loss experiences can initiate a rethinking and perhaps a transformation of one's values. Usually this transformation of values is toward Christ's ethical system—more people oriented, less materialistic, less status oriented. When people make these types of changes in their value system, they are becoming more "like Christ." They are growing spiritually.

SPIRITUAL GROWTH: CLINICAL INTERVIEW

Up to this point, we have approached spiritual growth from a biblical and theological perspective. It might be helpful, at this point, to illustrate from clinical material some of the ways that people grow spiritually. Following are excerpts from a group interview that I had with twelve original members of some of my first grief growth groups. Our conversation focused on how each person had changed and grown since our original group experience and since the death of his or her spouse some time before that.

Leader:
How have you grown since the death of your spouse?

Joan:
Oh, that's a big question. It's been incredible; I think I have changed more than anyone else in the group. Even though I am a professional occupational therapist, I had a low self-image. I never related well in a group, always feeling that what I had to say would be dumb or boring, and not nearly so important as someone else's comments. I never really trusted people except in a one-to-one relationship where I would share myself more comfortably.

Leader:
And now?

Joan:
Now I am very happy with and proud of myself. I am much more open and caring with people I have just met. I feel that this me was there all along; it was just locked up and now is unleashed.

Leader:
You and Ann are leading a group?

Joan:
Yes, Ann and I are leading a discussion group on the grief cycle. I am also in charge of the TLA ("To Live Again") office and telephone. I take the initiative and call many widowed people just to let them know somebody cares. I got elected to my parish council (Catholic). And I am a full-time mommy.

Leader:
Ann?

Ann:
Well, I would say I've just grown up a lot. I was such a dependent, helpless creature when Mickey died. I disgusted myself. (*pause*) Since his death, I've gone back to work. I pretty well had to. I hated it at first, but I came to like it, in fact, really enjoy it at times. I have all kinds of

confidence now. I can make speeches in public about TLA and make big decisions about the kids without being wishy-washy.

Leader:
You've got six kids, right?

Ann:
Yes, five of them are now teenagers.

Leader:
You do have your hands full.

Ann:
We've had some problems with the kids, right, Joan? (*Joan agrees*) Melvin has been arrested twice for drugs and Melodie is really bad in school. I think she isn't going to graduate. I feel so bad at times, for them . . . having no father . . .

Leader:
But?

Ann:
Well, I am not going to rush out and get married just so they can have a father and more things. I like myself too much now (*praise from group*). I'd rather be a little poorer and on my own. We'll manage.

Leader:
I believe you will. Linda, how about you?

Linda:
Well, I think I've finally buried Henry. It took me a long time, as you know. I just could not let him go, but last month on our eighteenth wedding anniversary I was in church, and all of a sudden for no reason I started bawling (Henry's funeral was in the church). Boy, did I cry. I couldn't stop myself. I had to leave church. Father was giving me dirty looks. I was so embarrassed, I haven't been back since.

Leader:
You sound as though you still have some grief work to do, especially around allowing yourself to cry.

Linda:

I know. Everyone here tells me that too. I did not cry much for months after Henry died. I kept handling it on an intellectual level—"He's dead; I must accept it and go on; I will not fall apart and be dependent on anyone again."

Leader:

And now, you're beginning to let the hurt out?

Linda:

It's sort of like something you said once, "delayed grief," as though I am just now beginning to grieve. (*supported by group*)

Jim:

Remember our motto: "The only way out is through!"

Mel (*later*):

I think the biggest growth area for me is in the area of priorities. Before Jane died, I spent so much time working, rushing here and there. It seemed to be so important to make an extra buck and get another account closed. Then when Jane died, I was shattered. My whole life was turned . . .

Jim:

Upside down?

Mel (*continuing*):

I looked at my four sons and began to cry, not for Jane or for them but for me—for the time we wasted together. I try to spend more time with them now, especially on weekends. We're all we've got for each other.

Nancy:

I can identify with that. Before Ted's death, I used to get so worked up over small things; now they don't seem to matter much. (*begins to laugh in anticipation*) I am always telling the story of my basement. It flooded last month, and my mother was running around in a panic, calling the plumber and doing this and that. That's how I used to be, but now I can't get worked up over such things anymore. They don't matter. Who cares? It'll dry out. My mother can't believe the change in me. The important thing to me is my family, taking time *every day* to spend time with them.

Bev:
We take time *now*, whereas none of us did before. The most important thing is to enjoy today. Today is everything. Tomorrow . . . well, tomorrow is always an unknown.

Jim:
I would describe it as being glad I'm alive—really appreciative of each day, looking for ways to make it special.

Bev:
I'd rather be with people I love, really caring, taking the masks off—that's what matters to me. It's too bad that I didn't see that sooner, before John died.

Most of these people can recount many ways in which they have grown as a result of their loss and grief. Most of these personal growth advances are not necessarily spiritual, although each would have spiritual dimensions. Obviously, people who have not grown are not at this meeting (which is partly why they have not grown), although Linda is still in the throes of a contaminated and delayed grief reaction.

The latter third of this excerpt, however, concerning priorities and values, does illustrate one avenue of spiritual growth—the revolution of values. Severe loss experiences are "eschatological occurrences" in the sense of making their participants aware of the shortness of time. So vivid is this awareness to these people that most of them have completely reversed their "ordinary" value hierarchy. In all of their cases, their new values were more humane. The sense of urgency that revolutionizes values was born in a loss experience. Again, this illustrates one avenue of spiritual growth that is initiated by loss.

Leader (*later*):
What other changes have occurred since the deaths of your spouses?

Shirley:
The biggest changes have been in TLA itself. We are over six hundred strong now with chapters in Delaware County, Philadelphia and Berks County. Can you believe that? (*digression on TLA's growth*)

Leader:
Each of you is personally in some kind of leadership role.

Ann:
This has been an important thing for me. TLA has given me a place to call home, something to take up my time and give me new hope.

Leader:
Why have most of you gotten so active in leadership roles?

Shirley:
We believe in TLA. We experienced what a difference it made in our lives; we wanted to help others to grow too, to really show people out there that there are people who care.

Grace:
I would say that it's given me a place to be needed. I really missed that when my Johnny died. He needed me, and then when the kids began to go their own way, they didn't need me anymore either. But TLA did.

Leader:
Each of you is active in some way. Would you say that being active is helpful to widowed people.

Bob:
To an extent. You can run away in activity, too, you know.

Dan:
But I think it's important. It's given me a new direction.

Leader:
Like a new purpose in life?

Joan:
Yes, but it's been a social outlet for me too. That's also important.

Leader:
I would suspect, too, that being involved in the hurt of other people has kept you honest with your own hurt.

Nancy:
Yes, I always learn something from every new person I talk to.

Ann:
When a new person first tells her story, you hurt all over again, just as though it were you.

Leader:
Does it ever end, the grief? Does it ever stop?

All:
No. (*all agree*)

Shirley:
I don't think I'll ever get over it, but I have learned to live with it.

Leader:
So you folks still hurt, ugh? I thought leaders are supposed to have it all together. (*laughter*)

Bob:
Right! Just as ministers are always perfectly practicing what they preach!

Leader:
Touché!

For each of these people, TLA has given them more than just a place to grieve and a social outlet, however important those things are. TLA has also given them a sense of purpose and meaning. For some it has filled in the gap of meaning, left vacant by the death of their spouse and/or the growing up of their children. Obviously, this situation is unique to this particular group of people, who were the founders and the current leadership of this organization. It does illustrate, however, the crisis of meaning that accompanies a grief reaction and one way in which people can resolve that crisis. These people are actively and emotionally involved in caring for other people. The strengthening and creation of new bonds of love is an excellent counterbalance to the severance of a bond of love. Active personal involvement in TLA provides an excellent blending of a sense of meaning and purpose and a loving involvement in other people's growth. In short, it's good therapy. Any similar organization (like a church) that is both meaning-oriented and people-oriented could provide the same growth potential.

Leader (*later*):
What role did your religion or faith play in your grief? Did it help resolve your grief or block it?

Joan:
I have always considered my faith as very strong and precious, despite my current doubts. Mickey was a strong Christian—he had been a Norbertine Brother until ill health forced him out, and he lived his faith. We saw our life as a part of God's plan, working primarily through him and secondarily through me . . . .He was in the hospital for eight months before he died, all of which time I was pregnant. I felt a lot of resentment early that he had to suffer so much, that I had to travel back and forth to the hospital, and that he wasn't taking care of *me* the way he had during our first pregnancy. (*later*) I think the conflict between my faith and my emotions helped delay my grief reaction. I was so sure of Mickey's happiness and my "job well-done" that I couldn't feel sad. How could I be sad when God had taken Mickey to such a wonderful place as heaven . . . or so I thought.

Leader:
How did that change?

Joan:
Well, I guess it changed through our group and these people. They cried and got angry at God and everything, but still had faith. Finally, I began to see my anger and let me come out.

Leader:
Are you still angry?

Joan:
No, not much. I am mostly doubting God now. All of this stuff about virgin births, resurrections of dead bodies and the rest, I'm not so sure it makes any sense anymore. At this point, I do feel that I am doing God's will in helping other widowed people and opening myself to all people. But the emotional closeness with God is not there. I feel as if I'm talking to a brick wall sometimes and am not really sure where I go from here. I suspect I am experiencing a religious crisis as my life is in transition, and that I will come out of it stronger yet.

Leader:
I hope so.

Linda:
I was pretty religious before Henry's death too. I was in the CYA as a youth. Henry and I used to go to Mass every Sunday. Then when he died, I just turned off of church. I don't know where God is anymore. I cried and cried, asking him "why" this happened, but no answer. Not a thing! Ever.

Leader:
Is that where you are now?

Linda:
Yes, I listen to you all, your wonderful experiences, and I just don't know. I don't feel anything.

Leader:
Give it time. You'll find it again in your own way . . . .

Bev:
I felt abandoned by God, too, at my husband's death. There were many long nights when I felt really alone in more ways than one. Then I had that mystical experience that I told you about, when John appeared to me at the front door, just as though he was walking in from work. It was a weird, weird experience, but I immediately knew what it meant. It was John's way of telling me that he's O.K. He's still present with

me, watching over me and the kids. From then on I knew God was on my side. I figured God allowed John to come back to do that, to show me he was O.K., so I figured God really does care.

Leader:
Both God and John are present with you. Both of them love you.

Jim:
You know, it's funny. Heaven used to be such a rational thing with me, before Marge's death. I mean, I believed in heaven, but it was a point of intellectual discussion. Now, I know heaven exists—I mean, I don't even know it, I "live" it. I feel it in my guts! It's not a question of knowing anymore. It's as automatic as being sure that I exist. Marge is there, at peace, finally after years of torment.

Leader:
Did you ever have a mystical experience like Bev's?

Jim:
No, not as such, but I know what she means. They give you comfort, and they're meant to help you. I believe God does those kinds of things, sends "experiences" and answers prayers, and even speaks through people, in order to help you.

Nancy:
For me, that's the way I see God best now—in all of you. At times, when we are really close, I feel God right here, along with each of our husbands and wives, just as if we were all one big family, laughing and loving each other. (*others agree*)

This excerpt illustrates the wide variety of ways that religion or beliefs can influence how a person handles a personal tragedy. In Joan's case, intense religious devotion actually momentarily blocked her grief process. Linda's previous religious activity did not contribute anything to the resolution of her grief either, although in her case all of the data is not in yet. Bev, who came from a moderate religious background, has actually grown stronger religiously because of her loss and grief experience. In general, the whole group agreed with Nancy that dogmatic religion is less a concern with them now, replaced by a more personal, experience-oriented religion. The key variable in determining whether religion is growth-producing or growth-blocking is probably still the quality of the religious content itself.

Leader:
How has your concept of God changed over the years since the death of your spouse?

Joan:
Having been raised in Catholic schools, I had a good idea of the fear of God as well as the love of God. I now feel freer to interpret my actions in regard to his plan for my life, rather than use a checklist approach . . . this is good.

Leader:
You feel more grace . . . more acceptance from God.

Joan:
Yes, that's it.

Linda:
I'm not sure I've ever known God. (*pause*)

Leader:
Say more.

Linda:
I guess I've gone from a Santa Claus image of God to being an atheist. Before, I always thought that God would give me anything I wanted, if I was just good. Well, I was good, real good, and all I got was death.

Leader:
You sound a bit angry.

Linda:
Now, I don't know. I'm not sure there's anybody out there at all.

Leader:
The Santa Claus business died, but so far nothing has risen to take its place?

Linda:
No, nothing.

Nancy:
I feel God's love strongly through other caring people. I consider all of the wonderful people who have been given to me, whom God sent to me in my time of need. I feel as though TLA was an answered prayer.

Leader:
So God is more present now for you.

Nancy:
And less up there beyond the clouds . . . but that too, I mean, that's where our husbands are, there with God. But God is also here among us.

Leader:
Is that promise in the Bible, about all things working for good with those who love God, is that true from your experience?

All:
Yes, maybe, no. (*varied answers*)

Leader:
One at a time, please.

Bev:
When I look back over my life and the life of this organization, I am amazed by what has been accomplished. I believe this all has been according to God's plan, that he is behind all of this. All of this came out of tragedy. All of this would not have happened without tragedy. Sounds crazy, ugh?

Ann:
I would have been a helpless dependent creature all of my life if Mickey stayed alive. It was almost as if God planned all of this, as though it was the only way he was going to get me to grow up.

Leader:
Then, did God cause death?

Bev:

No, I don't think so. There were times when I thought so, but now in retrospect I don't think so. It just happened . . . that's it. That's all there was to it. Then God came along and turned it into something good.

Leader:

Then God is less powerful than you once supposed, that is, he does not control every little event in life.

All:

(*confusion, mixed answers*)

Bev:

I suppose if that is true, that God is less powerful, he is more loving then. Instead of being distant, God is now closer than he ever was before in my life. God and I have had a thing together over the last few years, walking and talking together early in the morning. In spite of how low I was, I always thought God would get me through this, one way or another.

Leader:

That's quite a statement of faith. (*others agree*)

Linda:

I couldn't ever say that, but I really admire your guts.

Nancy:

Yes, Bev, I have admired your faith too. You've been the one person who has hung in there with the God stuff, even when the rest of us were shooting you down. It really means something to you.

Leader:

And to all of you in your own ways.

This excerpt also illustrates the wide variety of understandings of God and the variety of ways that one's view of God can influence the handling of a tragedy. Bev's spiritual growth process shows a definite trend away from the view of "God as Heavenly King" to "God as

Comforter." It is a transition that not everyone makes. Many, like Linda, cannot get beyond being angry at the King God for causing (or allowing) the death of their loved one. They cannot "see" God in and among the comforting love and concern of other human beings. From the experience of this author, it seems as if most people who do remain religious after a severe loss do significantly alter their understanding of God. This spiritual growth process is usually in the direction of a more compassionate, comforting and suffering servant model of God, in short, "God in Christ."

SUMMARY AND CONCLUSIONS

This chapter has focused on how St. Paul understood spiritual growth and its relationship to loss. Sanctification or spiritual growth was defined as the process of growing into the "likeness of Christ." It is by definition a multi-dimensional growth process. It includes becoming like Christ in one's beliefs, in one's attitudes, in one's values and priorities, and in one's faith. The fulfillment of this spiritual growth process is the actualization of humanity's God-given potential, expressed in the concept of the "image of God" and made visible, according to Christian belief, in the life and personhood of Jesus Christ. Thus, the sanctifying process represents God's intention for humanity in creation. God authors it, sustains it, and lures it toward completion.

Paul's eschatological understanding of loss offers an unique perspective on loss. Like most of his Christian contemporaries, Paul understood that human existence as he knew it was fading away. The new Messianic Age was already drawing and would soon fully arrive. For Paul, an "eschatological occurrence" in this life is any experience in which life seems short or in which death seems near. Obviously, loss experiences are very vivid examples of eschatological occurrences. Loss experiences are "little deaths." They are experiences in which people keenly feel their finitude.

Faced with severe losses (or the threat thereof), people often reassess their life and values. They judge themselves in light of their eschatological awareness. As a consequence, many people make significant revisions in their values and life-styles. Judgment becomes the mechanism of spiritual growth. Further, these "little judgments" in this life are related ultimately to God's final judgment. Judgment is a continuum from this age to the next. This is so because eschatology is also a continuum. The eschaton is something yet to come and something present in every loss experience. Therefore, loss can indeed be a catalyst for spiritual growth through its innate dynamics of judgment.

The paths of spiritual growth in times of loss are varied. This is so because spiritual growth itself is a multi-dimensional process. One can seek to become "like Christ" in one's beliefs, in one's faith, in one's loving attitude for others, and in one's values and priorities. In times of loss and grief, one can grow along any one or all of these avenues.

Loss is never a guarantee for growth—either emotional or spiritual. If it were, we would indeed all become masochists. Clearly, loss *can be* a catalyst for spiritual growth. What are the factors that facilitate the growth process, and what are the factors that block it? How can pastors facilitate emotional and spiritual growth in their parishioners in times of loss? What resources do we have available? In future chapters, we will focus on four of the traditional pastoral resources—community, rituals, beliefs and faith.

6. Communities of Faith . . . Communities of Healing

A little girl came home from a neighbor's
house where her little friend had died.
"Why did you go?" questioned her father.
"To comfort her mother," said the child.
"What could you do to comfort her?"
"I climbed into her lap and cried with her."[1]

You have just walked out of the hospital room where your spouse of twenty-three years lay dying, an imminent victim of a lingering battle with cancer. The attending physician says that she has but a few days to live. You're numb. You cannot believe that this is happening to you. In a trance-like state, you walk down the hallway, deep in thought, dreading what is in store for you in the next few days, weeks and months. You stop at the courtesy telephone. You instinctively pick up the phone and start dialing. Whom do you call? Whom would you reach out to? In your time of need, who will come to your support?

One of the main resources that people in crisis have available to them is other people—family, friends, their clergy and, of course, other Christians. At its best, the local church is a network of people characterized by friendship, compassion and genuine care for one another. We are socially and psychologically interdependent. We have a common commitment to God, to love of neighbor and to certain humane values. In such communities, "when one suffers, all suffer" (1 Cor 12:26).

How a particular congregation responds to the grief of one of its members is of critical importance for that individual—both psychologically and theologically. People who fail to respond to another's loss or respond with an attitude of non-support work to block the healing process of that bereaved person. Each of us has an important and direct contribution to make to the health of our friends. Theologically as well, how we respond to a bereaved person communicates something of the nature of God. Bereavement often includes periods in which the mourning person feels alienated and distant from God. During such "silences of God," all that the sufferer knows of God is revealed in the faces of those representatives of God that minister to him or her. Our love and compassion for the bereaved is the only tangible taste that they may have of the Bread of Life. Again, St. Paul describes this incarnational theology so well when he writes of the "Father of mercies and God of all comfort, who comforts us in our affliction, so that we may be able to comfort those who are in any affliction, with the comfort with which we ourselves are comforted by God" (2 Cor 1:3–4). For the moment, we are God for one another.

Community is an over-used word these days. By "community" I mean a network of affectional bonds between any group of people. Obviously, community in this sense is more than just the physical approximation of people. Obviously too, there are many types of community in modern life. Most people live psychologically in several communities simultaneously. Most people have an extended family community, a neighborhood community, a religious community and a community of people centered around their place of work, a club, or a school. These diverse communities may vary greatly in size, strength of affectional bond and relative importance to the individual. For the purposes of this discussion we want to focus on religious communities or what I call "communities of faith." This chapter will explore how a community of faith can be helpful in facilitating the emotional and spiritual growth of grieving people.

THE DECLINE OF COMMUNITY

In the past fifty years, several significant changes have occurred and are occurring in American culture that effect the presence and quality of community. Most sociologists agree that there has been a gradual but persistent breakdown of community as this society has become increasingly urbanized. As more people move into larger metropolitan areas, the sense of community that characterized small town life has been lost. There is less community, and what community there is has become harder to form and to maintain. There are several forces that have contributed to this weakening of community.

Mobility. While Americans have always been a nation of movers, the frequency of relocating has accelerated in the last quarter of the century. There are several different types of reasons why people relocate: the movement of rural, poorer people to the cities, the fleeing of other urban people to the suburbs, and the transferred executives moving from city to city. Alvin Toffler reported that in the year 1967, 36,600,000 Americans changed their place of residence, which at that time was more than "the combined populations of Cambodia, Ghana, Guatemala, Honduras, Iraq, Israel, Mongolia, Nicaragua and Tunisia."[2] Certainly, the relocation of the populations of these countries would be a major news event. Yet, such a movement of people, writes Toffler, "on this massive scale occurs every year in the United States" without notice. In the seventy major urbanized areas in this country, the average family changes residences every four to five years.

The result of this regular change of residence is that people are uprooted from their emotional-social support system. For some people, this is a positive choice; for others, it is not. In any case, the tempo by which human relations are formed and forgotten quickens. Alvin Toffler writes of this change in the pattern of friendships:

> Friendship patterns of the majority in the future will provide for many satisfactions, while substituting many close relationships of short durability for the few long-term friendships formed in the past.[3]

Since the turn-over in friendships is quick, there is a tendency to "keep friendships bland and readily disconnectable."[4] There is less commitment, less willingness to get involved. If people are to have a meaningful support system at all, they must be prepared to form friendships fast. Yet, for many other people, who do not make friends quickly, there are gaps, long periods when they are without any significant support system. At any given moment, large segments of the population may be without any meaningful, close social network.

Anonymity. With the increased urbanization and suburbanization of modern society, there is increased anonymity. We know one another less well and less intimately. This condition is due partly to the fact that there are just so many more people in a metropolitan area. We feel overwhelmed by numbers. We cannot be friends with everyone. Instead of a few close friends, we tend to have many impersonal acquaintances. We "know" the mail carrier, the grocery clerk, the bank teller or our child's teacher. We know them all in casual, functional ways, what Martin Buber described as "I-it relationships." We are less connected. America is a "nation of strangers," seeking the genuine intimacy of an "I-Thou encounter," but too busy, too mobile and too frightened to find it.

Changing Family Patterns. There is no secret that the structure of the American family has and is changing rapidly. Small town America was built around the extended family, but in recent decades there has been a gradual decline of the extended family pattern. Fewer people live in association with grandparents, uncles, aunts and cousins. Extended families are spread out, sometimes in the four corners of the country. The nuclear family is now the primary family unit. Then add to this trend the growing frequency of divorce and single parent families. The result is that families are less of a built-in support system for people than they used to be. In times of a major loss, of course, relatives still come from out of state for the funeral or wedding, but their support is limited and temporary. They are not normally a part of one's ongoing community of support.

Fragmentation of Community. In the large metropolitan areas, community has become fragmented. It is not uncommon for a person to work in the center of the city and commute daily from a suburban "bedroom community." With the growing number of women in the work force, both husband and wife may spend eight hours a day, every day, in separate communities. Meanwhile, their children spend eight hours in a third community: the school. Add to this segregation the other assorted communities, like church, neighborhood, shared interest groups and so on. Most people do not live in a single community. They live in several communities. They have their church friends, their work friends, their neighborhood friends and their friends that they know through their children's activities. Usually these various "friends" do not know each other. Their only association is through the individual, who functions like the hub of the wheel. Community is fragmented and thereby weakened and less available in times of crisis.

The combined results of these four forces is that there is less natural community. Community is more difficult to form and to maintain.

What community there is, is less in-depth, less permanent and less homogeneous. Our social network tends to be fragmented, spread out and temporary. If we want community, we must be intentional about it. We must work at forming and maintaining a social support system.

COMMUNITY, MENTAL HEALTH AND BEREAVEMENT

The research in the fields of community psychiatry and social psychology have long concluded that the presence of a close-knit supportive group of friends functions as a mental health preventative. In 1978, the President's Commission on Mental Health completed a year-long study of the emotional health of Americans. Their report highlighted the important role that "a small dense network with strong ties" plays in mental health. One's immediate support group, whether that be family, friends or congregation, is the first-line of defense in a crisis situation or in an emotionally stressful situation. The panel concluded:

> To be connected to others, to belong, to receive social support when it is needed, and to be able to give it in return, is an important part of mental health . . . . Social and community support systems can help to contribute to a sense of well-being and of competent functioning. They can aid in reducing the negative consequences of stressful life events. . . . [5]

Following up on this observation, they go on to note that in times of crisis, like bereavement, people usually turn first to their families, friends and neighbors. Moreover, people with emotional problems will turn to clergy or other religious leaders before seeking out a mental health professional directly. A person's closest friends are the ones that he or she turns to first in times of need. Friendship is a necessary ingredient of sound mental health. Without friends, one is more vulnerable to mental breakdown and the harmful effects of stress—a conclusion that is particularly true in the case of bereavement.

Social scientists Sheldon Blackman and Kenneth Goldstein are one team of researchers who have studied the close connection between an individual's mental health and his or her community. They offer a theory for what happens in a small, closely-knit community. They theorize that there exists in every community or group a system of reciprocation. In times of crisis, people in supportive communities exchange emotional support or "credits" with one another. Giving aid to another person in time of need earns one certain "credits" or an unspoken mutual understanding that he or she will receive that support back in a similar time of crisis. The more that people are involved in a system of reciprocation, the more they will give and receive support and the wider their network of support will become. In a sense, the more that one gives support, the more one will receive support someday when needed. Blackman and Goldstein note that a person's ability to tolerate stress is related to his or her involvement in this reciprocation network. They write:

> Failure to be involved in such a network of credits . . . increases
> the probability that disability will result from a given amount of
> stress, because no support will be available.[6]

Their conclusion suggests that people who have fewer emotional and social supports manifest more psychological and physical symptoms in crisis periods, and are thereby in greater danger of mental and physical illness during those crisis periods.[7]

Many of the early studies of the value of a small supportive community have been done among so-called "primitive" peoples. In modern urbanized cultures, the growing absence of small supportive communities or tribes presents a serious mental health problem. Many community mental health workers are now talking about how to "retribalize" modern society. James A. Sparks, in his simple, helpful book, *Friendship After Forty*, writes about this dichotomy between the increasing friendlessness of modern society and the critical role that friendship plays in good mental health. He concludes:

> Friends and friendship, to take a practical and realistic approach,
> are an important resource for maintaining good mental health and
> preventing emotional disability regardless of age.[8]

Sparks outlines the barriers to friendship and the qualities that nurture friendship. He makes a passionate plea for the lifting up of friendship by the church through the development of a theology of friendship and for a learning or relearning of the arts of friendship.

What is true in a general way is also true in the specific case of bereavement. A close-knit supportive community is one key variable in determining whether or not a grief-stricken person will successfully recover from his or her loss. Let's consider some sample research in this area.

In a study by John J. Schwab and associates,[9] widowed people were interviewed one year after their loss and their current grief reactions were classified roughly into two categories: resolved and unresolved. The "resolved" group reported that human relationships, especially those that accepted their feelings, were crucial to their healing. Friends supported them and gave them someone to "talk out their feelings with." Concerning the "unresolved" group, the researchers write:

> The apparent lack of social supports we observed seems to be contributory (to unresolved grief). Furthermore, many respondents reported that their friends and relatives showed a concern and willingness to talk about the loss for only a few weeks. Thus it seems that many did not have an opportunity to express their sorrow or ventilate their feelings over a period of time.[10]

People were a key variable. The presence of caring friends gives mourning people the opportunity to talk out their negative feelings.

Another study on the interrelationship of community and bereavement was conducted by David Maddison and Beverly Raphael, who studied conjugal bereavement in the context of a social network. They too classified the resultant grief processes into "good outcomes" (indicating resolution) and "bad outcomes" (indicating unresolved grief and deteriorating health). They found that among several factors, the availability of other people was a critical variable influencing grief's resolution. More specifically, they found that the quality of one's social network and social contacts during bereavement greatly influenced the outcome. They write:

> More specifically, widows who subsequently proceeded to a bad outcome tended to express the feelings that there were some people in the environment who had overtly or covertly opposed the free expression of affect, particularly those of grief and anger.[11]

This study recognized that there were other variables, like the widow's own long-standing mode of expression, the manner of death and the quality of the marriage prior to the death of the spouse. All of these factors, plus the presence of community, determined the difference between good and bad outcomes. Nevertheless, the willingness of other people to listen to the widow's feelings without judgment, "insensitivity, overt or covert hostility, absence of empathy and ignorance of a widow's needs" was a crucial variable.[12] Grief is facilitated when the bereaved person has an opportunity to "freely and fully express" his or her grief emotions. That opportunity is made possible by the presence of caring friends.

From this discussion, it seems clear that we humans are healthiest when rooted in small, supportive communities. When tragedies or crises do occur, the availability of a supportive community is a crucial factor in contributing to a positive adjustment. The trouble with this insight is that community cannot always be manufactured in times of need. Friendships must be cultivated prior to the crisis at hand, like an emotional-social insurance policy. Another trouble with this insight is that we live in an increasingly friendless culture. As previously noted, it is harder to form and to maintain adequate communities than it used to be. In this culture the local congregation still stands out as one of the few institutions offering community. From this perspective, the local church is now more important than ever. At its best, the local congregation is a community of people that care for one another. We are the family of God—the extended family that most of us no longer have readily available. The ongoing support of one's church friends is a valuable mental health preventative—and at times of loss, transition or tragedy, the support of other people becomes crucial.

THE HEALING QUALITIES OF EMPATHY

The disciplines of psychology and theology have long argued that love has healing qualities. In our modern culture, however, "love" is a badly misused word, employed to cover "a multitude of sins" from lust to patriotism. Theologians have tried to describe what they mean by love through the term "agape." Agape refers to a special type of love. Agape is love that is unconditional, total and deeply caring. It is the kind of love that God has for human beings and the kind of love that saintly men and women have reflected throughout the ages. Agape is accepting and forgiving. It is empathic and compassionate. It is caring for another person without regard for one's own gain or pride. Agape is found in God in its purest terms and in humans in lesser degrees of purity. Yet, to the extent that agape is embodied in people, this kind of love facilitates healing—the healing of mind, psyche and relationships.

Psychotherapists, too, have talked about the healing qualities of love. One of the first to define love psychologically and describe its therapeutic qualities was Carl Rogers. Rogers defines healing love as consisting of congruence, unconditional positive regard and empathic understanding. Congruence refers to that quality in the care-giver of transparency—true openness, honesty—when the care-giver reflects on the outside what he or she feels on the inside. Unconditional positive regard refers to an attitude by the care-giver that is non-judgmental, non-evaluative and accepting. Empathic understanding refers to a situation in which the care-giver feels and truly understands the other person's world as he or she experiences it. Carl Rogers summarizes:

> Thus the relationship which I have found helpful is characterized by a sort of transparency on my part, in which my real feelings are evident; by an acceptance of this other person as a separate person with value in his own right; and by a deep empathic understanding which enables me to see his private world through his eyes. When these conditions are achieved, I become a companion to my client, accompanying him in the frightening search for himself, which he now feels free to undertake.[13]

When a pastor or counselor embodies these three characteristics, that care-giving relationship becomes healing. These are the qualities of love that foster growth and healing.

Robert R. Carkhuff has spent his life studying the nature of the helping process. Key to this effort was his attempts, based on Rogers' work, to isolate the essential ingredients of effective helping, to be able to measure those qualities scientifically and then to develop a training program that would increase the effectiveness of counselors. Carkhuff argues that all significant relationships have the potential to be helpful. Ministers, teachers, parents and friends can be healing agents as much as any professional counselor can. Each care-giver, to the extent that he or she embodies these qualities, can be an instrument of healing. For Carkhuff, the three essential characteristics of effective helping are:

1. An effective therapist is integrated, non-defensive and authentic or *Genuine* in his therapeutic encounters.
2. An effective therapist can provide a non-threatening, safe, trusting or secure atmosphere by his acceptance, unconditional positive regard, love or *Non-possessive Warmth* for the client.
3. An effective therapist is able to ''be with,'' ''grasp the meaning of'' or *Accurately and Empathetically* understand the client on a moment-by-moment basis. [14]

Carkhuff has studied these qualities as they relate to the effectiveness of therapy or counseling. He concludes that ''the greater the degree of which these elements were present in the therapeutic encounter, the greater was the resulting constructive personality change in the patient.'' [15] Furthermore, these findings held true for a wide variety of counselors, ''regardless of their training or theoretic orientations . . . .'' [16] Counselors or care-givers that do not embody these qualities can actually be harmful to or at the very least blocking of a person's healing process.

The conclusion of Carkhuff's extensive research is that the mere presence of other people is not healing in and of itself. Rather, it is the quality of those relationships that facilitate healing. Bereaved people will grieve and be healed from their sorrow if the right conditions prevail. Bereaved people surrounded by a community of friends who embody these qualities will be healed and will grow. Bereaved people surrounded by people who are largely unaccepting, non-empathic and ungenuine will have their grief process blocked and thwarted. If we pastors are to be true instruments of God's healing to the bereaved, we must strive to embody these qualities. If we cannot embody such qualities, we should not attempt to involve ourselves intimately in the lives of hurting people.

It seems clear that, although the mere presence of a supportive community is important, grieving people need others who embody an attitude of empathy. Such an attitude invites the free expression of one's feelings. Careful distinction, however, must be made between empathy and sympathy, the latter of which is usually associated with loss and bereavement. Family therapist Norman Paul draws a distinction between sympathy and empathy, the latter which is therapeutic for grieving families. He defines "effective empathy" as when one person "recognizes that he shares kindred feelings with another person. . . ."[17] "The empathizer," he continues, "is not only aware of the other's various experiences but finds himself sharing the reliving of these experiences."[18] Of the contrast, he writes:

> In sympathy, however, the subject is principally absorbed in his own feelings as projected into the object's special separate experience. In sympathy, the subject is likely to use his own feelings as standards against which to measure the object's feelings and behavior. Sympathy then bypasses real understanding of the other person . . . ."[19]

In families where there exists unresolved grief and unshared feelings, Paul, as a therapist, seeks to reestablish empathy by intervention. Only in such a healing environment can the grief process begin anew and the related family disturbances be resolved. Genuine empathy is critical for the healing of grief. Sympathy is destructive to it.

One of the more helpful ways to understand this distinction between sympathy and empathy is in the terms of Transactional Analysis.[20] T.A. posits that there are three main "ego states": Parent, Adult, Child. These three states of mind are universal, but the content of each will vary from individual to individual. In general the Parent state is that part of a person's personality that acts like a parent, however that role has been defined and modeled. In the Child state people act, feel and embody features of their personalities when they were younger. The Adult state is the neutral, responsible, objective part of a person's psyche. The relative balance and uncontamination of these various segments of the psyche is the key to sound mental health.

In the T.A. system, sympathy is essentially a Parent-to-Child transaction. Sympathizers feel "sorry for the griever." They adopt an attitude of condescension or "poor you" toward the griever. There is an implied "I'm glad it's not me." There is an implied "put-down" in sympathy—that sympathizers are "one up." The sympathizer is the helper and the sufferer is the helpee. There is also an implied distance in sympathy. "I feel sorry for you," the sympathizer thinks, and "I'm sure glad that is not me." Sympathizers distance themselves just enough so that they do not have to feel the griever's pain. They can observe pain from afar.

On the other hand, empathy is essentially a Child-to-Child transaction. In empathy one feels *with* the other person. Empathizers so share the griever's feelings that they relive, to some extent, these same feelings. Empathizers hurt too. Most bereaved people want and need genuine empathy and are quick to detect the hollow tones of sympathy. Clichés, such as "Time heals all wounds," or "Keep your chin up, kid," or "I know just how you feel," or "God works in mysterious ways," are often perceived as sympathetic in nature and not truly empathic. Most bereaved people react coolly to such gestures of sympathy. It would be better if nothing was said at all.

Our task as pastors is to create in our congregations this kind of supportive community. These kinds of communities do not always just happen. Sometimes it takes special leadership and training by the pastor over a period of time to mold and to develop networks of support. Networks that embody the healing qualities of empathy, acceptance and genuineness provide an atmosphere in which bereaved people can do their grief work, and thereby travel the road toward restored wholeness.

THE SELF-HELP PHILOSOPHY

Even though groups have been around since the dawn of time, the scientific study of group dynamics is a relatively young science within the broader discipline of psychology. Within the last two decades, there has been a surge of interest and participation in group work, including encounter groups, group therapy, sensitivity training, growth groups and so on. One aspect of this group movement is the "self-help" or mutual-help group. There has been a phenomenal growth of mutual-help groups. Most self-help groups are organized around a specific problem or topic such as bereavement, drug abuse, mental retardation, overweight and the like. People willingly bond themselves together in an effort to help each other with that particular problem.

The premier model of the self-help organization is Alcoholics Anonymous (A.A.).[21] Since its inception in 1935, A.A. has grown to a size of some 750,000 members worldwide. In the A.A. approach, the alcoholic is treated by joining a local chapter of the Alcoholics Anonymous program. There is no resident expert or professional leader at an A.A. meeting. Each and every member of A.A. is an admitted alcoholic (non-drinking). The other group members have "been there." They know the new person's rationalizations, excuses and defenses. They can cut through his or her smoke screen to confront him or her with the truth of his or her disease. The A.A. group offers support for the member and also a firm challenge to "surrender" his or her disease to a Higher Power. This unique combination of support and confrontation is growth facilitating. Help comes not from a professional, but from the group as a whole. Healing occurs because the "patient" is now in a genuine community, a network of people that surrounds the individual with a supportive, caring and confrontive community.

Another helpful characteristic of an A.A. program, as well as other self-help organizations, is that after a certain period, the individual is involved in helping others. He or she is now giving as well as receiving. Literally, the health of the individual depends on the group and, in turn, the life of the group depends on him or her. There is no health apart from the community. Self-help groups focus on the importance of support, shared experience, personal responsibility, complete honesty, achievable day-to-day goals and mutual caring.

Another model program of the self-help variety is the Widow-to-Widow program, developed by Phyllis Silverman of Harvard University.[22] Silverman began her involvement with this problem when she was researching how well the mental health system worked for newly widowed people. She concluded,

> I learned that, for the most part, these caregivers were inadequate. Not only did they have little understanding of what a widow or widower needs, but more often than not, they would withdraw, advising the bereaved to keep a "stiff upper lip."[23]

She also concluded, along with Australian psychiatrist David Maddison, that during the first year of bereavement "most widows felt that other widows were the most helpful" kinds of caregivers.[24] Based on these two conclusions, she gathered five well-adjusted widows to be a crisis intervention team. In an initial pilot project, they called on approximately six hundred newly widowed women, under the age of sixty-five, during a three-year period. The program consisted of regular personal contacts with a widowed woman, followed by some group and educational programs. The researchers at Harvard University discovered that the Widow-to-Widow program filled an important gap in the mental health delivery system. Moreover, widows had a unique contribution to make to the total care of a newly widowed person, a unique contribution qualitatively different than the care provided by other professionals.

The Widow-to-Widow program is an excellent example of a self-help group that deals with a life crisis or transition. Widowhood is not so much a disease as it is a normal, albeit devastating, crisis. The task of a self-help group or program is to get the individual through this transition. As noted in earlier chapters, such crisis periods are times of heightened vulnerability to physical disease and mental breakdown. The temporary community provided by these programs offers the necessary support that enables the grieving person to pass through this crisis unharmed.

I have described two of the more noteworthy types of self-help groups. There are many, many others. A.A. itself has sparked other "anonymous-type" groups, such as Gamblers Anonymous (for compulsive gamblers), Neurotics Anonymous (for people with chronic emotional problems), Overeaters Anonymous (for overweight people) and Parents Anonymous (for parents of delinquent teenagers). Each of these groups are built on the A.A. model and the self-help philosophy. Other types of self-help groups include Parents Without Partners (for single parents and their children), Make Today Count (for cancer patients and their families), Compassionate Friends (for parents of deceased children), Recovery, Inc. (for former mental patients), and the National Association of Retarded Citizens (for welfare of retarded people). These are only a few of the many types of self-help organizations that can and are being formed throughout the United States. The President's Commission on Mental Health estimated that there were "over a half-million different self-help groups" in the United States.[25] Now, that's incredible!

There are many reasons for the amazing success of the self-help philosophy. Several reasons stick out, particularly as they relate to bereavement:

1. These groups develop community; a small, closely-knit community of caring people. People in crisis desperately need community; they need friendship. In our modern society, there is little enough com-

munity. Self-help groups build a community that will see a person through the long haul, and in the case of A.A., the group is designed to go on indefinitely.

2. Self-help groups are built around the importance of empathy, not sympathy. The group is made up of people who "have been there." A self-help group consists of people who truly understand the individual's pain and suffering. Self-help groups are built around the empathy of the fellow sufferer. There is great healing power in such an approach, particularly for grieving people.

3. Self-help groups generally offer more aid and more often than any professional or community resource agency. When a crisis hits, people need enormous amounts of support, time and presence. Very few professionals can offer that kind of availability. Yet, a group can. By sharing the workload, the group can surround the griever with twenty-four-hour care.

4. In the self-help philosophy, the members of the group "own" the group. There is no paid leader. Each member of the group helps to set the agenda, direction of the group, and is involved in the ongoing maintenance of the program. In this sense, each person is involved. He or she owns "a piece of the action." It is *their* program. Nowhere is this more explicit than in the fact that each member is called up to give to new members, to "pass on" the love that they have received. This is a very growth oriented approach to healing. This approach helps people assume more responsibility, in a time when they may be feeling helpless or controlled by their fate.

5. Self-help groups downplay the medical-disease approach of human problems. It is easy, in this overly medical culture, to see one's problems or a crisis as a disease. When people feel that they have a disease, they feel more helpless. They feel more dependent on their doctor to make them well. Yet when they see their troubles as a normal reaction to a crisis event, they can be more responsible for their life. Self-help groups reassure individuals that what they are experiencing is "normal." The self-help philosophy works to normalize the trauma associated with loss and death.

6. Bereavement, or any crisis, brings with it inevitable periods of hopelessness. People wonder if their pain will ever end or will they ever be happy again? In a self-help group, the mere presence of fellow sufferers, who have made it is a constant symbol of hope. The

individual is reassured that "they made it, so I shall too." The use of recovered alcoholics or well-adjusted widows is hope-facilitating. In turn, hope creates confidence, growth and healing.

These are some of the reasons why the self-help approach to bereavement is an excellent, growth-producing philosophy. Every ministry to the bereaved should include some of these key elements if it wishes to be truly effective.

PASTORAL CARE STRATEGIES

Community can be a key resource for pastors as they minister to the bereaved. The question now arises, "How best can pastors mobilize this resource?" Several general strategies emerge.

Developing Community

The crucial connection between a close-knit, caring community and the positive resolution of the grief process is well established. Every effort, then, to build a caring community in a congregation is, in effect, a grief ministry. Furthermore, God has an investment in caring communities. Jesus' promise that "where two or three are gathered in my name, there am I midst them" (Mt 18:20) speaks to this investment. The Spirit of God is active in the dialogue, sharing and caring that goes on among people in small groups. God has many things to teach us all that can only be taught through the voices, thoughts and loving confrontations of other people. I believe that God enjoys groups. God rejoices in and lures humans toward community.

One way to develop community in a congregation is through the development of a network of small groups.[26] Small groups are not new in the church or in religious communities. There is some evidence to suggest that in the history of Christianity there is a causal relationship between the emergence of small groups and periods of religious revival. The two most obvious examples of this relationship are John Wesley's use of Methodist class meetings in the eighteenth century and the early development of the monastic movement—both of which make good use of close-knit communities.[27]

Every congregation already functions on a foundation of small groups. Most local churches have a variety of regular committee meetings, circles, deacon meetings, study groups and prayer cells. In recent decades, however, there has been a renewal of interest in small groups in the local church. This interest has been sparked in part because of the general emergence of group work in the broader culture. Moreover, I believe that this renewed interest in small group work is also a sign of the deep hunger that many people feel for more authentic community. These are times in which the development of deep friendship is harder to find and to maintain. Small sharing groups in the church can facilitate this discovery of community.

Many churches are attempting to meet this need by developing a network of small groups throughout the parish. Most churches have numerous small groups which can be rejuvenated and strengthened. Other congregations are working to develop new forms of small group ministry. There may be a variety of expressions and formats. There are study groups, sharing groups, prayer groups, fellowship groups, spiritual growth groups, couples groups, mission-action groups and so on.

Most social scientists classify group function into two generalized types: task orientation and relationship orientation. Task orientation means "getting an agreed upon task completed" and relationship orientation means "meeting the personal needs of the group members for community." The really new element in small group renewal these days, compared to former years, is that the latter element is receiving more recognition. Groups are now being formed whose primary and only purpose is to build relationships, friendships and community. Moreover, many pastors have also found that task-oriented groups can be more effective, efficient and harmonious if a certain segment of time is spent building community among the group members. When the personal needs of people are balanced with the necessity of completing the task at hand, the group functions more smoothly.

One way of structuring a small group ministry is by connecting each group to a particular type of loss event or stage of the life cycle. Obviously, there can be groups for those bereaved by the death of a spouse. In addition, many churches have groups or programs for the newly divorced. There are many other types of losses around which a group might be formed. Or there might be simply a general "grief-growth group," available for anyone who needs the loving support of others during a time of transition. As previously noted, many of the normal transition events or passages of life involve an element of grief. Howard J. Clinebell, Jr. has proposed the development of grief-growth groups based on a developmental scheme.[28] Erik Erikson's sequence of eight developmental stages, for example, suggests groups, like Identity formation groups (for youth), Newlywed groups (to build intimacy), Creative Retirement groups, Parents support groups (for parents of teenagers), and a group for expectant or new parents.

Grief-growth groups built around a life-cycle scheme are inherently transitional in nature. They are formed to meet a particular life-cycle crisis. Once that that crisis is resolved, the need for the group theoretically disappears. This idea fits well with the growth group philosophy which prefers groups to "self-destruct" after a specific length of time. These groups or "little communities" are agents of transition. They enable people "to get from here to there." They assist people to emotionally and socially adjust to a new life situation. Moving from here to there always involves some element of "letting go" of the past, as well as some element of "welcoming" the future. In this sense then, all transitional communities could be called grief-growth groups.

Given the incredibly large number of losses in life, it is hard to imagine any individual or family that is not, at any given moment, grieving some type of loss. Even if there is no immediate obvious loss, there are lots of developmental losses that people may be anticipating, and there are lots of previous losses that perhaps they are not fully finished with. In a sense, humans always have some loss—past, present or anticipated—that causes them concern. One of the functions of a caring, small group is to share these feelings and to help people to stay current with their grief processes. Community is built when people share together, sharing feelings, dreams, fears, plans and joys. The more people share, authentically and honestly, the more that friendships are formed and deepened and, in turn, the more that healing is facilitated. Small groups are an effective and a relatively safe and rapid way of building community. Building community in turn is a type of grief ministry.

Lay Caring Teams

Another idea for mobilizing the resources of a community of faith is through the development of one or more teams of lay people who can minister to people in various kinds of bereavement.[29] Such lay caring teams can supplement the pastoral ministry of the priest or minister. I agree with David Switzer when he writes that "there is a generally untapped source of power in specifically selected and trained lay persons who have much to give by way of help to other members of the congregation . . . ."[30] There are many benefits to a congregation and to the pastor, who takes the extra time to select and train volunteer care-givers. Such teams can assist the ordained, professional staff with the ongoing and at times emotionally exhausting task of ministering to the grief-stricken. Moreover, lay caring teams can also, like yeast in the bread dough, mobilize the caring resources and loving actions of the entire congregation.

In recent decades there has been an increased interest and emphasis upon the ministry of the laity. Many people are again realizing that God calls all believers to ministry, not just the clergy. Each member of the body of Christ has been given certain "gifts." There are many people in churches with gifts that could be mobilized in a ministry to the bereaved. Those gifts might include the skills of listening and caring. They might include the practical skills of cooking an emergency meal, running an errand for a stunned family or even mowing their lawn. These gifts and others might derive from the very fact that the care-givers have gone through a similar crisis sometime earlier in their own lives. Such people may not realize that their own suffering is a potential gift to another person. What a marvelous idea! This is, of course, the backbone of the self-help philosophy and approach. The self-help principle is that former grievers are effective ministers to the currently bereaved, more so than any professional helper who has had no personal experience with this kind of suffering.

The ideal plan would be to gather a team of lay people, who are themselves well-adjusted widows and widowers, to minister to the newly bereaved. Some churches might also want to broaden this ministry to include people with experiences with other kinds of losses. Divorced people can minister to the newly divorced. Single parents can minister to the single parents. Young married couples can run the premarital preparation classes. One congregation developed a lay crisis team focused on job loss, a very frequent experience in some communities.

One of the immediate barriers to this sort of program is that lay people themselves do not believe that they can do it. "Our pastor," they reply, "has training in this sort of thing. It is his job." There are two answers to this objection. First, a lay caring team does not take the place of the pastor's personal ministry. It supplements it. Lay caring teams should be under the direct supervision of the church's pastoral staff. They are, after all, extensions of the pastoral ministry of the church. For the most part, the church's pastor would still take the lead in ministering to the bereaved.

Second, I must clarify the job description of the lay caring teams. Their job is not to be professional counselors. Their job is not to do the pastor's job. Their job is just to listen and to care—actually two very important functions. Practically speaking, a lay caring team may do anything and everything—from cooking a meal, to attending grief rituals, to just sitting and listening to the anguish of the downtrodden. The main point of the self-help approach is that the bereaved do not always want or need counseling, or advice, or exhortation. A lay caring team, particularly one that is made up of people who "have been there," can minister effectively and uniquely to the bereaved.

Next, lay people may object to this plan with statements such as: "I would not know what to say to a crying friend." Of course, the lay caring team will need to be trained, prepared and educated to perform this vital ministry. Proper selection of volunteers is crucial. Not everyone who wants to do this kind of ministry is suited for it. The professional pastoral staff or outside mental health professional, with experience in this area, can educate the volunteers in "how to be an effective caregiver." These lay teams will also want to learn something about the dynamics of loss, grief and bereavement. Actually, the most helpful type of learning, in my opinion, is learning from actual experience. I recommend that, as a lay caring team begins its work, they meet weekly with their pastor to discuss their experiences and to learn as they go. Caring and listening are often skills that are more effectively taught through actual experience than through lectures or readings.

There are many churches and congregations that are trying to develop this kind of lay caring ministry. When this program is first considered, there are a couple of practical issues that must be addressed. The first question is whether to use an existing ecclesiastical structure or to create a new entity. In the Presbyterian church, for example, it is the board of deacons that is supposed to oversee the pastoral care of church members. In reality most local Presbyterian deacons do not realize their task, or those who do realize their task are overwhelmed by how to proceed. The other problem is that often congregations elect as church officers people with leadership skills or "the real doers." Yet, some of the best care-givers in a congregation are not necessarily the leader types, people that would not naturally be elected to an office. This is why some congregations form separate structures to organize their lay caring teams.

The other practical issue that will need to be addressed soon is that of forming a communication network. Unfortunately, not all losses or deaths occur at convenient, prearranged times. Many pastors become frustrated in their efforts to minister to the bereaved because they are literally the last to know when a death has occurred. In my opinion, the pastor should be the first to know. In turn, there needs to be some effective communications network whereby the pastor or church office can mobilize the support of the entire congregation. People in a state of acute grief have many immediate and varied needs—needs that a church community can effectively respond to, if the right people know what those needs are. James Sparks has called the local congregation a "resource switchboard." The key to mobilizing that switchboard is communication, developing a simple, effective means of passing the word around. This is also an area where the lay caring team can play a vital role.

Grief Is a Family Affair

Community begins with one's immediate family. Of all of the people that potentially can minister to the bereaved, the immediate nuclear family is the first and closest. The nuclear family—parents and children—are the closest community in which most people live. People look to this community first in a time of sorrow.[31]

The family therapist who has done the most to draw attention to the role that grief can play in family health is Norman L. Paul. Paul works with families in which one member is seriously emotionally disturbed, usually a teenaged or young adult member. He understands mental illness not just as a product of an individual's abnormal development, but also as a product of a family system that is somehow dysfunctional. He observes that such families are always closed systems, that is, they are systems characterized by an attitude of non-recognition and non-sharing of painful feelings. These closed-systems families are unable to deal openly and therapeutically with loss and grief.

In his work, Paul found a close connection between families with one "psychoneurotic member" and a "maladaptive response to object loss."[32] The original loss may have been as long ago as fifty years, even before the birth of the identified patient. Yet the attitude toward loss remained unchanged during that time, and recent losses only evoked similar reactions. The family attitude can be characterized by denial, and this attitude is most severe in families with schizophrenic patients. Such families may be said to be fixated at the denial stage of the grief process.

Later then, as one or more children grow up and seek to disengage themselves from the family system, the family system works to block this normal development. The "leaving" of the children is experienced by the family as another type of loss. The natural maturing process is inhibited or "denied" by the family system, resulting in a disturbed young person. The resulting emotional illness is directly related to the family's inability to deal openly with grief—either in the form of an original loss or in the form of the new emerging developmental loss.

Paul's approach to resolving these difficulties is to assist the family to have a "corrective mourning experience." The term "operational mourning" describes this technique that Paul has been experimenting with for many years. In a sense, the family is learning to "relive" their grief and to, in effect, finish their fixated grief process. Moreover, in the process of doing such, they learn the skills to deal openly with grief. They learn to share pain. Paul has suggested that a part of the family pathology is its inability to be empathic with one another, the inability to share painful feelings. Grief that is not shared is grief that is not healed.

Recently, I was counseling with a middle-aged couple whose situation illustrates a similar theme. Tom and Jane were contemplating divorce. They were one of so many couples these days whose primary complaint is that they have "drifted apart" over the years. They reported that they have nothing in common anymore, nothing to say to each other, and no emotional intimacy. Jane feels that she is "in love" with a younger man, a relationship that provides her with a deep, intimate encounter. In the process of talking with her one day, I asked her to review the history of her marital relationship in the hopes that we might determine when and where the relationship began to drift apart.

She shared that when she and her husband first met, they were very
much in love. They talked incessantly into the wee hours of the night.
They had in common several important dreams—to own their own
home, to raise a family and to build a career. The building of a career
was mostly related to Tom's chosen profession as a football coach. He
loved the excitement, challenge and competition of molding a group of
young men into a successful football team. At that time, Jane shared his
dream and willingly devoted herself to his career and, as she said,
"played the role of the coach's wife." Tom went through a series of
coaching jobs on the high school level, most of which were very successful. Then he moved up to a junior college position, but here he lost
the magic touch. There were no winning seasons after two years, and at
the end of that second year he was fired. At first Tom did not tell his
wife that he was fired. He indicated that he had resigned, preferring to
return to high school coaching. He denied his deep feelings of failure
and rejection. He responded by trying even harder at his "new" assignment. Their grief was never shared. Only years later did Jane actually learn that Tom had been fired. She reported:

> I was crushed when I learned the truth—crushed for him; what a
> terrible disappointment for him; but crushed for me too. I had given
> everything to our dream. I thought that I was a part of this, but
> when he didn't share his pain with me, I felt excluded, rejected . . .
> as though it was just his career and his dream right from the start
> . . . . I think that is when I first left him. Our marriage was never
> the same again.

Jane learned that unshared grief was the seed that sowed the eventual
destruction of her marriage. In that moment when pain was not shared,
each began to live separate lives, lives that continued to drift apart until
they came to this current impasse. Unfortunately, this key insight was
too late in coming to save the marriage.

The story of this couple illustrates so clearly, however, the tremendous importance of grief being shared. In the very act of sharing
pain, healing begins. Couples that cannot share their pain miss an opportunity to minister to one another and to move their relationship to a
new depth of intimacy and love. In avoiding their common pain, a couple sets the stage for an ongoing pattern of denial, isolation, and es-

trangement, a pattern which in turn often leads to marital disintegration.[33]

This key observation on the connection between family health and grief should not fall upon the deaf ear of a church's pastor. All of a pastor's ministry to the bereaved needs to be a family-oriented ministry. Whenever possible, our pastoral visitation must be when the whole grieving family can be present. Pastoral conversations should encourage family members to share their memories, pain and sorrow with one another, as well as with the visiting cleric. To the extent that pastors can mobilize a family's own caring and empathic love for each other, we help to strengthen the family unit in a time of crisis. We help bring family growth out of loss. After all, families are our closest community.

THE PASTOR AS COMMUNITY

Clergy are still one of the few, if not the only, professional group with the "right" and opportunity to call on bereaved people in their home environment. Most mental health professionals and physicians are "trapped" in their offices. Pastors have a tremendous advantage and potential to go where the people are. They can reach people with help, who otherwise would never receive assistance. Pastoral visitation is a very important and valuable tool. Clergy need to use it effectively. Taking that extra time to visit with a family communicates to those people in the strongest possible terms that you care. They know that you cared enough to take time out of your schedule just to be with them in their time of need. Even before a single word flows from your mouth, your presence alone will speak to your caring. Do not underestimate the importance of personal pastoral visitation.

In large congregations, some pastors have become more administrators than pastors. More and more of their time is spent in meetings, writing reports and managing programs, and less and less of their time is spent "in the field" calling on their people. The telephone has become an all too convenient substitute. In addition, regular pastoral visitation requires more evening and weekend hours than in earlier generations, as more and more people of both sexes work eight hours a day. Many pastors understandably resist giving up another night to do calling. Yet, in spite of both of these considerations, there is nothing so important or so effective in grief ministry as personal pastoral visitation.[34] There is healing power in the mere presence of one's minister or priest in a time of sorrow.

What is also clear from the research is that pastoral visitation must not stop with the funeral or after a few weeks when the bereaved parishioner appears to be normal again. Yes, there is no question that pastors should contact the family immediately upon hearing that a death or loss has occurred, even if that death is not a total surprise. This is usually a time of acute grief, a very important time for a pastor to call, particularly if the loss has come unexpectedly. Here the pastor's role is largely one of listening, supporting, comforting and planning. Widowed people say again and again that one of the hardest periods in their bereavement is the weeks following the funeral and internment. After the ceremonies are over and the friends leave and the relatives return to their distant homes, the widowed person is left alone with his or her sorrow. He or she now begins to feel his or her loss in a deeper, more frightening way. Depression, withdrawal and despair are more likely symptoms during this period. This is another very important time to make a pastoral visit. This visit can be a more lengthy one—a time to really talk now that all of the activities and urgent decisions are over. This is a time when the deeper feelings—the fears, the loneliness and the despair—emerge. This is a time to talk more intimately about God and spiritual understandings of tragic events. Finally, a third good time to call on a bereaved person or family is one or two months following the loss. Remember that a significant loss takes up to a full year to recover from. Continue to make such people a part of your routine calling, depending of course upon the severity of the loss, their pace in the grief process and so on. In the following weeks and months, monitor carefully the activity, mood and temperament of the bereaved parishioner.

So much of a pastor's effectiveness with grieving people depends not just on being there, but on the quality of pastoral relationship with the bereaved. Most experienced pastors know that it is much easier to minister to a well-known, well-loved parishioner than it is to the family that only occasionally attends services. Yet, in both situations, pastors must strive to be persons who embody the healing qualities of love, honesty and empathy. Particularly the latter quality is indispensable in grief ministry. Empathy bonds the caregiver to the griever. Empathy lightens his or her sorrow. Due to empathy, the griever is less alone in his or her pain. Empathy builds trust which in turn encourages the griever to open up, share more and talk. Empathy encourages the release of feelings, the expression of sorrow. By accepting their feelings, pastors enable the bereaved to accept their own feelings. Empathy paves the way for spiritual counsel. Finally, but perhaps most importantly, an empathic pastor is a symbol of God's love for the mourner amid his or her sorrow. In a time when many of the symbols of faith seem meaningless, there is still the caring presence of God's representative. Whether we like it or not, pastors are ambassadors of God to the sorrowing family. As we communicate a loving empathy, we communicate the loving empathy of the God we serve. As we suffer with them, we embody the presence of a God who also suffers with and for all humans.

CONCLUSION: BREAKING THE INVISIBLE WALLS

Over the years that I have worked with dying and grieving people, I have noticed that whenever others begin to encounter death "invisible walls" go up between them and the grief sufferer. Nowhere is this more obvious than among terminally ill patients. As soon as a patient is labeled "terminal," people alter their attitudes and relationships to that person. Suddenly the patient is isolated, surrounded by invisible walls of fear. A physician who previously had a warm, hopeful bedside manner now treats the dying person like an interesting case or a personal failure. The visits of all of the hospital staff are now less frequent and less lengthy. Friends and family may "breeze in," inform the patient how he or she is doing, promise to stop by next week and never return again. Clergy pay their customary calls, hiding behind structured prayers and formalized rituals. What conversations there are between the dying person and his or her community are stiff, formal and avoiding. There is an unspoken contract that "we are not going to talk about the obvious."

Studies indicate that most dying patients want and need to talk about their death. They need to say "goodbye" to their closest loved ones. They want to make sense out of their approaching demise. Death is one of the biggest, most significant and emotionally complex events of a person's life. Only by talking about it and talking through it are dying people able to accept the inevitable and transform this, the last event of their lives, into a growth experience. Yet the invisible walls go up as soon as others realize that they are dying. The dying are abandoned by their closest loved ones and professional care-givers in their time of greatest need.

I have seen a similar dynamic with people grieving the loss of a loved one as well. When John Jones lost his wife in a car accident last month, his relationship to others changed. Now he is "Mr. Jones, the widower." Invisible walls go up between him and his former friends as a certain alienation forms between John and his community. When friends call on him at the funeral or at home, conversations are peppered with clichés: "I know just how you feel," or "Mary was such a good person," or "We know she is at peace now." Conversations become formal, structured and polite. No one dares to mention "it" by name. They avoid talking about "death." In the weeks following, people gradually resist going to see Mr. Jones. They rationalize, "I don't know what to say to him," or "How do I act?" or "What if he breaks down and cries in front of me?" These are legitimate questions. They are also reflective of our own fears and discomfort with death. Then as the months pass, another type of estrangement colors John's relationship to his community. People begin to realize that John is now single again. He is available. The single or married women of the church gradually resist calling on him or talking too intimately with him. Another invisible wall goes up. His former couple friends do not know how to relate to him and gradually cease inviting him to couple events. Now Mr. Jones is isolated, alone in his grief.

These invisible walls of which I speak are those that appear whenever death touches our lives. Most people go to great lengths to avoid talking about or encountering death. It is easier to avoid pain and to hide the feelings associated with the finite. We prefer to focus on life, on youth, on vitality and on our endless future. "Why talk of death? It's depressing." "Why attend funerals? They're a barbaric, archaic custom!" The invisible walls are there, the walls that divide the living from the dead and the bereaved from their community. Isolated by such walls, grief is a lonely experience.

In the joys of the wedding feast at Cana, Jesus was surrounded by many people, but in the anguish of Gethsemani even his closest friends abandoned him. Yet, I believe that God did not intend grief to be a solitary journey. God intended grief to be shared, and the great amount of research, some of which has been alluded to in this chapter, gives further testimony to this fact. Community can be healing to grieving people. The availability and quality of a griever's friendships can be one important factor that contributes to that person's restoration to life. In short, pain shared is pain healed.

If we are to be such a community to one another in bereavement, then we must have courage. We must have courage to break those invisible walls . . . to talk openly about death . . . to feel another's pain . . . to cry together . . . to reach out to fellow sufferers . . . to touch their deepest sorrow and to be touched by their sorrow; and in that touching, community occurs and healing begins.

7. Grief Rituals

"Ritual is assumed to both communicate and to achieve."[1]

Christopher Crocker

Most of the crises, losses and separations of life are surrounded by rituals. Those rituals may be informal habits or formalized dramatic productions. Most of these rituals, particularly the more formalized ones, are presided over by the clergy. How clergy create, fashion and conduct these rituals can be very important. Rituals can be vehicles of God's healing work or shallow, deadening and inhibiting relics of an age gone by. In this chapter, we want to understand the psychological dynamics of rituals. We want to explore how rituals can be effective channels of healing. We want to discover new strategies for making rituals more vital and growth producing.

Ritual is any formalized, customed and symbolic behavior. It is by definition repetitive with a recognizable form or script. Rituals get their power precisely because they are repetitive and are therefore familiar to the participants and loaded with previous meanings and emotional connotations. Rituals are always social behavior, but not necessarily always done in a group. Rituals grow out of the life of a community, group or culture, as the collective attempt of the community to give meaning and structure to its experience of life.

Ritual always includes a symbolic power, "a pointing beyond itself." This power arises from the history of the ritual, its function in the life of the community, its repetitive character, but, most of all, from its religious-mythical symbols. The ritual script attempts to describe in symbolic terms the group's understanding of some aspect of life. In this sense, ritual is communicative. Those meanings may be explicit and verbal, or they may be implicit in the symbols. The extent of the power of the ritual depends in part on how commonly understood are the symbols and meanings of the ritual. Rituals that have lost their meaning are rituals which the participants no longer understand or rituals in which the symbolic meanings no longer communicate.

One way to classify rituals is by their timing and frequency. There are daily rituals, like one's "morning constitution" or a daily devotional. There are weekly rituals, like the Sunday worship of a Christian community. There are annual rituals, like birthdays, anniversaries and civic holidays, such as the 4th of July. There are seasonal rituals, like Passover, harvest festivals, or Easter. Finally, there are once-in-a-life-time rituals that grow out of the developmental transitions or crises of a person's life-span. Such rituals would include: funerals, weddings, graduations, baptisms, and so on. These occasions ritualize the passage of an individual from one stage of life to another and, in fact, to some extent get the individual from "here to there." They are transitional in nature. They are rites of passage. They are also types of grief rituals in that all such transitions involve elements of loss and grief.

RITUAL AND ITS DECLINE

During the last hundred years, Western culture has gone through a period of rapid social change. These changes in the social fabric have in turn changed our definitions of reality and human relationships. Modern people experience life and define life differently than their forebears did. Rituals, which are one way of expressing meanings, definitions and identities, have not changed at the same pace that society has as a whole. Ritual formation and modification is a much slower process. It is well that it should be, because rituals gain much of their power and influence precisely because of their continuity. They are our security in a changing world. Margaret Mead writes:

> Ritual offers a way in which people express their tremendous dependence on this continuity for their sense of identity, and their ability to draw on their own memories of those around them, and the faith of those around them. It is by drawing on memories that a sense of identity, security and continuity is assured.[2]

Institutions that attempt to change rituals quickly and frequently in an effort to keep pace with societal changes rob their people of the sense of rootedness, identity and continuity that rituals provide. Yet the roots of ritual must always be in the people's experience. When rituals cease to be popular, they cease to be authentic.

Nowhere has social change caused more of a gap between people's experiential meanings and their rituals than in the area of marriage and sexual roles. Society has gone through and continues to go through a period of intense social change in terms of the culturally accepted role and status of women. Correspondingly, our understanding of marriage is in transition. Gone is the courtship etiquette, the prescribed engagement periods and the romantic customs. The traditional ritual associated with marriage, the wedding ceremony, no longer means what it did to our parents. In the traditional marriage ritual, for example, the father of the bride "gives away" his daughter to her intended husband. This ritual expressed symbolically the transfer of male authority over and responsibility for the female from father to husband. It is a ritual that fit former times and former understandings of women and men. "Giving away the bride" is no longer a meaningful ritual to many couples. It is equally unsatisfying to older couples who are about to enter their second or third marriage. It does not reflect their meaning of marriage and of the wedding event. Some couples have attempted to revamp this ritual; others have dropped it altogether. In any event the ritual no longer reflects everyone's experience and therefore, to that extent, no longer serves as an effective vehicle of transition.

A similar ritual crisis is occurring at the other end of marriage: the divorce. While divorce dates back to the dawn of civilization, the frequency and wide-scale acceptance of divorce has accelerated in the last fifty years. Now nearly one-half of all marriages will end in divorce. In the vast sweep of human evolution, this change is occurring in a relatively short period of time. It is little wonder that ritual development, which is by its nature a slow process, has not kept pace. To date, Western society has not developed an official divorce ritual, although many people have proposed such. Some marriage counselors and psychologists argue that the absence of a meaningful divorce ritual creates more confusion, frustration and pain for divorcing people than would otherwise be necessary. A clear, simple, universally-accepted divorce ritual would aid people to separate "cleaning," with less feelings of failure and rejection, and with more of a sense of community. Such a ritual might also help people facilitate their grief, thereby facilitating their entry into their new life-stage.

Another factor that has contributed to the decline of ritual in modern society is the trend toward secularization. The growing movement toward secularization is, of course, not new. It can be traced as far back as the fifteenth century and perhaps before that. Yet it seems that its momentum has accelerated greatly since the Second World War. We live in an increasingly secular culture. In former times, many of the traditional ways of understanding life were essentially religious. Yet, as humankind has become more self-sufficient, knowledgeable and masterful of the environment, we seem to need "the God hypothesis" less and less. God gets pushed back to the "boundaries of our knowledge," as Bonhoeffer suggested some forty years ago. We explain life and its problems increasingly in terms of secular causes. We need fewer rituals, because there are fewer religious explanations of life.

Furthermore, those religious rituals that do survive this secularizing process become increasingly secular themselves. The case in point, of course, is Christmas. Christmas was once a highly religious and uniquely Christian holy day. Yet it seems increasingly obvious that Christmas is being secularized into a commercial celebration of "religion" at best, and of materialism at worst. The current debates in American courts over whether local governments may be allowed to display a crèche on public property, as many have for centuries, illustrate this change. The general direction of emerging legal opinions is that the manger scene is too Christian, and therefore prohibited, but Christmas trees, Santa Clauses, and wrapped gifts are permissible. The courts have determined that these Christmas symbols are no longer Christian—an interesting idea.

Another issue at work in the decline of ritual in modern times has been the increasingly pluralism of Western culture. Western society is no longer a homogenous culture, if it ever was. It is a mixture of differing religious traditions, ethnic backgrounds, family customs and social-political philosophies. Furthermore, within each major religion there are numerous denominations which further fragmentize the American religious framework. Each of these denominations has its own set of rituals that give expression to the theological meanings of that group. In short, there are no official or universal rituals. There are only competing sets of rituals, traditions and customs. Most funeral directors know this fact all too well. In death, there are military funerals, Catholic funerals, Mormon funerals, Masonic funerals, Protestant funerals and even new humanistic funerals. Each ritual competes for preeminence over the deceased.

As more and more people intermarry, the rituals of each family or tradition become blended. Their uniqueness is lost in the melting pot called America. The end result is usually a watered-down ritual or no ritual at all. More and more people live without any meaningful set of weekly, annual or crisis rituals. They live without the social structure that defines who they are and facilitates their life-stage transitions. This fact, along with the breakdown of community, leaves people vulnerable to a higher rate of mental and physical illness in times of transition, adjustment and crisis.

The Absence of Ritual and Grief's Dysfunction

The triple impact of rapid social change, secularization and pluralism has contributed to a decline of formal rituals and their use in modern society. Yet, we see from anthropological studies, especially in primitive societies, that ritual is the primary vehicle for the expression of grief emotions. What then do modern men and women do with their grief feelings? The answer is increasingly clear: nothing. Most modern people live with unresolved grief processes, resulting in increased use of mental health services, clergy services and medical services.

For many scholars there is a direct correlation between the increased absence of ritual and the steady rise in the need for psychological services in modern society. Secular humans are gradually substituting psychotherapy for ritual as the primary way of facilitating their normal grief reactions. Geoffrey Gorer, an English anthropologist, believes that the disappearance rituals in contemporary British and American societies is a serious problem. "Mourning," he writes, "is treated as if it were a weakness, a self-indulgence, a reprehensible bad habit instead of a psychological necessity."[3]

Rituals provide the guidance that encourages people to grieve.

Rituals teach people how to grieve. The growing absence of rituals means that there are more and more people who literally do not know how to grieve. People no longer have a clear ritualistic guidance that enabled them in the past centuries to grieve without embarrassment. Edgar N. Jackson compares primitive to modern societies when he writes:

> Primitive man faced his grief directly and worked out a system of personal social rituals and symbols that made it possible for him to deal with it directly. Modern man does not seem to know how to proceed in the expression of this fundamental emotion. He has no generally accepted social pattern for dealing with death. His rituals are partial and unsatisfying . . . .[4]

The ill effects of the absence of ritual is nowhere more startling than with children. Modern children, unlike their counterparts in centuries past or in less-developed countries, are systematically "protected" and shielded from death, dying and grief. Often modern children grow up not ever having personally seen or participated in a funeral. I frequently encounter teenagers or young adults who have never been to a funeral in their entire lives. They do not know what to do or how to act. They are embarrassed. They tend to avoid the subject. So, when a severe loss occurs, they are emotionally confused, bewildered and inhibited. They feel sorrow, but do not know how to express it in socially acceptable ways. They tend to hold in their pain, resulting in more complications. Family therapist Norman Paul writes:

> It is ironic that the culture which has provided Karen (case study) with a better standard of living, health and education than most of the world's children has simultaneously deprived her of another vital need—the opportunity to complete her grief within a socially acceptable context. In some, more primitive societies, every death is an occasion involving the entire community including the smallest children. All participate in rituals and ceremonies that mark the passage from life to death. . . .[5]

In a sense then, rituals serve educational purposes, teaching each new generation how to express its strong emotions in socially acceptable ways. Without such rituals modern humans are emotionally ignorant and inhibited, and therefore prone to great difficulty in successfully resolving their grief.

There are other sets of data that suggest a connection between the full use of rituals and successful grief resolution. Colin Parkes' London study, for example, attempted to assess the degree of emotional upset in the first three months of bereavement.[6] Parkes isolated three groups of widows. The third group that tended to avoid their feelings and express as little emotion as possible was more closely related to a higher incidence of physical and emotional illness. In this group, the tendency to avoid the full and free expression of emotions was reflected in several ways. This tendency was a part of a larger "family style," and one of the expressions of that style was a marked tendency to be "engaged in little formal mourning." No one "visited the grave or crematorium except on the occasion of the funeral." Parkes believed that this lack of involvement in ritual was one element in this group's dysfunction. Parkes concludes: "The absence today of social expectations and rituals facilitating mourning is likely to contribute to the occurrence of pathological reactions to bereavement. . . . "[7]

Vamil D. Volkan is another scholar who has studied the relationship of ritual and grief resolution. He has pioneered a method of therapy for people with unresolved grief called "re-grief therapy."[8] In his studies of pathological grief, he confirms the conclusion that "it is characteristic of our patient's experience that the funeral rites did not go well. Our findings here suggest the importance of this kind of ritual, among others, and the benefits of full participation in it."[9] Volkan's patients did have rituals available to them, but these ritualistic observations failed to facilitate the grief process. Perhaps grievers did not participate fully in the ritual. Perhaps the rituals were conducted poorly. Perhaps the rituals just did not mean anything to the participants. In any case, the absence of ritual and/or the misuse of ritual can contribute to unresolved grief.

The decline of ritual and the use of ritual is widespread in our modern societies. A few scholarly voices are beginning to be alarmed by this trend and to question its wisdom. Rituals should and can be effective vehicles for the healing of grief wounds. The question now before us is "How?" How can pastors, the primary ritual leaders in our society, revitalize rituals in ways that will make them effective pastoral tools?

The Rite of Passage

The term "rite of passage" was first coined by French anthropologist Arnold van Gennep in 1909. His work has been one of the landmark studies in the modern study of rituals. In his study of "semicivilized" societies, he noted that the life of an individual in any society is "a series of passages from one age to another and from one occupation to another."[10] Each life cycle transition, whether childbirth, career advancement or death, is marked by a well-defined ritual, which he termed a rite of passage. He writes:

> Transitions from group to group and from one social situation to the next are looked on as implicit in the very fact of existence, so that a man's life comes to be made up of a succession of stages with similar ends and beginnings: birth, social puberty, marriage, fatherhood, advancement to a higher class, occupational specialization, and death. For every one of these events there are ceremonies whose essential purpose is to enable the individual to pass from one defined position to another which is equally well defined.[11]

Van Gennep noted that these rites of passage were generally quite similar not only in a given society, but even across societal lines. These rites seemed to be a society's way of recognizing and facilitating the transition of an individual from one status/role to another.

Having identified a common ritual form, the rite of passage, van Gennep sought to analyze its structure, hoping to gain perspective on how it functions to facilitate an individual from one life-stage to another. He took his clue from a detailed analysis of the territorial passage: the transition from one country to another or from one province to another. The ceremonies surrounding a territorial passage seemed to be easily classified into three successive stages: separation rituals, transition rituals and entering rituals. Van Gennep found that this same tripart structure was operative in all rites of passage. He concluded that there were three phases to all rites of passage: separation, transition and reincorporation. While there were various individual rituals associated with each phase, the overall pattern remained consistent through all of the common life crises.

From an analysis of several common life-cycle transitions, the tripart formula was easily apparent. For example, van Gennep understood the betrothal and marriage process as a unified pattern of separation, transition and reincorporation. The beginning of betrothal was marked by separation rites, involving leaving the parents' home and/or leaving one's own sex group. The betrothal itself was a kind of transition or neutral period, concluded by the wedding which was a rite of incorporation into a new life status. Van Gennep carefully noted that this process was as much a life-cycle transition for the next of kin as it was for the bride and groom. Similarly, pregnancy and childbirth together constituted an extended rite of passage. He writes:

> The ceremonies of pregnancy and childbirth together generally constitute a whole. Often the first rites performed separate the pregnant woman from society, from her family group, and sometimes even from her sex. They are followed by rites pertaining to pregnancy itself, which is a transitional period. Finally come the rites of childbirth intended to reintegrate the woman into the society as a mother, especially if she has given birth to her first child or to a son.[12]

Also, a funeral which might at first glance appear to be just a rite of separation actually included rites of transition and reincorporation when considered together with mourning rites and customs. Especially for the immediate next of kin, the death of a parent can mark a significant life-cycle transition from child to parent, from heir to head of family, etc. Rites of separation include the funeral-burying process. The mourning process is best understood as a transitional period during which all normal societal functioning ceases. Reincorporation rites which mark the end of the mourning period include such things as the removal of black clothing, the return to normal (or new) duties, the erection of a monument, etc.[13] In each of these three examples—marriage, childbirth and death—there were always three parts: separation, transition and reincorporation.

There are several interesting and relevant insights of van Gennep's work. First, van Gennep suggests that every life-cycle ritual involves some element of separation. This is so because every life-cycle change is a transition, a change from one role or status to another. In order for people to make this transition, they must leave something behind. They must let go of the status, attachments and relationships of the dying life-stage. Separating is not easy nor always welcomed. Rites of passage are designed in part to help people separate, to say their "goodbyes," so that they can get on to the next life-stage. Each of these life-cycle transitions, then, involves an element of loss, and, to that extent, an element of grief. Each of the rites of passage is structured in some manner to deal with grief.

Second, it seems clear from van Gennep's work that all rites of passage involve a transition, a movement from "here to there." Van Gennep's model of the territorial passage is an apt description of most rituals in the life cycle. There is always some movement, some change, some "passage." In death the deceased changes status, but, more importantly, the next of kin also changes status—for example, from son to head of the clan or from wife to widow. In wedding rituals the couple changes status from single to married. In adolescent puberty rites (of which there are very few in our society) the individual changes status from that of a child to an adult. Rituals surrounding occupational changes carry the person from one job status and authority to another. Moving or relocating rituals are designed to facilitate a family's physical transition from one place to another. Even in birth rites the woman goes from wife to mother and the man goes from husband to father.

While van Gennep was largely concerned about rites of passage, other types of ritual could also be viewed as being agents of transition. The sacrament of penance or the Eucharist can be understood as designed to carry an individual from sin to new life. Daily devotionals or rituals can be understood as carrying one through the day. Viewed in this way, every major religion has a ritual system based on life passages, a system that is designed to carry the individual from birth to death. Rites of passage have to do with facilitating the transition of the person(s) from one stage to another. In fact, most rituals have at least some of this transitional quality.

Third, van Gennep and other anthropologists believe that these rites of passage actually facilitate a person's transition from one life stage to another. Rituals do this in new two ways. First, the rites communicate to the individual's community the new status or role. Rituals are after all social behaviors. They are ways of publicly acknowledging and celebrating the individual's transition. They are the group's way of bestowing new responsibility or authority upon the individual. Without social communication, the individual could not assume his or her new status, regardless of how much he or she might feel ready for it on the inside. In this sense, rituals have a descriptive function. They describe what has happened.

Rites of passage also have a prescriptive function, in that they prescribe certain behaviors, emotions, attitudes and changes. Social expectation can be a powerful determinant. In the process of the rites themselves certain behaviors and emotions are prescribed. For example, in grief rituals people are expected to cry, to weep and to wail. To modern ears, there may be a certain artificiality to this kind of social expectation. Yet such expectations gently and persistently encourage mourners to express their grief feelings. If mourners did not participate in these rites or if there were no such rites, there would be no opportunity to grieve. After the rite of passage is completed, the individual is now expected to cease grieving and to behave in a manner suitable to her or his new status. Ritual prescribes the ending of the grieving process as well as prescribing its commencement.

In this larger sense, rituals serve an educational function. Rituals teach people how to grieve. In most semi-primitive societies this teaching begins very early as children participate fully in the rites of their community. Besides teaching how to express emotions, rituals also teach or prescribe the behaviors or responsibilities associated with each new life-stage. Someone has said that ritual is the vehicle that carries a person along life's journey. Ritual, particularly rites of passage, do this both by communicating the accomplished fact and by actually facilitating that change. They describe and they prescribe.

RITUAL AS A GRIEF FACILITATOR

Rituals serve many purposes. When anthropologists and sociologists study ritual, they see that ritual serves to bond a community of people together and to recognize changes in social status. When theologians look at rituals, they see that rituals reflect the values and theology of a given community of faith. When educators look at rituals, they notice that rituals teach people the wisdom, values and history of a given culture. For purposes of this discussion, however, I want to look at rituals through the eyes of the psychologist or pastoral psychologist. From this perspective, ritual also performs a very important function. This function can be simply stated: Rituals facilitate grief.

In the grief process there are two polar dynamics: structure and release. These dynamics have been described previously as remembering and forgetting, as pain and mitigation and as confrontation and comfort. A healthy grief process oscillates between these two poles. Both elements, held together by a dynamic interplay, seem to be necessary for healing. In order for rituals to be effective vehicles of sorrow, they must provide mourners with both dimensions of this process, both structure and release. Let us consider how rituals might do this.

First, rituals provide for emotional release for grieving people by giving them the occasion to deal directly with their loss and with the emotions involved therein. Rituals, when they are done therapeutically, force people to confront the reality of a loss and their emotions surrounding that loss.

Once people confront the reality of their loss, the inevitable emotions associated with that loss will spill forth. Ritual is supposed to encourage its participants to express their emotions, fully and freely. Audrey Gordon, writing about Jewish mourning practices, comments:

> The intention of all mourning practices should be the fullest possible outpouring of grief and the opportunity for the family and community to reknit after the loss of one of its members so that they may continue to be able to love and work.[14]

Rituals provide for a catharsis. Without the ritual event, we can too easily avoid our pain and go on for years, carrying our sorrow within us. In short, the purpose of ritual is not to control emotions, but to release them, a simple but profound principle that falls upon too many deaf ears.

Edgar Jackson has referred to the expressive function of rituals as the "therapy of acting out."[15] We are accustomed to thinking of "acting out" as a negative thing, that is, a thing that we should avoid. On the contrary, argues Jackson, in ritual we act out our feelings all the time. Ritual always involves some sort of drama, movement or dance. The processional or parade is one of the more common types of ritualistic movement. In other words, we express our feelings not just through tears, but through action, words and music. It seems a shame that most modern rituals make less and less use of music and movement. The words of the poet and the melody of the lyricist can describe the deepest feelings of the heart at a time when no words will do. And at other times, feelings can be so strong or sorrow so deep that only the dance or the parade can express the pent-up energy. Lack of music and movement contributes to the deadening and dysfunction of ritual. The purpose of ritual is to enable people to release or to act out their grief feelings.

A hospital chaplain once told me the story of John, a fifty-three-year-old terminally ill father and husband. John was a dominant, independent man who had "ruled the roost" at home and, outside the home, had built a successful family retailing business. It was no easy matter for John to come to terms with the fact he "might" die. In the course of caring for him, John remarked one day to the chaplain that he had some things that he wanted to say to his sons, but felt it difficult and awkward to do so. The chaplain suggested that he invite John's family to come to the hospital and share with them in worship and the Eucharist. The family was invited, and, interestingly enough, they all came as requested. The communion table was set up on John's bed, on a hospital tray over his feet. The family—his wife, two sons, a close personal friend, his daughter and her husband—gathered around the bed. The minister donned his priestly garb and the service began. Prior to the sacrament, the chaplain reflected on Matthew 5:23–24 which instructs believers to be reconciled with others before coming to the altar of God. In that spirit, he invited those assembled to share anything that they had always wanted to say to one another—words of love, forgiveness, gratitude or hurt. Initially there was silence; then gradually feelings emerged:

Dad, I love you . . .

I remember the time you taught me to ride a bicycle . . .

Daniel, I never told you this, but I'm sorry I badgered you so much about going into the business. I should have laid off. It really wasn't your cup of tea, was it?

Dad, sometimes I have loved you and sometimes I have hated your guts . . . but, I guess now I just want to say "thanks." (They embraced.)

Wayne, I guess I never told you that I was really proud of you when you graduated from college. You really did well, son.

Then John's wife said:

> You know, honey, there is something I never told you. Do you remember that stray dog we adopted when Wayne was seven? Well, he wasn't a stray . . . we just knew that you wouldn't let us have a family dog otherwise.

Laughter filled the room. The tears gave way to smiles. They celebrated together. Then they celebrated with God. It was a simple occasion, a powerful occasion and a deeply personal occasion. In this case, ritual became a vehicle for the release of feelings and a channel of reconciliation. John lived another two months and conversations continued during that time, but for this family the occasion of ritual stands out as a precious moment in their common life together.

The second way that ritual can facilitate grief is by providing a structure in which to grieve. At first this sounds odd, as though I am saying the exact opposite of what I just said, but when people are dealing with strong emotions, they need structure. We tend to resist releasing our strongest emotions, be they sorrow or anger or anxiety, because we are literally afraid of them. We fear that we shall be overwhelmed by our emotions, that we will lose control and that we will then be embarrassed or rejected by others.

Rituals can provide a safe structure in which to emotionally let go. After all, in rituals the releasing of emotion is expected. No one will laugh at or ridicule us for showing some emotion within the context of ritual. In addition there is the support, safety and dependency of a group of people. These people are our friends, who understand and accept our terrible feelings of anguish, fear and sorrow. In most cases our friends even share these same feelings.

Another aspect of the structure that ritual provides has to do with words and meanings. Rituals always include meanings—meanings that make sense out of the experience of loss. These meanings are handed down from generation to generation. There are comforting words, words that reassure us, words that provide hope for tomorrow, but, most of all, words that make sense of raw emotion. Language helps us understand emotions and helps us structure emotion in ways that enable it to be assimilated. In this way the raw experience is balanced with the tradition. The emotional is balanced with the cognitive. Feelings are tempered with insight.

One of the best examples of how the interplay between release and structure function in a grief ritual is in the orthodox Jewish mourning practices.[16] The Jewish mourning system, in response to a major loss, is made up of successive periods of mourning, each stage having certain prescribed practices and behaviors. There are five successive periods of mourning in all. The first period is between the death and the burial. Here the anguish is most intense and all social and religious affairs are canceled. The second phase is the three days following the burial. This is the period of weeping and lamentation. Mourners remain at home and visitors are discouraged. The third phase, called the Shiva, includes the seven days following the burial. Now, visits to offer consolation are encouraged, but still the mourners are prohibited from conducting business as usual. The Sheloshim is the thirty-day period following the burial. Here mourners may leave the house (after the Shiva is over) and gradually resume some normal activities. The fifth mourning period is the full year following the death of the loved one. During this period all normal routine is restored, but officially mourning does not end until the first year anniversary of the death of the loved one. At that time there is the unveiling of the monument. During each of these periods, there are extensive and detailed instructions for the mourners regarding how to mourn. Gradually as each successive phase emerges, the restrictions are lessened.

While the structured mourning system is anathema to many modern people, there is great wisdom and good psychology in its approach. The structured grief ritual encourages the fullest expression of grief in the initial periods. Many of the prescribed behaviors, like the Keriah ("rending the garment") or the prohibition of physical comforts or the prescription to withdraw socially, are designed to facilitate grief feelings. They are designed to evoke emotion, and to evoke it as intensely as possible in the early phases. These customs are designed to help mourners do their "grief work" fully and completely. However, besides the emphasis upon release, the ritual also embodies a clear structure. There is a starting point, successive stages and a visible ending point. At each stage, the mourner is "moved along." He or she is not allowed to get stuck along the way. The structure includes clear boundaries and limits. Without a structure, grief is at best more difficult.

STRATEGIES FOR REVITALIZING RITUAL

Since ritual can be such an important vehicle for grief, pastors must work to revitalize ritual. What are the guidelines that should govern the therapeutic use of ritual? There are no easy answers to this question. The answers that emerge come in sets of polarities. Striking the right balance between these polarities is the key to making ritual an effective tool of pastoral care.

1. Control vs. Release

Most ritual reflects elements of both control and release. The same ritual can be used to control people's emotions and to release people's emotions, depending on the intention of the officiating pastor. Both elements—control and release—are important in the grieving process. The structure of the ritual, embodied in the words, the format, and the meanings of the ritual, provide the control. Balanced with the need for structure is the need for emotional release. If ritual does its job, people will leave the event saying, "It was a moving experience" or "I feel better now" or "She really spoke to me." To this end, I encourage pastors to customize rituals to facilitate the free emoting of the participants. I encourage the use of "loaded" words, the telling of stories that "touch" you, the use of hymns that run deep in tradition. Further, I encourage pastors to give people the opportunity to express feelings.

The use of Scripture in pastoral care and ritual is one of the most bewildering subjects.[17] There is such a diverse hodgepodge of advice in the Bible that pastors can pretty much quote verses according to their own whims. Scripture can be used to control feelings and used to release feelings. I once went to a funeral where the minister peppered every paragraph with a Scripture verse. He bombarded the audience with "The Bible says . . ." or "The Lord teaches. . . ." His thematic passage was: "Grieve not, like those who have no hope" (1 Thes 4:13), which he quoted six times. It seemed to me that he was preaching more than consoling. I left that funeral with a gnawing feeling that the minister was frightened to death—afraid that someone might break down during the service. Sure enough, it was one of the few funerals I have ever been to where no one, not even the immediate family cried. No one dared!

In contrast to this controlled event, I remember a splendid funeral conducted by a very skilled pastor who used as his thematic text the story of Jesus and Lazarus. He focused our attention on Jesus' tears when he heard of his friend's death (Jn 11:35). He noted that Jesus loved Lazarus so much that even outsiders noticed it. He went on to speculate about what kind of experiences they must have had together in order to develop that kind of love . . . and grief. We imagined together the memories, the work performed, the roads traveled, the family ties, the arguments fought and forgiven between Jesus and Lazarus. As he described the friendship of Jesus and Lazarus, each of us could also see in the Scripture our friendship to the deceased person lying before us. Each of us also had memories, ties and roads traveled with the departed. At one point the minister asked a few of us to share those thoughts in one-word sentences. In that context it was easy to share our grief for the dead person. However deeply we hurt, we knew that Jesus shared our feelings. And as Jesus' love helped return Lazarus to life, so, too, our love for the deceased would bring forth new life. Death is never completely victorious. This pastor used Scripture therapeutically. He painted a picture of the experience behind the Scripture incident. That experience touched our experience some two thousand years later, thereby making the Scripture come alive for us with empathy and hope.

2. Observation vs. Participation

Rituals include elements of both observing and participating. Probably modern rituals have increasingly leaned toward the observation side, with less and less participation. We have become a nation of observers. Television teaches us so well to observe life rather than to participate in it. So it is that the chancel has become a stage and the congregation is increasingly referred to as an audience. People leave the ritual saying to the minister, "That was a wonderful service, pastor," which translated means, "It was a good show." It is difficult to involve people fully when they are caught in this observation mentality.

Participation is the key to rituals becoming grief facilitating events. There are many ways to gain more participation in rituals. Congregational singing and responsive readings are a start. Inviting select members to read or lead portions of the ritual is another. I have found that when the leading figures, other than the minister, can share how they are feeling, it is very powerful. When the grieving spouse reads his or her favorite poem, there isn't a dry eye in the house. When the new mother tells of her dreams for her newly baptized baby, it touches every heart in the room. When the relocating family can rise up in church and say goodbye to their "extended family," it means a lot to all concerned. Obviously not everyone can participate in a given ritual. Most of the participation is vicarious, but vicarious participation can be powerful, especially when the leading characters share some of their deepest feelings.

3. Novelty vs. Continuity

When the minister begins a funeral or memorial service with the words, "The Lord is my shepherd; I shall not want," tears begin to flow before the words are out of the minister's mouth. Why? Certainly not because anyone in the congregation has seen a shepherd in the last twenty years. They cry because the Twenty-Third Psalm has been said at every loss event in their lives, and at every occasion of fear or trouble. It is the Psalm they heard at Grandpa's funeral. It is the Psalm that their mothers recited to them as children before they went to bed at night. It is the Psalm that they muttered silently to themselves before they went into surgery last year. This is the tremendous power of continuity in ritual. Much of the power of ritual to emote feelings lies in its continuity. In this way, the current loss in linked up with all other losses in our lives. The present grief triggers old griefs. In an anti-tradition culture, as American culture is, we must not underestimate the therapeutic power of continuity.

Previously, I talked about the custom of "giving the bride away" and how it originally grew out of a cultural understanding of the status of women that is today no longer widely accepted. In spite of being an anachronism, I continue to be surprised by how many brides-to-be want their "Daddy" to walk them down the aisle and give them away. The therapeutic value of this ritual lies in its continuity, not in its cultural meaning. In other words, the woman has emotional business to do with her father and needs the ritual to structure that interaction. Understanding this need, I have attempted to revise this rite, keeping the intention to do business, but restructuring its meaning.

One of the more common revisions of this ritual that I have used is to view this custom as a time for the couple, both of them, to say "goodbye" and "thank you" to their respective parents. In order for a couple to be fully committed and loyal to one another, they need to disengage from their family of origin. Conversely, parents sometimes need help learning to disengage from their children's affairs. We are all too familiar with newlyweds who cannot let go of a parent or a parent who still interferes in his or her child's marriage. The wedding ritual can help people disengage by first publicly announcing in the ritual that this is what is occurring (as an accomplished fact), and, second, by helping the parties to finish their emotional business with one another (facilitating the fact).

The minister introduces this section of the wedding by saying:

> Today we are creating a new family. We are taking from two families David and Susan and bonding them together into a new family. After this day, their loyalty, devotion and affection will be first and foremost to each other, not to their respective parents. This is the way it should be as "the two become one." Before we do this, however, we want to pause to acknowledge with thanksgiving the love, devotion and patience of their parents. In this regard, David and Susan would like to say something. . .

At this point, the couple may turn to their respective parents and say a few words, give a gift, hug one another or in some other way say "thank you" and "goodbye." This is often a touching moment. After these words are said, the ceremony proceeds. This revamped ritual is a nice blending of descriptive and prescriptive functions of ritual.

4. Universal vs. Particular

There are formal and informal rituals. Formal rituals are usually not very personal. Informal rituals, such as retirement dinners and office birthdays, are often very personal. Weekly or seasonal rituals tend to be less personal and more universal. There is a need in all rituals, even the most formal ones, for personal elements. This is particularly true of life-change rituals. After all, a funeral is about a particular individual. A wedding is about a particular couple. A baptism is about a particular child. Even a graduation ceremony is about a particular group of people. Good rituals combine elements of the personal and the universal. In fact, rituals at their best tie together the particular and the universal. They link an individual's experience with the universal experience of all humankind. His funeral or her wedding reminds us of our funeral or our wedding. Their experience is our experience—and the experience of generations before us. It is a particular person's ritual, but his or her ritual is shared universally by all people.

For the average pastor, the problem with personalizing ritual is largely a problem of time. A personalized ritual requires that the minister know the family well or is willing to take the extra time to get to know them. It requires that the pastor take extra time to meet beforehand with the central figures of the ritual and work with them to customize the event. Many busy pastors do not have this kind of time. Many other pastors, who are in large downtown churches which get a lot of walk-in requests for weddings and funerals, are in even greater binds. Doing rituals for one's congregation is one thing, but how much time can a pastor afford to give to these walk-in requests? As cold as it sounds, there is an issue here of cost effectiveness as well as pastoral integrity. Churches in this situation must choose between charging fees to pay for the pastor's time or releasing the minister from his or her regular duties to perform such rites. The choice is not an easy one to make. Personalizing rituals helps ritual events to be more therapeutic, but personalization requires extra time.

CREATING RITUALS

In this day and age when there are so few ready-made rituals and when people are not ritualistic-oriented, pastors must often create their own rituals. This need is especially true in the context of pastoral care and counseling. Rituals, as simple as a prayer or a short devotional, can be tools that facilitate our feelings, solidify our gains, clarify our meanings or commit us to some action. The most therapeutic use of ritual occurs when the need for ritual and the content of the ritual arise out of the process of pastoral care.

A priest friend of mine whom I was supervising in the skills of pastoral care relayed to me the story of calling on a family in his parish within the first few months of his arrival at that church. About eighteen months prior to this time, the family had lost their eldest son in a tragic automobile accident. They had two other children, who were now thirteen and ten years old respectively. While visiting with the family, the young priest made several inquiries about their deceased son. The son, Roger, had been very popular and successful in the local high school prior to his untimely death. The parents proudly noted that he was on the football and baseball teams and was president of the sophomore class. Sensing the minister's interest, the parents invited the pastor to see Roger's room, which the parents said was "exactly as he left it." Sure enough, to the minister's surprise, Roger's clothes were still in the closet. The mother reportedly dusted the room every day and even changed the bed linen weekly. The walls were still crowded with Roger's posters, awards and various photographs. The parents were very proud to show off their dead son's room and to tell the new priest of his accomplishments.

The pastor was shocked and deeply concerned by what he saw that day. To him the room had become a "shrine." The parents were worshiping their son's memory and idolizing his accomplishments. They had refused to give up what was lost. He decided to continue to call regularly on this family. After considerable caring and counseling, he was able to persuade them of the "inappropriateness of their shrine." Then he did something that I thought was wonderfully creative. He proposed that he and several friends of the family assist them in the "packing up" of Roger's things and that they ritualize this "special" occasion with prayer, song and worship. They spent the following Saturday together, cleaning, packing, sorting out, crying, praying and remembering. It helped to have friends there. And it helped to turn this painful process into a special day through ritual.

They had previously decided that many of Roger's things were to be given to the local state hospital where retarded youth could make use of them. Everyone went with the family to the hospital and again blessed the "giving away of their precious gifts." When all was said and done, the occasion was closed with a benediction, as if to say that this whole day's work was worship. The occasion functioned as a symbolic ending to the parents' self-imposed mourning period. It also served well, in the words of the priest, "to reorient their worship away from the idols, and again to the living God." The pastor's creative use of ritual helped to enable and empower the family to "let go" of the past and to re-enter life's mainstream.

Let me offer one more illustration, this time from my own experience. Recently my family moved across town to a new and larger house, one that will accommodate our growing family and its needs. While we were all excited about the change and looked forward to spreading out our junk, as the time of moving came closer my wife and I were increasingly aware of our growing sense of loss. This was the first house that we had ever owned. We had invested more of ourselves in fixing it up, designing it, and decorating it to our tastes. We had come to really "own" this house. Yet in spite of the growing sense of loss, we were both too caught up in the chaos of moving to share much about our feelings.

Several days later, however, we had occasion to return briefly to our empty house to make a couple of minor repairs. We were both struck by how different it looked. Suddenly it seemed very empty, lonely and cold. We were compelled to walk through the empty house, pausing in each room, reflecting silently and together on our memories of each room. We remembered the birth of our second daughter in one room, cold winter evenings by the fire in another room, a dissertation that got grudgingly written in another, periods of marital conflict and renewal in another, a backyard where our beloved family dog is buried. Each room held its memories. We both felt a deep need to say "thanks" to God, and, oddly enough, to the house as well. Our brief ritual helped us to get in touch with those deeper feelings of grief and gratitude that had been lingering within us.

Sara Ebenreck, writing in a delightful magazine about rituals, called *Family Festivals*, tells a similar story. When her family moved out of a home, they too took time to say thanks by walking through their old house (as a family), remembering special times in each room. In addition, they reflected on the people who had come before them in that house and on the people who would follow them there. They finished their ritual by asking God for a blessing on their move. She summarizes her experience:

> Our ritual brought us tears and smiles—and a sense of peace. By putting our thanks into words, we felt ourselves part of a larger cycle of that home that had held people before us and would hold others after us. Asking God's blessing helped us see that new life would grow here as well as in us as we "let go."[18]

Moving is one of the most common and one of the most under-rated loss events in modern life. Moving involves a complex set of losses/changes, including the change of schools, houses, friends, churches and jobs. When most families move, there seems to be little time for rituals, much less for deep conversations. The situation is confused, chaotic and frustrating. Nevertheless, moving is an important loss-transition event, and time should be found somewhere to ritualize the occasion.

Rituals, like the two described above, are ways of bringing feelings to the surface, ways of expressing ambiguous emotions, ways of helping people to "let go" of the past and to "welcome" the future. Rituals can be effective tools for the facilitating of grief work. In the ebb and flow of pastoral care and human interaction, we must be ready at times to ritualize the lived moments and thereby facilitate the healing of wounded spirits.

CONCLUSION: RECOGNIZING THE DRAMA

When you stop and think about it, the story of salvation is quite a drama—the events of Eden, the family plots, the miracles, the scandals, the rise and fall of nations, the coming of the Christ, his betrayal, his triumph, the heroics of the early church and the eventual consummation of the Kingdom of God. For Christians, this theological drama is at the core of our being. Christians, as well as Jews, have a strong sense of history and of the progressive series of divine encounters with humankind.

Similarly, each person has a story to tell, a personal drama of his or her battles, betrayals, victories, sufferings, and joys. Losses and griefs make up a significant part of those dramas. As we work with grieving people, we must be keenly aware of the sense of drama in their lives. We must not see them just as a case or as a generalized type, but as unique individuals with their own encounters with God, temptations, defeats, and victories. We must place whatever present loss we are dealing with in the context of the whole sweep of a person's life. We must grasp the whole, the flow of their lives, the process of their struggles toward salvation.

Getting a sense of the drama of life is necessary before we can effectively use ritual. This is so because ritual grows out of the dramatic moment. Once we get this sense of the drama of life, ritualizing becomes easy. We employ ritual to give meaning and structure to the dramatic moments of life, moments when ordinary words and ordinary behavior just won't do. Grieving and growing are two processes filled with dramatic moments. Through ritual we link each person's drama to the larger dramas of humankind and salvation. Rituals grow out of the sense of drama in life.

8. Do Beliefs Make a Difference?

"Your pain is the breaking of the shell that encloses your understanding."[1]

Kahlil Gibran

Each human being has a variety of beliefs about the world, life and human nature. These beliefs range all the way from the formal ecclesiastical creeds to the informal "pearls of wisdom" that our grandmother handed down to us. The issue before us in this chapter is whether or not these beliefs help a person to grieve and to grow in times of loss. What is the role of belief in the economy of the grief process? Do believers have any psychological advantage or disadvantage compared to non-believers? Most pastors, as well as many laypeople, will find these questions to be of keen interest.

The next two chapters have to do with beliefs and faith and their respective roles in bereavement. For purposes of distinction, I am defining beliefs as a set of cognitive meanings held to be true and faith as a pre-cognitive sense of trust. To clarify further, belief is an accepting as true certain facts or conditions about a given subject or subjects. We believe that it is true that "God exists" or that "there is life after death" or that "everything works out for the best." Belief and believing is largely a cognitive activity. There is always a "that clause" to every belief statement, "I believe that. . . ." Beliefs are, therefore, subject to discussion, debate and examination, but not all beliefs are verifiable by scientific methods. Beliefs are logical only within the individual's own frame of reference. They make sense to the individual and fit with his or her experience.

Faith is best described as trust in some reality or belief beyond oneself. For most people, this is a faith in God. Faith is trustful self-surrender. Faith is loyalty. Faith is pre-cognitive or trans-cognitive. It is something that one "senses" or intuits. Faith or trusting is not primarily a cognitive activity. One cannot think oneself into faith. One can examine beliefs and believe up to a certain point; then one must make a "leap of faith." This leap of faith is based solely on trust.

Admittedly, this distinction between belief and faith is an arbitrary one. Other people could easily argue, and would have to agree, that belief and faith are inseparable. One must always have faith *in* something. One cannot trust just in general terms, without an object of trust. Neither can one believe that something is true, without being called upon to make a faith decision. If one believes that God in Christ is true, for example, then one must respond in faith. To do less than that would be to deny the truth of those beliefs. In other words, beliefs call for some action, some obedience, some commitment on the part of the believer. It is difficult to separate faith from beliefs or beliefs from faith. Yet, for purposes of definition, we are going to focus primarily on beliefs in this chapter and on faith in the following and final chapter.

OPERATIONAL BELIEFS

Beliefs can take a wide variety of forms and formats. There are formal beliefs, embodied in the creeds of a church or the constitution of a nation. We rise in worship and proudly confess, "I believe in God . . . the Creator of all life . . . in Jesus Christ, Lord and Savior . . . in eternal life . . . in the forgiveness of sins." On the Fourth of July we pledge again that we believe in "one nation under God, with liberty and justice for all." These are formal beliefs. At the other end of the scale are our operational beliefs.[2] These are the beliefs deep within our hearts by which we actually live. These are the beliefs, some of which may be semi-conscious, that govern our lives. These operational beliefs may be expressed in words or they may be only implied in our behavior. On Sundays we sing, "Jesus loves me, this I know," but during the week we operate on the assumption that "I'll never amount to much anyhow." On holidays we may believe that "all people are children of God," but during the week we run our businesses on the principle, "Get the other guy before he gets you." The problem of hypocrisy is the problem of the gap between our formal theology and our operational theology. We profess one set of beliefs, but live by another.

Albert Ellis was probably the first spokesperson for what has become known as cognitive therapy. Ellis' Rational Emotive Therapy (RET) begins with a simple yet profound assumption that "you feel as you think." He argues that our emotions stem from our thoughts, ideas, opinions and beliefs. He writes:

> ". . . human emotions do not magically exist in their own right and do not mysteriously flow from unconscious needs and desires. Rather, they almost always directly stem from ideas, thoughts, attitudes or beliefs and can usually get changed by modifying our thinking processes.[3]

According to Ellis, most of our thinking is formulated in sentences, phrases or belief statements. In other words, we talk to ourselves when we think. Thus, some of our most basic operational beliefs about ourselves and life can be formulated into short catch phrases or sentences. Sometimes we see the more popular of these phrases on bumper stickers or sweatshirts. By isolating these basic ideas and evaluating their rationality, Ellis argues that we can interrupt our negative behavior patterns and even change our basic personality structure.

These "internalized statements" may be beneficial or destructive to our well-being. Many of the most illogical of these beliefs are common enough to be catalogued. Ellis cites several of the most universal of the self-defeating "beliefs" as:

> The idea that it is a dire necessity for an adult to be loved or approved of by almost everyone for virtually everything he or she does.

> The idea that one should be thoroughly competent, adequate and achieving in all possible results.

> The idea that it is terrible, horrible and catastrophic when things are not going the way one would like them to go.[4]

These are but a few examples of the many irrational ideas or beliefs that can make up a person's operational theology. A person's operational beliefs may also be constructive and health oriented. When people feel deep within their souls that "I'm O.K., you're O.K.," or that "I am lovable and capable," or that "God doesn't make junk," a person will probably have positive feelings and life-giving behavior patterns. In either case, the key to living "the most self-fulfilling, creative and emotionally, satisfying life" lies in intelligently organizing and disciplining one's thinking.[5]

Since the pioneering work of Albert Ellis, the school of cognitive therapy has rapidly become a major force in modern psychology. People like Aaron T. Beck, Maxie C. Maultsby, Victor Raimy and pastoral counselor Paul A. Hauck have expanded the theory and application of cognitive therapy.[6] All cognitive therapists, however, still argue for the same basic tenet that how one thinks determines one's emotions, and that only by changing one's beliefs can most emotional disturbances be resolved. In recent years cognitive therapists have made their most significant contribution in the area of depression. Using this context, let us consider Ellis' ABC Theory of Emotions. Paul Hauck writes:

> An emotion is a physical reaction to a mental stimulus. If we have angry thoughts, we feel angry. If we have alarming thoughts, we feel tense. If we blame ourselves, the result is depression. Ellis has labeled this process the ABC Theory of Emotions. A is any event outside of ourselves. B is our attitude, opinion, belief—in short our thinking about A. And C is the emotional reaction we have as a response—not to A, the event, but to B, the opinion about it.[7]

People are normally aware of only the A and the C: the initiating event and their resulting depression. Therefore, they conclude that "I am depressed because I lost my job." They imply a causal relationship between the external event and their feelings. They imply that they are mere emotional victims of circumstances. What cognitive therapists point out is that there is an intermediate step (B) in that process: how they think about the external event. Actually, it is these opinions or beliefs about events that lead to depression. The external event (A) is losing one's job. The belief (B) is, "I am a worthless person," or "I must be an incompetent person." The resulting feeling (C) is depression. Alternative beliefs that would not lead to depression would be, "I did not perform as well as I could have on this job," or "My abilities are better suited for another kind of work." Another way of describing this process is noting that depression occurs because people draw certain conclusions about their being from their actions. Because "I cannot do something well," the depressed person says to himself or herself, "I am not a good person." They confuse statements about their doing with their being. They confuse beliefs about their performance with beliefs about their intrinsic worth. They confuse an evaluation of their deeds with an evaluation of their personhood. The result is depression.

Cognitive therapists support the idea that it is our beliefs—our operational beliefs—that determine much of our behavior and emotions. As we consider the role that beliefs play in grief and bereavement, we must focus on those beliefs that really govern our lives and for the moment leave aside those formal creeds that may or may not touch our souls.

OUR BELIEFS AND OUR HEALTH

Walt is a thirty-five year old husband, father and businessman who describes himself as a personnel "trouble-shooter" for a large corporation. He had been involved in some marriage counseling at our agency. When his wife did not wish to continue with that process, he contracted with me to work on "his persistent and growing depression." Walt had an M.A. in psychology and was a bright, sophisticated client. He always thought of himself as a responsible, straight and moral person. He liked to be the good guy, the helper. He prided himself in being a good listener, a good provider and a good father.

It was not always easy for him to ask for help, but in this case he was desperate. He felt that he was losing his marriage, a situation that he reasoned caused him to be depressed. During their courtship Walt had helped Jane "straighten her head out" after a couple of bouts with alcoholism. In the latter half of their twelve-year marriage, she began to grow more as a person, working outside the home, developing more interests and activities independent of her husband, and seemingly, from Walt's perspective, "not needing him anymore." There seemed to be a direct relationship between her increasing independent style and his increasing depression.

Yet the missing link in his depression-forming process was the role that beliefs played. One of Walt's operational beliefs could be summarized as: "I am worthwhile only when I am needed." Sure enough, he was needed less and less at home. He was still a valued employee at work, but that was not enough. The real cause of his depression was not Jane's growing up, for he knew logically that this process was good for her. The more exact cause of his depression was his belief that he was no longer worth anything.

Depression has a way of compounding itself. Another corollary to Walt's belief system was that he was worthy only when he was understanding, caring and compassionate. Admittedly he had a difficult time allowing himself to feel and to express angry feelings. When he would begin to feel depressed or angry, you could hear him saying to himself, "Walter, you should not be depressed. You have everything going for you," or "Walter, you have nothing to feel angry about. You should be more understanding of Jane." This kind of internal discounting of his own feelings fed the depressive cycle. As he internalized his own feelings, he got only more depressed. Gradually he dug his depressive hole deeper and deeper.

Walt's case is an interesting example, because his pattern and sick belief system is not unlike those that many people have who are in the helping professions. Clergy, counselors, doctors and teachers get a great deal of their self-worth and identity from helping others. However, when they cannot be helpful or provide for others as they believe they should, they feel less worthwhile. They blame themselves. The result is depression. While this is a generalized discussion, the pattern is common enough to warrant our attention. It is one of the built-in risks of being a helper-type person.

In the terminology of Transactional Analysis, a script is a blueprint for a life course. "A psychological script," writes Muriel James,

> is a person's ongoing program for a life drama which dictates where the person is going with his or her life and the path that will lead there. It is a drama an individual compulsively acts out, though one's awareness of it may be vague.[8]

Scripts vary widely just as dramas do. Scripts can be sagas, comedies, tragedies, romances, adventure stories or even dull plays. Different scripts contain varying degrees of constructiveness or destructiveness.

Various forces can influence and mold our early script formation. There are national scripts, such as "We Americans have Yankee ingenuity." There are ethnic scripts, such as "We Italians are hot-blooded." There are family scripts, such as "We MacDonalds are a cut above." But the largest single influence on a child's script formation is that of the parents, who consciously or unconsciously script their child by repetitively saying things such as "She is just like her Aunt Sally" or "He is really going to go somewhere in life" or "Danny will never amount to anything in life." Children, like radar, pick up these early programming messages and unconsciously plot out their life courses. Not everyone has just one script, of course. Sometimes people have several competing scripts, or a counter-script, or even a series of successive scripts. A script is essentially a semi-conscious belief we have about ourselves, our life and its future course.

Psychiatrist, M. Scott Peck uses a slightly different image to describe the same concept. He calls humans "map-makers."[9] A map is "our view of reality with which we negotiate the terrain of life." From our earliest days we are constantly making and hopefully occasionally revising our maps. Like the use of road maps, life maps guide us through life. They tell us what to expect ahead, whether to anticipate obstacles and how to get to our desired goals. Obviously our maps or scripts must be accurate. If they are based on reality, they will guide us well. We will see the world as it really is. If maps are inaccurate or "outdated," they will guide us down unhealthy paths and distort our interpersonal relationships.

It is always amazing to me how powerful such operational beliefs as "scripts" or "maps" are in our lives. Scripts have a tendency to be terribly self-fulfilling, either for good or for ill. For example, consider the young woman who was regularly told: "Men are beasts, and they will always leave you stranded." After she married at the early age of seventeen, she became increasingly jealous over little "signs" that her husband was cheating on her. Her insecurity and distrust grew. She became convinced that he was about to leave. Her husband reacted with growing anger, defensiveness and intolerance. Eventually, after six years of nagging, distrust and conflict, he did in fact leave, unable to stand the constant jealousy and criticism. She got her wish. Her script became fulfilled, and with great reassurance she can tell her young daughter, "See, men are nothing but beasts and will always leave you stranded." Admittedly, this is an oversimplified story, but the pattern is recognizable in many forms. There is a strange security in maintaining and fulfilling one's beliefs, even if they are self-destructive beliefs.

In the musical play, "Man of La Mancha," the aging Don Quixote sets upon a campaign to restore the age of chivalry, to battle evil and right all wrongs. When Quixote and his squire Sancho arrive at a distant roadside inn, which he claims is a castle, he meets Aldonza, the local servant girl and part-time prostitute. Quixote sees her as his Lady, the ideal of womanhood, whom he will worship and defend evermore, his "Dulcinea." Aldonza is confused and angered by Quixote's refusal to see her for what she is. Later her resistance increases and she questions Quixote again and again, "What do you want from me?" to which Quixote responds in the famous song, "The Impossible Dream." Her initial efforts to change her script are met with hostile violence at the hands of her usual patrons. Disillusioned, Aldonza denounces Quixote and his foolish "dreams."

In the dramatic climax of the story, Quixote, having come to his senses, is nevertheless dying. Aldonza pleads with him to become Quixote again and restore his former vision of her as a Lady. He briefly returns to life and to his vision, only to die moments later. Yet Aldonza, having seen the vision once again, refuses to acknowledge that Quixote has died. "Don Quixote is not dead," she states. When questioned by Sancho, she replies, "My name is Dulcinea." Quixote's belief in her, as a Lady full of value and worth, literally transformed her. She changed her beliefs about herself because he believed that she was something more than she was. This story illustrates the tremendous power of beliefs to hold us prisoners, and the redemptive power of another person's loving belief to change our beliefs about ourselves. What we choose to believe, especially about ourselves, can be life-giving or life-destroying.

MEANING AND SUFFERING: SOME SAMPLE RESEARCH

On first impression it seems obvious that our beliefs about God, our life course and the purpose of suffering would influence how we handle a severe loss or how we face death. The popular bookshelves are filled with "inspirational" literature written by people who have suffered tremendous losses, only to be sustained by faith, the love of God and the knowledge of life everlasting. No doubt too, we have all heard our share of sermons exhorting us to "have faith" in times of crisis and suffering. Yet the amount of research that has dealt with this important subject, particularly in empirical ways, has been relatively slight. Admittedly it is a difficult subject to "get a clear handle on."

Studies of the experiences of prisoners-of-war do provide some data concerning the role of a person's belief system in times of crisis.

The modern study of prisoner-of-war experiences began after World War II and focused on the German concentration camp experiences. Many writers [10] have agreed that it was of the greatest importance for a prisoner-of-war in these camps to have some spiritual life, defined broadly as any religious, political or humanistic philosophy of life. Such beliefs helped a person cope by giving him or her convictions to cling to in the face of torture, and by giving him or her a sense of meaning in the face of suffering. Interestingly enough, one key variable was not the content of the beliefs, but the degree of commitment and devotion to one's beliefs. Thus DeWind writes:

> It is, therefore, no mere accident that the convinced Christian as well as the Communists, who would seem to be their psychological opposites, should have shown the greatest power of resistance in camps, and even managed to set up certain forms of anti-Fascist organization. [11]

Having a belief system and adhering to it intensely formed a psychological defense against the constant oppression of mind and body. The value of the belief system was in its ability to provide meaning, offer strength and encourage hope, even in a hopeless situation.

Viktor E. Frankl, reflecting upon his three years in a German concentration camp, notes that a prisoner's belief system was critical to his or her survival. [12] Without it, prisoners would be overwhelmed by the inevitability of their death and literally "give up" and "give in" to their captors. The daily confrontations with death and suffering challenged the prisoners' beliefs and forced them to make an existential decision about their attitude toward suffering. He writes:

> Whenever one is confronted with an inescapable, unavoidable situation, whenever one has to face a fate which cannot be changed, e.g. an incurable disease, such as an inoperable cancer; just then one is given a last chance to actualize the highest value, to fulfill the deepest meaning, the meaning of suffering. For what matters above all is the attitude we take toward suffering, the attitude in which we take our suffering upon ourselves. [13]

Suffering challenges one's beliefs. Suffering is the acid test of faith. For many, their beliefs come up short and fail to provide the necessary meaning. For others, however, death or near death experiences can function to strengthen, refine and enlarge their beliefs. Frankl notes that some people, implicitly through their beliefs, did not become helpless victims but found an increased sense of personal responsibility and freedom, even amid complete imprisonment.

From this experience with suffering and meaning, Frankl generalized his insights into a new system of psychotherapy. He called his system logotherapy (logo = meaning), which assumes an innate human "noetic" or spiritual dimension expressed most visibly as the "will-to-meaning." Whether in a concentration camp or not, Frankl reasoned that all people must deal with suffering, loss and death. Finding and maintaining a sense of meaning is one irreplaceable ingredient in a person's overall health, and in times of loss it is essential.

The Vietnam War and the American prisoner-of-war experiences there offered modern researchers another opportunity to study the role of a person's belief system in separation and loss. The Center for Prisoner of War Studies in San Diego has studied the effect of prolonged separation and loss upon the families of prisoners-of-war and missing-in-action service personnel.[14] In a study by Edna J. Hurietes and associates the authors divided two hundred and fifteen wives of POW/MIA servicemen into two groups: those who found religion helpful in coping with the absence/loss of their husbands and those who did not.[15] The former group was associated with greater age, greater activity in church affairs, less tendency to date and fewer guilt feelings. One of the most interesting correlations was between religion and "moving on." The term "moving on" was defined as psychologically "letting go" of the husband's role in the family and making significant adjustments to life without him, such as beginning to date, a change of residence, beginning full employment and so on. The authors write:

> Religion and "moving on" to a new life may be mutually exclusive; in this case, if the wife holds onto religion, she may feel too much guilt associated with beginning a new life for herself. Perhaps those wives who had reported that religion was of no help were also those who had moved on towards a reorganization of the family and a closing out of the husband's role, but not without feelings of guilt and emotional ups and downs which at times included contemplation of suicide.[16]

This study [17] seems to indicate that in this situation religion served more as a defense mechanism, rather than as a facilitator of the grief process.

Religion reinforced and strengthened the widow's desire to hang on to the possibility that her husband would soon return. Their beliefs in God, in America and so on, helped them endure. In such cases where their husbands did return, their beliefs were justified, but in cases where the men never returned, their beliefs only prolonged and denied the necessary grieving and "moving on."

The Pueblo incident in which eighty-two United States servicemen were captured and imprisoned by North Korea served as another clearly definable incident in which researchers could study the role of a prisoner's meaning system. Charles V. Ford and Raymond C. Spaulding, who gave psychiatric tests and interviews to the returning prisoners, reported that formal religious beliefs were not a significant variable in determining good or poor adjustment to the imprisonment.[18] They did report that "when crew members were asked about the methods they used to cope with their incarceration, they frequently stated that they maintained a faith in their commanding officer, religion and country."[19] In a follow-up study "faith" was described as "a confidence in the leadership of the crew and the belief that the U.S. government and Navy would not abandon them."[20] This "faith" or belief in the United States appeared to be more frequently associated with the well-adjusted group. It is interesting to note that Korean efforts to "brainwash" the American prisoners-of-war, as with the efforts of the Chinese Communists in the Korean War,[21] were aimed at "reforming" the prisoner's belief system. They assume, probably through countless years of experience, that the content of a prisoner's belief system and his devotion to it are key factors in determining one's cooperation or resistance to imprisonment.

It is clear from this survey of some of the literature that a person's belief system is an important variable in determining his or her adjustment to severe loss, death and hardship. Belief, of course, must be understood in its broadest sense, as any religious, philosophical and/or political belief that provides one's life with a sense of meaning. It also appears that the strength of a person's convictions mattered as much as the content of those beliefs. What is not clear, however, is the role that beliefs play in facilitating or blocking an individual's ability to "move on." In some cases, especially where the loss is perceived as temporary, religious beliefs help the individual endure the hardship by defending him or her from the painful finality of the loss. In other cases, especially where the loss is perceived as final, beliefs must be used in a different way, to give comfort and meaning amid the process of grieving. Clearly, religion can be an escape or a comfort.

LOSS AND THE ECLIPSE OF MEANING

"One characteristic all human beings have in common," begins James Fowler in a recent featured *Psychology Today* interview, "is that we can't live without some sense that life is meaningful."[22] Human beings are "meaning-making animals," perhaps the only one of God's creatures to have this need for a sense of meaning. We need to feel that our lives have purpose, worth and intrinsic value. We need to sense that our work and activities are not in vain. This need for meaning is what Abraham Maslow called a "higher need." The basic human needs for food, sleep and even love normally take priority over the need for meaning. Yet, as more and more people have their basic needs relatively satisfied, most of the time, the need for meaning assumes greater importance in the hierarchy of a psyche's priorities. Without a sense of meaning, people stumble through life in varying degrees of directionless behavior or in what Viktor Frankl called "noogenic neurosis." If the modern trend toward meaninglessness continues, this spiritual illness may one day replace cancer as the "number one killer."

As we look at the need for meaning from the perspective of grief theory, as described in Chapter 2, we see that meaning can best be understood as related to attachment. Humans find meaning in those things to which they are emotionally attached, or, conversely, they attach themselves emotionally to those things that they perceive as meaningful. People build their personal meaning systems around their particular constellation of emotional attachments. If one's emotional attachments change, as they inevitably do in times of loss, then a person's meaning system also must change. To the extent that our meanings or operational theology is built around our earthly attachments, there will be inevitable "lapses of meaning" when those attachments are ruptured by loss.

Consider an adolescent boy who finds a great sense of meaning in playing football. Everything in his life "lives or dies" on each week's game. He adopts the philosophy, rituals and myths of the coach, the team and the school for which he plays. He believes, "My life has meaning because I contribute to the larger cause of my team." Yet, ten years later as an adult, this same person no longer finds much meaning in playing football. He no longer needs football in order to find meaning. Perhaps now his sense of purpose and worth is embodied in his work. He adopts the values, rituals and customs of the "organization man." He believes, "My life now has meaning because I contribute to the development of this product or because I earn x-amount of dollars per year." Yet, still many years later, when this same man retires, his sense of meaning must be revised again. His adjustment to retirement depends, in part, on what meaning he gave to work and whether he can find a new sense of meaning apart from work. Perhaps now our fictitious man will come to believe, "My life has meaning because I have fathered many fine children . . . or because I can help others . . . or . . ." We can see clearly the tremendous importance of finding a sense of meaning that transcends the predictable losses of the human life-cycle.[23] My point here, however, is simply that we humans invest ourselves in various attachments and thereby give to our lives meaning and purpose. As these attachments are lost, either in the normal course of human life or by tragic accidents, our meanings are altered. There is in bereavement, then, an "eclipse of meaning" when the old meanings no longer work, but new meanings have not yet emerged.

This same observation, that meanings change over the course of one's lifetime, has been made by other scholars, writing from differing perspectives. Colin M. Parkes has desecribed the changing pattern of one's meaning system over the life-span as changes in one's "assumptive world."[24] James W. Fowler has summarized his years of study and research in faith development in a book entitled, *Stages of Faith*.[25] As the title suggests, Fowler argues that people grow through several well-defined stages of religious faith during the course of their lifetimes. Building on the psycho-social stages of Erikson and the cognitive structure analysis of Piaget and Kohlberg, Fowler delineates six stages of faith development, based not on the content of faith but on the structure of belief.[26] These stages are only roughly correlated to chronology, and many adults never get beyond stage three or four in Fowler's scheme.

Erikson has offered another perspective on the role of meaning in the life-cycle.[27] He has suggested that the need for meaning is focused primarily in one life-stage: the last one. As a person approaches death and the termination of life, the conflict between ego integrity and despair emerges. Erikson describes ego integrity as "the acceptance of one's one and only life cycle as something that had to be and that, by necessity, permitted no substitutions . . . and in such a final consolidation, death loses its sting.''[28] The opposite, despair, arises when we realize that our life cycle was not meaningful and that there is no time left to do otherwise, no time to repeat it over again. Kübler-Ross, who has worked so extensively with people who are living in this crisis, dramatically describes her awareness of this same point:

> We could not convey to our colleagues that we are all dying—that we all have to face our finiteness long before we are terminally ill. This perhaps is the greatest lesson we learned from our patients: Live, so you do not have to look back and say, ''God, how I have wasted my life.''[29]

While the need for meaning reaches its zenith in the Eriksonian eighth stage, Kübler-Ross has suggested that it is also present throughout the life cycle. The triggering factor appears to be any transition, loss event or near-death experience.

Daniel J. Levinson and his associates have studied the issues involved in a man's mid-life crisis. As a man enters into the mid-life transition, they note:

> He is likely to review his progress and ask, ''What have I done, where am I now? Of what value is my life to society, to other persons and especially to myself?'' He must deal with the disparity between what he is and what he has dreamed of becoming.[30]

As previously noted, middle age involves several subtle but important losses. There is in those losses an intensification of the awareness of time. This awareness initiates a ''crisis'' of meaning, in which a man or a woman must reevaluate and redefine his or her beliefs about life, himself or herself and God.

Every loss is a reminder, then, of the shortness of time and, ultimately, of death itself. In this sense every loss is an eschatological occurrence (see Chapter 7). Therefore, each loss will initiate a temporary crisis of meaning, in which we must reevaluate our life and its meaningfulness in light of the current loss. Sometimes such reevaluations result in a positive but radical conversion of a person's life, values and priorities. Other times, such a reevaluation results only in a more desperate clinging to the old meanings. In either case, bereavement brings with it an eclipse of meaning, a time when the old meanings, tied up with what is now lost, no longer function, but new meanings have not yet emerged. Amid bereavement, there are inevitable periods of meaninglessness. Our job as pastors is to help grieving people through these periods of meaninglessness and to help them discover new meanings that fit the new life-stage that they are entering.

FINDING PURPOSE IN SORROW

Painful and persistent suffering is bad enough, but the real anguish of suffering is often found in its meaninglessness. More than twenty-five hundred years ago, a man named Job stood under the curse of meaningless suffering.[31] The horror of Job's situation was not just that his children died or that his cattle died or that his body was covered with boils, but that his sufferings were pointless. He could not find a reason or a purpose for why God had afflicted him so. His so-called comforters came to him and offered several possible explanations, most notably that Job was being punished for some unknown wicked deeds. Job loudly protested that he had been a good man, a pious man and a righteous man. He could see no logical reason for his plight. At best his anguish seemed to be the result of a cruel cosmic "bet" between God and Satan.

Many of us will suffer for a cause. The Indians who followed Mahatma Gandhi into the arms of British soldiers willingly did so because they believed that their suffering had purpose. Those Americans who fought in World War II willingly suffered, and some died, because they felt that their cause was just. Some people voluntarily give up one of their kidneys in order to save the life of a friend or a relative. They endure pain and a future life of limitation knowing that there is purpose in their sacrifice. Sorrow becomes bizarre, absurd and so much more painful, when the mourners cannot see any good purpose or reason for their loss. Meaning has a crucial role to play in mitigating the anguish of grief.

The question of the purpose of loss and suffering is not a new one to the human race. Over the eons of human inquiry mourners, theologians and philosophers have suggested many possible answers to the meaning of suffering. Some of the broad categories are:

1. Loss is punishment. We suffer because we have done something wrong, unwise or sinful. This was a very common idea in biblical times. It is found clearly in the Book of Job. It appears in the New

Testament as well, where Jesus refutes it on several occasions (Jn 9:2; Lk 13:4). The question "What did I do to deserve this?" is often the first thought that many people have when tragedy strikes. Interestingly, there is some truth to this impulse. At times, sinful behavior does sow the seeds for future suffering. Hatred is the foundation for violence and war. Alcoholism leads to death. Deceit eats away at marital trust. Environmental pollution contributes to illness. Inhumane, unhealthful or sinful behavior often carries a built-in judgment. This is especially true when suffering has been caused by human error. Yet, to say that God willfully uses suffering to punish humans for their misdeeds is another matter. Loss has no such divine intentionality.

2. Loss is for a greater cause. In an evil world just causes often require human sacrifice. On occasion we can choose to suffer, knowing the importance of the cause. At other times we look for a cause after-the-fact, hoping to console ourselves with the knowledge that our loss is not without purpose. After the massacre bombing of U.S. Marines in Beirut last year, Americans cried out for some explanation why our soldiers were in Lebanon. What the shocked and grieving citizens wanted was some reassurance that their native sons did not die in vain, that they gave their lives for a higher purpose, a greater good. Believing such, we are comforted and can endure our grief work easier. There is no greater anguish than knowing that our loved ones gave their lives for nothing.

3. Loss is to help others. One of the main causes that makes sense for most people is that of helping others. Barney Clark voluntarily became the first recipient of an artificial heart, partially because he wanted to live, and partially because he knew that his suffering would help others to live a more full life. When he died after one hundred and twelve days of "artificial" life, he was recognized as a public hero. His suffering had meaning. Similarly, many bereaved people form or join self-help programs to help other people who have the same problems, diseases or losses as they have had. Other mourners write books of their experiences, and in the very writing of the book itself they give meaning to their loss and to the death of their loved one. In giving to others, people find meaning and purpose.

4. Loss benefits the sufferer. In bereavement sometimes we comfort mourners with the exhortation, "God is testing you!" By such ad-

vice we are saying that this suffering or this loss will strengthen your faith, improve your character or make you more compassionate. It is hard to believe that God would take the life of a loved one, bring on a devastating hurricane or cause a plane to crash, just to test our loyalty. Yet here, too, there is some truth to this meaning. Most often, in retrospect, grievers look back on their affliction and say, "Yes, I have grown," or "Yes, my faith is stronger now," or "Yes, I am a better person." These are meanings that come only in retrospect, meanings that emerge only in and through the process of healing. It is hard, if not cruel, to forecast such purposes at the moment of loss.

5. Loss is a part of life. When we really stop and think about it, one of the reasons why we find death so difficult to understand is that it is a relatively uncommon experience in Western civilization. We do not see as much death, loss and suffering in our daily lives as did people in former generations. Most of us in the prime of life expect health, happiness and vitality. When loss occurs, it disturbs our expectations. It ruptures our beliefs about life. We scramble to find some explanation.

There are other cultures and many people within our own culture who routinely expect loss. They accept loss and grief as a normal part of life. They assume that loss has no special meaning, no special explanation other than being "a given" of human existence. There is some truth, and maybe even some meaning, in this argument. Loss is a part of life. It is also, more precisely, a part of love. Any meaning that is to be found in loss is found in its connection with love. We give life meaning by loving others, but as soon as we do, we are vulnerable to loss. Loss is an unavoidable part of love. As long as we are human, we shall lose. The only way we cannot lose is to cease to love and to cease to be human.

When I was doing my early clinical training, I was taught to pay attention to feelings at all cost. So when a sorrowing mother protested, "Why did this have to happen to my child?" I interpreted her "real" message to be, "I am angry at God," and I responded accordingly. My clinical educators seemed to be saying that the only dimension of the human psyche that mattered was feelings and that there is no realm of meaning, or, if there is, it is not relevant to grief work. Certainly, there are times when "why" questions cover up great anger, and that anger must be dealt with. Yet I have come to be convinced that finding purpose in one's suffering is a crucial part of the grieving process. In fact, I would argue that a person's grief work is not complete until he or she has found (or has created) some meaning in his or her loss. Just as our emotional life can be wounded by a loss, so too our meaning systems can be shattered by a loss. Just as our emotions require healing, so too our belief systems require a similar healing. It is as if a person must grieve simultaneously on several different levels—a feeling level, a meaning level, a social level and, for many, even a physical level. We are, after all, whole people.

Melodie was a thirty year old woman who had given birth to two children, a girl and a younger boy. When the boy, John-John, was about nineteen months old, he fell into the family swimming pool and died. It was a horrible sight to discover him there, floating face-down in the clear blue water. It was an exceedingly painful loss for Melodie and her husband to bear. As a couple they did not deal with their mutual pain well at all. It became the wedge between them and a festering wound that eventually led to the death of their marriage.

When I first met Melodie, it was some two years later. She had contracted with me to do some counseling around her persistent weight problem and chronic but mild depression. We explored both of her losses quite thoroughly. She reported, and it seemed to be true, that she had done most of her grief work over John-John's death. The one thing that still "bugged" her, however, was "Why?" "Why?" she would ask. "I still don't see any point in his death. Why did God have to take him, just at the start of his young life?" All of the usual religious reasons for accidental death and undeserved suffering did not make much sense to her. Her son's death seemed completely pointless, beyond comprehension, totally repulsive to her spirit.

While I heard her concern about the meaninglessness of John-John's death, I continued to focus, as a good counselor should, on her feelings. We did do some processing of residue grief feelings, which seemed helpful at the time, but still she regularly kept coming back to the same theme, "Why, why did my baby have to die?" The question haunted her, and at times I began to fear that she was becoming obsessed by it. Finally I began to really listen to what she was telling me, and we recontracted our counseling "to discover together some meaning in John-John's death."

We began to read together: Bible, consolation literature, personal accounts of loss, theology, etc. We discussed our findings each week.

Always we made our discussions very personal—does this idea touch Melodie and her loss and does it help make sense out of John-John's death? The process intensified over weeks to what is called the "impasse stage." The resolution came in an unexpected form. She said that the answer came to her one night, just before sleep, in the form of a single statement: "John-John had to return to the water." She immediately remembered that her son had loved the water. He was fascinated by it, and several times prior to his death she had stopped him from playing too near the pool. She interpreted all this to mean that in John-John's former life (reincarnation) he had lived in the water and that he had an unfinished task from his former life. His soul was born into this earthly life in order to complete that unfinished task, and then, upon completing it, he returned to his home, the water.

Her emerging mythology was a product of her own personal struggle to find a purpose to her son's death. Her resolution was uniquely her own. She found great relief in this explanation for what had seemed to her, up to that point, to be unexplainable. I chose, after some careful thought, not to challenge her unusual explanation. Even though it was not particularly Christian, I saw the grace of God in her process. Her myth was a gift from a comforting God. Finally, her soul was at rest. She found some purpose, some meaning in her terrible tragedy.

We humans, particularly in times of loss, need to find some purpose in our suffering. A part of the necessary healing that all mourners must go through includes this discovery or rediscovery of meaning in their plight. When the normal sources of meaning fail us, we look for meaning anywhere that we can find it. And at times, when meanings do not readily emerge, we must work to create our own meanings. We need some explanation for our loss. Melodie's persistent and stubborn determination to find meaning in her son's death, only testifies to the deep human need we all have to find purpose in our sorrow.

Loss and the Nature of God

One of the most common beliefs that nearly ninety percent of all Americans share is a belief in God. Yet, while most Americans say that they believe in a Supreme Being (whatever that is), there are probably as many different beliefs about what that Being is as there are individuals. Each person's perception of God is slightly different and unique.

Some people see God as a Heavenly King governing the affairs of the world; others see God as a Sovereign Lord demanding obedience from earthly subjects; others see God as "the Force," an impersonal universal power for good; and still others see God as a forgiving Father, nurturing the growth of children. To some extent, each of us perceives God in the light of our own personal histories, prejudices and temperaments. How we view God influences greatly how we understand and cope with loss.

Belief in God, like all meanings, goes through a temporary eclipse in times of bereavement. Suffering, especially sudden, unexplainable, undeserved suffering, leads most people to question who and what God is. Is God really in charge of the world? Is God really caring? In traditional theological debates, this dilemma has been referred to as the problem of evil. I prefer to call it the problem of the nature of God. In its simplest form, the problem of the nature of God is usually structured something like this:

A. God is all-loving.
B. God is all-powerful.
C. Innocent people suffer.

In order for there to be a resolution of this problem, one of the three propositions must not be totally true. The first possibility is that God is not all-loving and occasionally wills unwarranted loss to humans. Perhaps God has a mean side, or perhaps God gets angry with humans and, from time to time, does punish us or allow us to be punished. The second possibility is that God is not all-powerful. Perhaps God is not in total command of the situation. Perhaps there are corners of the universe where chaos or Satan still reigns supreme. Perhaps, God does not have the power to prevent every evil. The third possibility is that those whom we perceive to be innocent or righteous are not really so worthy. Perhaps everyone who suffers really does deserve what he or she gets. Of these three possible resolutions to the conflict, the first two solutions involve significant changes in the nature of God. Thus, finding meaning in loss inevitably involves a discussion of the nature of God.

Alfred North Whitehead, the noted British philosopher, once distinguished between the two natures of God with the phrases "God as Caesar" and "God as Fellow-Sufferer."[32] These terms adeptly describe the two different sides of God.

God as Caesar. This image of God is that of Divine King, Sovereign Lord and Creator of the Universe, who sits upon a heavenly throne from where every event on earth is willed. All creation is this God's Kingdom. God is omnipotent (all-powerful) and omniscient (all-knowing). Nothing happens, therefore, anywhere in God's realm that is not allowed or willed to happen. This side of God is above the world, apart from human history and aloof from human suffering, tragedy and loss. God's primary activity is that of a legislator and judge. God issues commandments and calls for obedience. In creation, God establishes the laws of nature and usually does not violate them. God is also the judge of these laws. In this form, God is eternal, changeless, the ''unmoved mover.'' God is the same ''yesterday, today and forever.''

God as Fellow-Sufferer. There is another view of God—that is, as companion, as friend and fellow sojourner with each human being. This God is involved in the world and, therefore, knows intimately the pain and suffering of all living beings. This is the tender side of God, the feeling side of God, the God who listens to prayers and who suffers with and for people. This God feels what we feel, weeps as we weep. This God is our comforter who helps us in our trials, rather than the one who brings on our trials. This God is the forgiving parent, rather than the punishing parent. This God is involved in the process of life, rather than watching from above it. This God is the one who is still creating, molding and fashioning the world, through the lives and actions of all believers. This is the God of the cross, the God of the manger, the God of the Incarnation, the God who champions the cause of the meek, the poor and the bereaved. In this form, God is changeable or, at least, able to be influenced and accessible to humans.

These two images of God are quite different. In classical theology these two views of God are presented as two aspects of the same divine nature, God's transcendent nature and God's immanent nature. Yet in the daily lives of people, especially those in bereavement, these two sides of God seem more like two different gods. Loss and bereavement are often a time when the image of God as Caesar fades and is gradually replaced by a new experience of God—God as Fellow-Sufferer.

As children, most of us are raised with an image of God as Caesar or as the divine parent. We associate God with our early familial experience of authority. In the eyes of children, parents do seem all-powerful and all-knowing. Our parents are the just rule-makers, the enforcers and, at times, the punishers of disobedience. All of these earliest experiences of authority get transferred onto God. God is seen as all-powerful, all-knowing, a rulemaker and a judge. The view of God as Caesar works fairly well throughout our childhood and adolescence. It is an image that emphasizes the orderliness, security and justice of all of life.

When a loss or death occurs, people with this view assume that God willed this loss event the way God wills all events in the world. God caused it or, at least, allowed it to happen. God chose not to prevent it. Yet, this God must be loving or, at least, just. Therefore, people with this point of view must rationalize this apparent contradiction by postulating that "people deserve what they get" or that "the innocent will be compensated in heaven" or that "God did this for our own good," or that "now the deceased will be at blessed peace with God."

This understanding of God does not hold up well as life matures, and there are an increasing number of losses and, occasionally, pointless tragedies. In fact, in my opinion, this view of God adds to the suffering of mourners. They are likely to spend all their time looking toward heaven, waiting for God to answer their "why" questions, while at the same time failing to see that God is already next to them. In and through the process of grieving, many mourners find God to be a Fellow-Sufferer, a God of the process, a God who comforts them even in their greatest sorrow. This God or aspect of God is not learned in Sunday School or in theology classes. This is a side of God that must be experienced and lived through. It comes with age, and it does not come easy. It is a vision of God that is born in suffering and fashioned by personal anguish.

I have known so many personal friends who were committed and enthusiastic Christians in high school and college, only to be practicing agnostics years later when we rediscovered each other. What happened in that interval? Perhaps an unwelcomed divorce, a sudden tragedy or an untimely death shattered their belief system and, in the pain and confusion of bereavement, they threw out their old beliefs. When it became apparent that God did not "promise a rose garden," they gave up the notion of God with their baby clothes and acne medicine. Their old image of God died, but in their haste for easy answers, they overlooked the God who shared their pain, "God as Fellow-Sufferer," the God who transforms pain into new life.

CONCLUSION: THE QUEST FOR MEANING

I must confess that I have a bias. I believe that ultimately life is meaningful. I believe that meaning is built into the very fabric of human existence. The Creator has given us a few hints over the centuries, in the form of revelations, as to what that ultimate meaning might be. Yet, as we look at life and how it is lived on a day by day, year by year, and even a moment by moment basis, we find that meanings change, evolve and develop. The meaning of this hour, the direction of my life, and the purpose of pain all change over the course of our lifetimes. The meanings that make sense to a child are not the beliefs that guide the adolescent or the ultimate concerns of the adult.

We all have many meanings and fragments of meanings that coexist in our souls. Each of us lives with different levels of meaning, ranging from the formalized creeds to the cultural mottos to the semiconscious "scripts" about our lives. Taken all together, these meanings make up our operational theology, our most sacred and basic assumptions about life, ourselves and God.

As our lives change, evolve and mature, and especially in times of transition or in moments of loss and tragedy, the present meanings do not always make sense. Every change initiates a rethinking of our beliefs. What does this event mean? What does my life mean now that this has happened or now that I have turned forty years old? What can I learn from this event? Where is God in this process? It seems to me that we humans are constantly involved in a quest for meaning.

The modern search for meaning is certainly made more difficult by the rootless culture in which we live. The traditional structures, rituals, and institutions from which most people derive meaning have themselves cracked, changed or been badly shaken by the earthquakes of rapid social change. We are more and more "on our own" to find whatever meaning we can in life. And to make matters worse, there are many false prophets and secular priests who offer us ready-made, rigid belief systems, which our allegiance to is designed to line their wallets. Yet, while I share the concern for the absence of meaning in our times, there is something terribly healthy about being on a constant quest for meaning. I believe that sound mental health is found more in the process of the search for meaning than it is in any particular set of beliefs.

I realize that encouraging people to search for meaning needs to be balanced with our need for commitment, stability and loyalty to a particular belief system. A commitment to process, if taken to the extreme, would result in religious anarchy or nihilism. Yet, having said that, I would still wish that we would hold onto our beliefs a little less tightly, that we would be more playful with our meanings, that we would consider faith to be a "working hypothesis" more than a proven fact. We must commit ourselves to those beliefs that we cherish most, and we also must realize, simultaneously, that our most cherished beliefs need to grow as we change. We must invest ourselves in the process of growth and change, in the process of discovering and rediscovering meaning, especially those meanings that transcend loss.

Jesus once promised, "Ask and you shall receive, seek and you shall find, knock and it shall be opened to you" (Mt 7:7–8). Among other meanings, this verse suggests that we must ask before we can receive, that we must seek before we can find, and that we must knock before it will be opened to us. Nowhere is this dynamic more true than in the realm of meaning. We must ask, seek and knock. We must be persistent in our quest for new levels of meaning, for new depths to our beliefs and for experiencing new aspects of the God we worship. Only in the quest for meaning shall we find meaning.

9. Faith And Loss

"A Christian is someone who can leave home, without taking the furniture with him."[1]

David C. Duncombe

One day several years ago, I was flying on a commercial airline from Los Angeles to Chicago to attend a convention. As we approached Chicago, the weather became increasingly cloudy and threatening. We were apparently passing through a series of thunderstorms which, on occasion, gave my prepared lunch a jolt off its tray. The pilot announced with carefully chosen words that O'Hare Airport had been temporarily closed due to severe thunderstorms, and that we were in a holding pattern, waiting for the airport to reopen (which, of course, he expected within a few minutes). I do not recall how long we circled above Chicago, but it seemed to me as though it was one of the longest waits of my life. Even though we were supposedly above the turbulence, it was a rocky wait. I could see nothing but black clouds and flashes of lightning out of my window.

My anxiety rose steadily as the time dragged on and on. I began praying, meditating, deep breathing—anything that would work to calm me down. Soon I was silently screaming to the pilot, "Just set this plane down, will you? I don't care where—just set it down!" Since my plea went unnoticed, I decided to get up and try pacing in the back of the cabin. I remember speaking to one of the stewardesses there, inquiring how she coped with these occasional anxious rides. She responded with absolute calmness, "Oh, I don't worry much with Captain Allen. I have great faith in him and his crew. They are some of the best in the fleet."

192

Gratefully, I can reassure you that I did make it to Chicago that day, and even home again, a few days later, all in one piece. And I am sure that my anxiety was made worse by my lack of exposure to airline trips and turbulent weather. Nevertheless, the occasion gave me cause to reflect a bit on faith and, in particular, on the stewardess' remark, ''I have great faith in him.''

It occurred to me that there are many things that we have faith in, that we take for granted. I have faith that the bank will deposit my check. I have faith that the chair on which I am sitting will hold me up. I have faith that the sun will rise tomorrow. Conversely, I do not have faith that my car will start, especially when it has been doing so only intermittently. So much of our ability to have faith depends on a history of faithfulness that we have with the given person or object. The stewardess had a personal history of trustful experiences with airplanes and with Captain Allen. It was easier for her to have faith, whereas I, without that history, was more distrustful. Our ability to trust is rooted in history—a developmental history, if you will.

It occurred to me, too, that my inability to have faith had to do with my own sense of not being in control. In situations where I am in control, where I can do something or where, at least, I have more knowledge of what is going on, I feel more trustful. In this situation, above the clouds over Chicago, I had no control. There was nothing that I could do, and I had very little knowledge of the situation outside of Seat 15A. In such situations, faith came a little harder. There are many situations in life, like this one, where things are essentially out of our control. Foremost among them are loss events. As much as we might wish to, we cannot control loss, death or tragedy. Therefore, in these situations faith takes on a dimension of courage.

In this final chapter, we want to focus on the role that faith plays in facilitating grief and growth in the human personality. You will recall that, in the last chapter, we made a distinction between belief and faith, defining the latter quality as a pre-cognitive sense of trust. Faith is a commitment, a loyalty, a trust. Beliefs are the content or objects of our faith. Obviously, people can have faith in many things and can have many different types and degrees of faith.

It has been my experience that bereavement does call forth from us a special kind of faith, and that without this special kind of faith we do not grieve or grow well. This type of faith is best described as ''faith as trust" and "faith as courage." It is to these two themes that this chapter now turns. In so doing, we will be reviewing the thinking of two of the more noteworthy and influential scholars of our generation, both whom have given to faith a central place in their thoughts.

FAITH AS BASIC TRUST

Erik H. Erikson is one of the earliest and most well-known of the life-cycle theorists. His scheme of eight developmental stages is widely accepted and readily understandable to laypeople and professionals alike. Erikson has also written the most of any theorist on the presence and role of trust in the human personality. He has suggested that within the first year of life the human infant "experiences" a conflict between basic trust and basic mistrust.[2] By "basic trust" Erikson means an attitude toward oneself and the world that "senses" them to be basically trustworthy, that is, consistent, predictable and good. This condition, however, never exists in the absolute. The resolution of this primary conflict, like all succeeding conflicts, results in a ratio between basic trust and basic mistrust. According to Erikson, indications of a relatively positive resolution are "an infant's ease of feeding, depth of sleep, the relaxation of his bowels," and a willingness to let the "mother out of sight without undue anxiety or rage."[3] Furthermore, through the relatively positive development of basic trust, the infant's ego develops the first basic strength or virtue—hope. Hope is "the enduring belief in the attainability of feverish wishes, in spite of the dark urges and rages which mark the beginning of existence."[4] In this way, then, basic trust is "the cornerstone of a healthy personality."[5]

According to Erikson, this "sense of" basic trust or mistrust is pre-cognitive. It represents an attitude or stance toward life itself. It is not something that is acquired through rational means. It is beyond and prior to any particular belief system, although religion can contribute to its depth and regular renewal. Erikson has suggested that the development of basic trust "becomes the capacity for faith."[6] Faith is the religious expression of basic trust. Similarly, hope which is the virtue emerging out of a relatively positive resolution of this initial conflict is "the ontogenetic basis of faith."[7] Without this basic hope, any formal religious expressions of hope would be impossible.

Erikson has suggested that the institutional expression of basic trust is organized religion. He writes:

> The parental faith which supports the trust emerging in the newborn has throughout history sought its institutional safeguard . . . in organized religion. Trust born of care is, in fact, the touchstone of the actuality of a given religion. All religions have in common the periodical childlike surrender to a Provider or providers who dispense earthy fortune as well as spiritual health . . . ."[8]

Organized religion serves to strengthen and renew a person's basic trust through the mechanisms of creeds, rituals and values. All adults need this periodic renewal of faith (or trust) for their own mental health and that of their children. Infants "learn" to trust their world in large measure from their parents' capacity for trust. Erikson observes that "many who are proud to be without religion" are actually jeopardizing their children's capacity for developing basic trust, because an infant's basic trust finds its roots in the adult's faith.[9]

Moving beyond the infancy period, Erikson has suggested that basic trust continues to play a role in later adult life stages. He has suggested that, with each life-crisis, the earlier stages are relived and the later stages are previewed. He outlined in detail how this dynamic worked in terms of the identity crisis.[10] He has not, however, provided a similar outline of how this dynamic might work in terms of basic trust. Perhaps the dynamics of loss and grief can offer some hints on how basic trust serves to facilitate later development growth.

In previous chapters we noted that all life-cycle transitions involve losses which are experienced in greater or lesser degrees of severity. With each passing stage of life a person's constellation of emotional attachments changes. Some loved ones, some valued objects or some cherished ideas are lost. Sometimes these losses or changes come suddenly and dramatically. Sometimes they come gradually and predictably. In order to remain healthy, a person must regularly grieve or let go of his or her attachments to these lost objects. By so doing, people prepare themselves to love new people and to attach themselves to new ideas, places and times. Each lost attachment, however, represents security. Attachments are the means by which we maintain our personal identity and security. Every change in our attachments, however suddenly or gradually, represents insecurity. Change is "risky": letting go of the old, the familiar and moving toward the new, the unknown. Even when the transition is gradual, there are "in-between" periods when we have only partially let go of the old and only partially embraced the new. At these moments the risk is felt most keenly.

Otto Rank has suggested a similar understanding of development changes. He has argued that each developmental change or loss has a psychological push and a pull—"a pull back to the womb" and "a push toward self-dependence."[11] These two psychological forces, which find their roots in the "birth trauma" itself, color all subsequential life-cycle changes. He writes:

> The inner fear, which the child experiences in the birth process . . .
> has in it already both elements: fear of life and fear of death, since
> birth on the one hand means the end of life (former life) and on the
> other carries also the fear of the new life.[12]

He suggests that both of these fears, the fear of losing the past and the fear of the new, are in fact the same primary fear—the fear of separation. Journalist Gail Sheehy has borrowed this distinction, describing "the push-pull" that underlies all steps in human development.[13] "In every life-cycle transition," she notes, "the 'Merger Self' beckons us back towards the comforts of safety and the known, while the 'Seeker Self' urges us to confront the unknown and make changes."[14] Noting that developmental growth inevitably involves a risk, she writes:

> Growth demands a temporary surrender of security. It may mean a
> giving up of familiar but limiting patterns, safe but unrewarding
> work, values no longer believed in, relationships that have lost
> their meaning. As Dostoevsky put it, "taking a new step, uttering
> a new word is what people fear most." The real fear should be of
> the opposite course.[15]

The question now emerges: If risk is an element in all developmental growth, what enables a person to face that risk? Erikson's concept of basic trust provides a partial answer. A loss experience, especially a severe one, is a blow to our sense of basic trust. Loss is usually experienced at first as an unpredictable, random and evil event. It momentarily heightens our sense of basic mistrust. In Eriksonian terms then, each loss initiates a momentary "reliving" of our first develop-

mental conflict between basic trust and basic mistrust. A healthy adult
with a stable sense of basic trust will weather the present crisis by re-
lying on a storehouse of previous trustful life-experiences, beginning
in the first year of life itself. An unstable person with a weak sense of
basic trust will have a more difficult time recovering from a severe loss.
He or she will cling to any security—real or imagined—to support his
or her shattered sense of trust. Thus, basic trust is a key resource that
faciliates a bereaved person's ability to grieve and to grow.

FAITH AS COURAGE

Paul Tillich's understanding of faith has influenced a wide cross-
section of Christianity and represents a viewpoint that is informed by
psychological insights. In his little book, *The Dynamics of Faith*, Tillich defined faith as a "state of being ultimately concerned."[16] Every
person, he argues, has certain things, values, beliefs or causes to which
he or she has ultimately, passionately and willingly devoted his or her
life. Ultimate concerns are those things that give our lives meaning and
purpose, the causes to which we are highly committed, the values
around which we structure our priorities. According to Tillich, ultimate concerns, like all beliefs, offer a threat, a promise and a demand.
The threat refers to what might happen if we fail to devote ourselves to
a given belief. The promise refers to the rewards promised for such devotion. And the demand is reflected in the action, deeds and behavior
that the belief system demands from us. All of these dimensions of an
ultimate concern—the threat, the promise and the demand—are themselves ultimate in their nature. They are no small matters.

The content of one's ultimate concerns may vary widely. Some
may believe in the traditional God or ethical code of the Jewish and
Christian Scriptures. Others may be committed communists, socialists,
republicans or nationalists. Others may build their ultimate loyalties
around such themes as personal success, occupational achievement,
public recognition, avoidance of conflicts, the approval of others, ath-
letic prowess or other "script"-like phrases. In these latter examples,
we may be only dimly conscious of our ultimate concern. Nevertheless, it is still equally operative and can be terribly powerful.

For Tillich, faith is an act of the total person. By this he means,
among other things, that we organize and structure our lives around our

ultimate concerns. All other projects, concerns and priorities are secondary to this primary purpose of our lives. Our ultimate concerns give
"depth, direction and unity to all other concerns" and to the whole
personality. "A personal life which has these qualities is integrated,
and the power of a personality's integration is his faith."[17] We organize
our lives around our beliefs. That is the nature of belief and particularly
of ultimate beliefs. Being without ultimate concern "is being without a
center."[18]

Faith is also an act of the total person in the sense that it transcends
both rationality and emotionality. Faith is a function of the whole person. Particularly concerning rationality, Tillich notes that faith is often
mistakenly viewed as "an act of knowledge with a low degree of evidence." The implication is that if we just had enough knowledge, we
could know with certainty and we would need no faith. This view of
faith corresponds more directly to "belief rather than to faith . . . one
believes that one's information is correct." Belief is based on evidence, whereas faith is an act of self-surrender, loyalty and commitment.

Faith then, by its very nature, always includes an element of uncertainty. All doubt cannot be removed. True faith accepts elements of
uncertainty. The word that Tillich uses to describe this acceptance of
uncertainty is courage. Courage is a necessary part of faith. He writes:

> Courage as an element of faith is the daring self-affirmation of
> one's own being in spite of the powers of "non-being" which are
> the heritage of everything finite. Where there is daring and cour-
> age, there is the possibility of failure. And in every act of faith, this
> possibility is present. The risk must be taken.[19]

All faith includes an element of risk. All faith includes an element of
doubt. All trust includes an element of mistrust, to use Eriksonian
terms. Thus, faith can be described as having an "in spite of" quality.
"There is no faith," writes Tillich, "without an intrinsic 'in spite of'
and the courageous affirmation of oneself in the state of ultimate concern."[20] It is easy to read the morning newspaper or to stand at the fresh
grave of a loved one or to listen to the scholarly debates of philosophers
and, in those moments, to doubt the existence of a loving God. In such
moments, faith becomes trust in spite of one's feelings to the contrary.
Faith, as so understood, includes an element of courage.

Faith, particularly when understood as trust, is often placed in jux-
taposition to fear. Fear and faith are opposite states of mind. Tillich distinguishes between fear which has a specific object and anxiety which
is more general and is related to the threat of non-being. Fear takes
many forms: fear of loss, fear of rejection, fear of pain and even fear of
the moment of death. Fear can be overcome by love, trust and support.
Anxiety, on the other hand, is more generalized than fear. It is an intrinsic part of human existence and, as such, cannot be overcome.
Anxiety, or ontological anxiety, is a part of the human predicament and
can only be responded to with courage, courage rooted in God, whom
Tillich calls the "Ground of Being."

Tillich distinguishes between three types of anxiety: the anxiety
related to fate and death, the anxiety related to the loss of meaning and
meaninglessness, and the anxiety related to guilt and condemnation.
All three of these anxieties belong to human existence as we know it.
In addition, all three of these anxieties are most acutely present in bereavement. In a sense then, loss demands from us a special kind of
faith, a faith as courage. Faith as courage, as it responds to each of
these anxieties, acts in spite of these ever-present anxieties. First, faith
is the courage that affirms us as unique and worthwhile, even in the
face of our anxiety about death and fate. Second, faith is the courage
that accepts God's forgiveness of our sins, in spite of our awareness
and feelings of guilt. Finally, faith is the courage that accepts our one
unique life as meaningful and purposeful, in spite of our occasional
feelings of meaninglessness.

We are accustomed to thinking that if we just had enough faith, we
would not have any doubts. Some soldiers are accustomed to thinking
that if they just had enough bravery, they would not have any fears in
battle. Some grieving people are accustomed to thinking that if they
just had enough faith, they would not feel any sorrow. All of these "accustomed" ways of thinking are unhelpful. In contrast, faith as courage suggests that faith is trusting God *in spite* of one's doubts, that
bravery is action *in spite* of one's fears, and that faith is hope in a new
tomorrow *in spite* of one's present sorrow. Sometimes faith is the courage to trust in spite of feelings to the contrary.

In this regard I am reminded of the scene in the Garden of Gethsemani when Jesus struggled with his own impending death. Gospel
writers record that Jesus describes himself as "troubled even unto

death'' (Mt 26:36) and that he prayed so hard that ''sweat poured off of his head, like great drops of blood'' (Lk 22:45). People familiar with the symptoms of anxiety/fear will recognize that Jesus is having a moderate anxiety attack. He is scared to death. He is anticipating his suffering and pain. He is torn by the conflicting choices between whether to continue to allow his execution or to go home to Nazareth (''let this cup pass from me''). He is already beginning to feel an estrangement from God, a spiritual loneliness. Perhaps, too, he wonders if all of his suffering will have any purpose or meaning. All of these feelings are intensely present. Yet, in spite of these fears, Jesus trusts in the God whom he has known as Father. In the agony of Gethsemani, we see a man who is terribly afraid and also a man who is terribly courageous. Faith is courage, the courage to trust in spite of the feelings to the contrary. Faith is courage in the face of fear.

TRUST AND HUMAN HEALTH: SOME SAMPLE RESEARCH

In recent years there has been a renewed interest in the role that trust plays in creating and sustaining human health and wholeness.[21] One segment of this thought comes from humanistic psychology. In his book, *The Transparent Self*, Sidney Jourard argued that self-disclosure is a vital ingredient of a healthy personality. A healthy person, says Jourard, is a person ''who displays the ability to make himself fully known to at least one other significant human being.''[22] By self-disclosure Jourard means the ability to reveal to another person one's innermost feelings, desires, dreams and thoughts. The ability to disclose oneself is related positively to more mature, open and healthy personalities. Conversely, people who cannot disclose themselves are more prone to mental and physical illness. ''People's selves stop growing when they repress them,'' claims Jourard.[23]

Self-disclosure, however, is a risky business. Others may not care about, accept or even listen to the self that we are so timidly revealing. In addition, some people may not return our trust and, in fact, use our personal ''revelations'' to hurt us . . . and we all have been hurt in this way. So it is, then, that most people have learned to be cautious about when, where and with whom they reveal themselves. This resistance is a part of the general human resistance to all pain. Yet, it is this resistance that blocks the healing process. Only through self-disclosure can we be healed of the inner wounds of the spirit.

What makes self-disclosure possible then? The obvious answer is an atmosphere of trust. When people experience another person as trustworthy, then they are more likely to reveal themselves. Jourard writes:

> . . . it has been found that disclosure of one's experience is most likely when the other person is perceived as a trustworthy person of good will and/or who is willing to disclose his experience to the same depth and breath.[24]

Jourard formulates the principle that trust begets self-disclosure and that self-disclosure, in turn, begets more trust. Other researchers have described this principle by saying that people who are themselves trustworthy tend to trust others, and that people who easily trust others turn out to be very trustworthy themselves.[25]

Most people who have studied marriage or who are keen observers of their own marriages have noted that trust plays a crucial role in sustaining a healthy relationship. Marital fidelity is built on mutual trust and fidelity and is, of course, more than the mere absence of adultery. Spouses who are themselves trustworthy tend to trust their mates and, by so doing, tend to create an atmosphere of trust and openness in which love can grow. The opposite of trust is distrust, suspicion and jealousy—a trinity of demons that have destroyed many a happy home. People who cannot easily trust, who are prone to be distrustful of others, find it difficult to sustain a long-lasting marriage. Marital trust is sometimes like a delicate crystal. Traumas, betrayals and infidelities can shatter the crystal into a thousand little pieces. Trust, like the crystal, is rebuilt ever so slowly by each person taking small mutual steps toward one another.

When a trustful atmosphere exists in a marriage, spouses are more inclined to disclose themselves, to reveal their inner beings, and thereby to build a deeper, more intimate type of love. In a sense, love can be defined as a wanting to fully know the beloved and a wanting to be fully known by the beloved. Love flourishes in self-disclosure. Love requires vulnerability. Without trust vulnerability becomes mere foolishness. What a marvelous experience it is when one's trustful vulnerability is met by love, when trust meets trust.

Another segment of the literature on trust and faith in human health concerns itself with the role of trust in promoting healing. Examples of the important role that faith plays in healing range all the way from the dramatic "faith healings" of someone like Oral Roberts to the simple trust enjoyed by a small town, family physician. Both types of healers depend on an element of trust in order to perform their healing arts. Nor is the importance of trust limited to physical ailments. Several people have documented that trust is an indispensable quality in all psychotherapy.[26] Without a basic trust between therapist and client, no healing occurs, regardless of the techniques employed.

Dr. Jerome Frank, through a series of studies of Johns Hopkins Medical School, has attempted to define faith in medical terms and to study its role in healing.[27] He has suggested that faith, medically understood, has four components: expectancy, suggestion, personality structure and status. Each of these factors plays a role in making faith effective in healing. Faith *expects* certain things to happen, and that expectation is usually *suggested* by a person perceived to have *status* medically or religiously; and the patient's degree of openness to this faith depends, in part, on his or her *personality structure*.[28]

One of the interesting and controversial types of studies regarding the role of faith, as so defined, has to do with the "placebo effect." A placebo is a harmless drug, without any medical value, that is administered to a patient with the suggestion that it is a valued and effective medication for his or her ailment. There have been a wide variety of amazing results from such "suggestions." For example, in one study involving patients with bleeding peptic ulcers, notes Dr. Frank, seventy percent of them showed "excellent results lasting over a period of one year," when treated with distilled water and when assured that the medication would cure them of their condition. The control group, which received the same inert injection, but they were told that this medication is only "experimental," showed only a twenty-five percent reduction in symptoms. Similar results have been achieved when placebos were administered to chronic mental patients, as if they were tranquilizers. The illnesses that are most effectively treated in this manner are those that have a strong psychological base. "The effectiveness of the placebo," writes Frank, "lies in its ability to mobilize the patient's expectancy of help . . . ."[29] He speculates that an attitude of "expectant hope" activates the patient's own healing processes, which in turn facilitates the restoration of health. Faith, defined medically as expectation, plays a crucial role in the healing processes. Medical science can no longer ignore the power of faith as one ingredient in the healing of a person's body and soul. In fact, I would suggest that people do not heal at all, without some element of faith. With this principle in mind, let us turn to a specific discussion of bereavement and the role of faith in the healing of grief wounds.

The Role of Faith in Bereavement

Every normal, healthy person has a certain "basic trust," a sense that life is stable, good and orderly. This basic trust is the cornerstone of a healthy personality. It is the pre-cognitive soil out of which all conscious religious faith grows and continues throughout one's adult life, undergirding one's ability to trust. In times of severe loss a person's sense of basic trust is momentarily shaken. This shaking of the foundation may occur suddenly, as in an untimely death of a loved one, or it may occur gradually, as in the suffering that comes with a repeated or prolonged illness. In either case, whether by explosion or erosion, one's basic trust is momentarily gone. Life seems cruel, random, chaotic and unfair. A person's only reasonable response to such a life is mistrust.

Fear plays a major role in bereavement. One could write a whole book just on the role that this crucial emotion plays in grief and in growth. Every time we love someone or give ourselves to a cause or allow ourselves to become attached to something, we run the risk of losing that attachment. There is a hidden element of fear in all love. Thus our trusting/loving of others always carries with it what Tillich called an "in spite of" quality. We love in spite of the fear of losing. We trust in spite of distrust.

Fear does strange things to people. Probably the most typical and pervasive impulse that people have when they are afraid is to want to control. On a political plane, governments become more controlling when their leaders become more fearful. On a social level people become more controlling of others (manipulation) when they are afraid of being rejected, hurt or ignored. And on a personal level we become repressive (controlling) of our own emotions when we are afraid of the painful emotions that are stirring within us. The opposite of control is freedom. The opposite of fear is trust, trust in the governed, trust in others and trust in our own healing processes. The essential polarity is between fear—leading to control—and trust—leading to freedom.

When a significant loss or series of losses shatters our basic trust, we are momentarily overwhelmed by fear. Our primal mistrust of life resurfaces in our consciousness. We are afraid to love again, afraid to grow or to change, afraid to try a new venture, afraid to believe in God's goodness, afraid to depend on others and afraid to let go and really cry. We cling to the past, to our defenses and to the mechanisms of control.

Yet a part of the grieving process must be a reestablishing of our basic trust, and a replacing of fear with love, and a displacing of control by freedom. Thus it is my contention that faith plays a crucial and major role in the recovery of a grieving person. The reestablishment of a sense of faith is the key to full recovery, but it is also the only means to getting there. Little by little, the grief sufferer must take small steps toward rebuilding his or her sense of trust. At first it is hard and very scary. It takes courage to take trusting steps in the face of a distrustful experience. Slowly, however, trust is reformed within the soul, until finally the once bereaved person is fully recovered. It is as if with each loss we must relive our first developmental crisis between basic trust and basic mistrust. Each severe loss or series of losses forces us back to the origins of life, when each of us entered the unknown world alone. Bereavement has a way of forcing us to enter a similar unknown, new world.

There are three specific dimensions of this basic trust (or faith) that must be rebuilt in the process of grieving. The restoration of each is necessary in order for full healing to occur.

Faith as Trust in Oneself

To be an effective griever, to heal oneself fully and freely, one must have an innate faith in one's own healing processes. This trust is most clearly focused in the ability to trust one's own feelings. When we are in a state of acute bereavement, there are thousands of strong, mixed emotions that swirl around within us. It can be frightening and confusing to feel all of these intense conflicting emotions. This is especially so for people who are not accustomed to strong emotions, or for people who are dealing with their first major loss experience. The face of the bereaved widow or widower often reveals graphically the anguish of these hours. There is the push toward controlling the explosion that is within, and there is the pull driving them to release the energy within or to burst.

Psychologists often speak of the "wisdom of the body" or of what Fritz Perls called "organismic self-regulation." By this phrase they mean that the psyche has a certain wisdom of what it needs at any given moment. People who are in tune with this wisdom and who follow it are usually healthier personalities. In grief, the wisdom of the body is so clearly to cry—or maybe it is not. Maybe our feelings are to be angry, or to be depressed, or to be relieved, or to be indifferent. The best advice is, simply put, to "let it be." Whatever we are feeling, let ourselves be it. We must trust our feelings.

I hear so many people who are holding in their sorrow, who claim that they cannot release it. They say, "I'm too afraid. If I let it all out, I think I will go crazy." The fear is that if they release their control over their feelings, they will never again regain that control. The fear of "going crazy," as it is popularly expressed, is the fear of being overwhelmed by the emotional, irrational forces within. The temptation is always to try to control those forces.

Susan was raised as an only child in a midwestern family. When she was twelve her mother died suddenly due to a rapidly-developing cancer. She had her own difficulties adjusting to her loss, and it took her many years before she could allow herself to fully realize the impact of that loss. In one of these latter grieving periods, she was saying to me that she was now beginning to get in touch with a secondary loss that is coming to disturb her almost as much as her mother's death. That loss was the loss of her father. Susan's father's way of coping with the death of his wife had been "to throw himself into his work." He was a salesman who worked on commission for a large machinery company. He had a tendency to be very hard-working anyhow, but after his wife's death, Susan reports that it was even "more so." She remembers that he seldom came home for dinner during those years and that he often worked Saturdays as well. "He had never worked Saturdays when mother was alive," Susan noted. He was consumed by his work now. He virtually resigned the care of his daughter to her grandparents, who became permanent house guests following the funeral.

Susan remembers that "we never talked much about mother after her death. I guess that it was too painful for Dad. We began to live separate lives—Dad in his work and I in my world of school and friends.'' Susan was not aware that her difficulty with her mother's death was complicated by this "double-whammy," as she called it. On that fateful day when her mother "passed on," she lost her mother, yes, but she also lost her father!

Wayne E. Oates has written a delightful little book, entitled *Confessions of a Workaholic* which every pastor should read.[30] Oates recounts his own personal struggle with his addiction to work. He notes that workaholism is the foundation of a way of life, upon which much of America's values are built. Unlike alcoholism, which is usually viewed with scorn, workaholics are praised, admired and handsomely rewarded for their addiction by corporations and institutions. Yet, like alcoholism, the addiction to work can noticeably "disturb bodily health, personal happiness and interpersonal relationships." It too can lead to an early death.

Workaholism, like all obsessive-compulsive behaviors, is fueled by fear. Compulsive people are hyped-up, energetic people, who are always on the run. They need to be busy, to get lots of things done. They have great difficulty being alone, being present in the "here and now" and paying attention to their own feelings. They are do-ers, not be-ers. When I meet such people, I often wonder what it is that they are running from, for it does appear as though they are running.

Some people are just naturally compulsive types, but others use their compulsiveness to avoid inner painful feelings. Compulsiveness is a way of controlling or running from oneself. This compulsiveness, which is usually considered a defense mechanism, might better be called an "escape mechanism." Workaholism, particularly increased workaholism, may be an escape from grief. Compulsive people tend to become even more compulsive when they sense that their control over their emotions is "slipping away." Their first response is to work harder and harder. They cope with the increasing insecurity with increasing work.

Compulsiveness of course, can take many forms besides workaholism. One can be addicted to alcohol, to gambling, and even to food. Particularly in the case of alcoholism and food, the culture supports and even encourages their overuse. The media daily bombards us with the message, "When upset, bored or anxious, drink and eat to feel better." Pastors need to be alert to the level of compulsiveness in their parishioners. Increased compulsiveness or addictive behavior might be one clue that a person has a real or anticipated loss in his or her life, one that he or she apparently is not dealing with.

The solution to compulsiveness is awareness, full awareness. The way out of this self-destructive trap is to simply stop and listen to one's inner feelings. The way to health is to trust one's feelings, trust them enough to allow them to be. Release the control, let your feelings surface. Let the pain emerge. Only when the pain enters the light of the day does healing begin.

Faith as Trust in Others

As has been said so often, bereavement is one of those conditions that, if you wish to recover from it, you must be willing to express your feelings. Talking out one's grief normally requires other people. Mourning is a social activity. We must share our sorrow with at least one other human being. Talking helps us to release the intense pent-up emotions of bereavement and, where our loss is gradual and complex, talking helps us to identify our subtlest of feelings. Only by so sharing our feelings in all of their diversity and complexity can we find wholeness. Successful grieving, then, requires a basic trust in other people.

For many, trusting other people, especially with one's weak, vulnerable emotions, is not an easy matter. Certain individuals who have been raised to be more private and aloof will resist sharing with others. Other people, because of previous hurts, rejections or distrustful experiences, are reluctant to confide much in others. Trusting other people has some built-in risks. Sometimes it takes a lot of courage to ''reach out and touch someone'' or to be touched by someone.

The inability to trust others finds its roots in fear. One of the fears that blocks us from grieving is the fear of being weak. Grief is perceived, and correctly so, as a weakness. When we are grieving, we are temporarily weak, deprived and emotionally incapacitated, needing the support of friends. In our culture men, probably more so than women, find it very uncomfortable to appear weak. Men resist crying, especially in public. It is unmanly, unmasculine and un-''macho.'' In bereavement, the cultural message aimed at both men and women is that we should ''keep a stiff upper lip'' and should bear our sorrow stoically. In a culture that prizes competition, rugged individualism and rationality, there is little freedom to cry. There is some truth to the proverb, "Pride goes before destruction and a haughty spirit before a fall" (Pr 16:18). Too much pride, self-sufficiency and individualism blocks a person from trusting others and condemns him or her to work out his or her sorrow in isolation. Yet, people who can "surrender to weakness," as Everett Shostrom has put it, are more healthy, more trusting and, I believe, more able to grieve.

The other form that fear takes in bereavement that prevents us from trusting others with our pain is the fear of rejection. If we do reach out, there is always the possibility that the other person may not respond with warmth, or may not have time for us, or may not want to hear our "garbage," or may just walk away. Some people deeply feel such rejections and respond to those slights by withdrawing further into their own private worlds where they can lick their wounds. As most people know, rejection is partially "in the eye of the beholder." Some people feel rejected at the slightest provocation. Others seem to have a thicker skin that enables them to resist hurts easier. Most of us, however, do not like rejection of any kind, especially when we are already hurting, as in the case of bereavement. This is especially so when we are sharing some of our deeper, more tender, more vulnerable and less attractive emotions. We fear that rejection, and yet we hunger for the comforting support of our loved ones.

William B. Oglesby, in his book *Biblical Themes for Pastoral Care*, reminds us that one of the symptoms of fear is "hiding."[31] When we are afraid, we hide from others, from ourselves and from God. This duality of fear and hiding is a pervasive theme in Scripture, starting with Adam's fear of being "found" in the Eden forests to Jesus' disciples who "all forsook him and fled" on the night he was betrayed (Mk 14:50). The Divine response to this human tendency, notes Oglesby, has always been: "Fear not!" for "I am with you." God seeks to "reach out" and touch fearful hearts, thus overcoming our self-imposed isolation. Companionship, sharing and intimacy—be it the God-human kind or the human-human variety—is the antidote for fear. So it is in bereavement as well.

Several years ago in the heyday of encounter groups, I was participating in a group program with a man with whom I later became a good friend. Hal was in his thirties, married, with two lovely children. He was on the quiet side, an emotionally reserved individual. He described himself as "the engineer type"—rational, aloof, critical and more comfortable with ideas than with people.

Hal was originally "sent" to the group by his wife because she wanted more emotional closeness and intimacy from him. She described their marriage as one that was very satisfying in every outward, conventional way, but at a deep level of intimacy it was a very lonely relationship. Hal came to the group indicating that he, too, felt "something lacking" and wanted to try to be more expressive of himself. In the course of several months, his progress was limited at best. He spent much of his time in the group observing, analyzing and distancing himself. Frustration began to build among the other group members. "Here we are sharing our guts," they would note, "and Hal just sits there and doesn't share anything of himself."

On one occasion the group had Hal on the "hot seat," firmly, gently and sometimes angrily trying to get him to open up and share something more of himself. The confrontation went on for seemingly hours. The frustration and tension were mounting in Hal, as well as in the rest of us. Finally one perceptive woman, who had remained somewhat removed from this process up to this point, stepped forward. She tuned into a deeper level of my future friend. She went to him, sat in front of him "Indian style," holding his hands for several moments, just looking into his eyes. She asked one simple question, "Tell me, Harold, who hurt you so bad that you are so afraid to love?" Moments passed—it seemed like hours. Then tears began to well up in Hal's eyes and gently run down his cheeks. "My father," he replied, "my father left me." Suddenly a flood of grief burst forth, and we all just held him while he cried.

Later, as we debriefed this experience, we learned that Hal's father had died, quite unexpectedly, when Hal was thirteen years old. The young Harold was close to his father and missed him terribly. He had grieved some then and, from all outward appearances, had "gotten over it." Yet, at another level, the residue of his loss remained. His personality had changed following his father's death. His way of relating to people was now more cautious, more reserved and more protective. He was now less talkative and more private. It was as if he went into "hiding"—fearing to share that nagging pain deep within his soul. It was also as if he was saying, "I'll never be that hurt again. I will never let myself be that vulnerable again."

Hal's story has stuck with me for years. It was a dramatic and intense encounter. It was also a vivid illustration of the deep fear we all, to some extent, have of sharing ourselves with others and also, concurrently, of the deep need we all have to trust others with our pain. It often takes a great deal of courage to place ourselves fully and completely in the hands of others. What is faith, then, if not this courage to trust others in spite of the twin fears of rejection and of being seen as weak? Only through such faith do we find healing.

Faith as Trust in God

Most of us live day to day with a basic trust in God. By this I mean that we assume, at an almost unconscious level, that life is basically good, predictable and orderly. We generally know what to expect of tomorrow. We trust that life is essentially good, which is, in my terms, an innate trust in God, the Creator and Sustainer of all life. When a severe loss occurs, however, and especially when that loss is sudden or untimely, our sense of the goodness of creation is shattered for a time. Similarly, people who suffer with chronic illnesses or handicaps also wonder how fair is this life that God authors. Even the so-called minor, gradual losses can have a cumulative effect, leading to the same momentary mistrust. In such times, our perception of reality, our sense of life's orderliness, is shaken. Our trust is weakened. We are temporarily braced, waiting for the "other shoe to drop."

A part of the grieving process is a reconstruction of this basic trust in God. To be healthy we need to believe again that life is predictable, orderly and fair. We need to renew our assumption that the creation is good—that the future has possibilities. I do not mean to suggest that everyone loses faith in God when a loss occurs. Yet everyone does have his or her trust in God shaken to a greater or lesser extent. For some people, this period of doubt is short-lived. Such people draw upon a foundation of faith and bounce back relatively soon. For others, however, the shattering is permanent. They never recover a sense of God's goodness. They live out their days in a shadow of dread, despair and nostalgia.

The story of Abraham has always been an example of faith par excellence. Both Jewish and Christian believers have looked upon Abraham as the "father of faith." Why is this so? The saga of Abraham begins when God says to him, "Go from your country, your family and your father's house to the land that I will show you, and I will make of you a great nation" (Gen 12:1–2a). Scripture then records that, based on that command alone, Abram (as he was then called) went. In reading this story of Abraham, what strikes me is the simple phrase, "he went." He left his extended family, his inheritance, his land and his father's people and . . . went! Some of us might make a major move if we knew where we were going and what the advantages might be for us, or if we knew more about the One who was commanding us to move, but Abraham knew none of these things. As the author of Hebrews describes it, "he went out, not knowing where he was to go" (Heb 11:8b). His faith was based on few tangibles. It was a more risky faith, a more courageous faith than that which is usually required of us. Compared with later biblical heroes, Abraham did not play "yes . . . but" games with God. He did not ask for extensive reassurances, nor was he offered any. He did not make up any excuses, nor was he granted any. He did not ask for a lot of securities, not did he get any. He just went into the unknown future with only a promise to lead him. Because of his "leaving," people of three world religions all point to Abraham as the founder of faith. He had a trust in God that transcended temporal losses.

The example of Abraham is a good illustration for those who suffer grievous losses of one kind or another. A major loss, among other things, thrusts mourners into a new future. Suddenly the wife is a widow. Suddenly the worker is among the unemployed. Suddenly a family is homeless. Suddenly "the two are one." Suddenly a whole person is handicapped. Suddenly (or perhaps not so suddenly) one is facing an unknown future. Losses, whether welcomed or unwelcomed, thrust people into a new life situation. Like Abraham, most of the props, attachments and possessions that gave us security in our old lives must be left behind. The old identities, the old fame, and the previous successes are useless in the new future. We must develop new skills, new identities and new modes of living. We too must enter the future with nothing but a promise.

When an unknown future is thrust upon a person, some resist going. Fear overcomes faith. They cling to the past. They idealize that which is now lost. They deny the reality of the change that has occurred in their lives. They pretend to be youthful when they are aged. They pretend to be still married when their spouse has gone. They pretend

Mom is still around when she has been dead for years. They pretend they are still a lawyer even though they have again failed the bar exam. They keep pretending. When the fear of the unknown frightens us, we all are tempted to cling to the past or to whatever securities we have available.

In order for a person to successfully grieve, he or she must have a certain basic trust in God and, in particular, in God's future. A part of the grieving process, by definition, is a leaving behind of the past and an entering into the future. What makes this entering into the future possible? I believe that it is a basic trust, a faith in the future and, by implication, in the One who is there. The fear of the unknown is frightening, but faith is trusting that the future can be good in spite of ever-present fear. Faith is trusting that the future belongs to God and that God is already there, working to bring new life out of old.

As with the other dimensions of basic trust, the restoration of faith in God is both the goal and the means to achieve that goal. Each and every new step that a grieving person takes shows an implicit trust in the future. When a widow makes her first step to cope alone, when parents first learn to live without their deceased child, when the divorced woman makes her first tentative plans to date again, when an amputee makes his or her first efforts to walk—as each of these people takes these steps, however small these steps might be, they are implicitly saying, "I trust in the future. I believe that the future can be as good as the past that I have lost." By so trusting, step by step, the future unfolds before them and new life emerges out of old.

Jürgen Moltmann's book *Theology of Hope* attempted to put the study of the "last things" into first place in Christian theology. He argued that hope is an essential ingredient and companion of faith. He writes:

> Hope is . . . the expectation of those things which faith has believed to have been truly promised by God. Thus, faith believes God to be true, hope awaits the time when this truth shall be manifested . . . faith is the foundation upon which hope rests, hope nourishes and sustains faith.[32]

Hope is possible, for Moltmann and for all believers, because God is essentially a God of the future. The future belongs to God. The proper domain of the Divine is not some heavenly court in the sky, but the future. In this sense God is eternal, that is, God transcends time. This belief that the future belongs to God makes hope possible for the bereaved.

The psychology of hope is a fascinating subject, one that is receiving more scholarly attention in recent years.[33] Psychologically hope is largely expectation. Studies in medicine and psychiatry have documented that a person's expectation of the future is actually one determinant of the future. People who expect health are more likely to realize it. People who expect illness are more likely to realize it. Recovering surgical patients heal faster with a hopeful attitude. Prisoners-of-war who ''believed'' that their situation was hopeless gave up and, in some cases, literally died. Students perform better academically when they have hope of achieving success. Ezra Stotland talks about a ''therapy for hope,'' in which he describes a more hope-centered way of providing psychotherapy for chronic mental patients and documents that they show considerable improvement under such treatment.[34] Hope is admittedly a subjective subject, but writers and scholars are increasingly suggesting that it is a ''necessary condition'' to human healing and wholeness.

The ability to hope is grounded in a trust. Hope, of course, is not optimism. Hope realistically faces the current dilemma, tragedy or suffering. Yet hope hopes in spite of that current situation, no matter how hopeless. In this sense hope has an element of courage in it too. Hope can do such, because genuine hope is grounded in a God of the future. Hope can do such also because hope is grounded in God's faithfulness. Faithfulness is an essential characteristic of God's nature. It is revealed in God's propensity to make and keep promises. Throughout the Old and New Testaments, God is a ''God of the promise.'' ''God reveals himself,'' writes Moltmann, ''in the form of a promise, and in the history that is marked by promise.''[35] God can make such promises because God owns the future.

In a sense then our trust in God needs to be viewed from a developmental perspective. Our ability to trust God in times of loss depends on the history of our trusting relationship with God. If we have confronted other unknown futures and we have found that new life emerged out of old, then we can face the current loss with more trust. Developmental psychologists and grief scholars will confirm this proposition. How we have dealt with previous losses colors our ability to deal with the current loss. Successful grieving experiences and successful trusting experiences combine to build a storehouse of trust feelings. If we can look back on our life and point to times when God brought life out of death and trust out of fear, then we are more likely to trust in the present moment. In fact, that is not a bad pastoral counseling strategy: to help bereaved people identify previous successfully grieved losses, perhaps those that were less severe than the current dilemma, and then to help them draw strength and insight from yesterday's success. The God of yesterday, and of yesterday's fulfilled promises, is also the God of tomorrow. God keeps promises—we can trust that. A basic trust in God, as so defined and discussed in the past few pages, is essential to grief's resolution.

Conclusion: To Love Again

Many years ago I had the privilege of working with a group of widowed people who called their organization T.L.A. ("To Live Again"). Over the years I have occasionally confused these words and have sometimes mistakenly referred to the organization as "To Love Again." In a sense this latter formulation speaks to the central issue of our entire discussion of grief and growth. In a sense too, the phrase speaks of the pivotal theological problem of human existence.

The purpose of grief is to enable a bereaved person to love again. If the grief process is allowed to do its work, a person will be released from his or her attachment to that which is lost and thereby be able to reinvest himself or herself again in new "loves." In a sense we humans cannot help ourselves regarding love. We form emotional attachments to people, places, things and ideas surely and as naturally as we breathe. It is part of our humanity. Yet the painful truth of human existence is that loss is also an inevitable part of life. Inevitably we will lose those things that we love most. Everything, everyone that we dearly love in this hour, will eventually one day be lost to us by death, by estrangement, by aging. Loss comes in many forms. Each of us, then, in the lonely hours of our bereavement, must and will make that personal decision, that existential decision, whether to love again.

Someone has said that "to fear death is to fear life." There is some truth to this adage. We can come to so fear death, loss and everything finite that we will cease to invest ourselves at all. We will cease to love. After all, why love if we are only going to lose the thing we love eventually? Is there an alternative?

The only alternative that I know of is to love with abandonment and to live life to the fullest, knowing that grief is as much a part of life as is love. The only alternative is to tell ourselves, as many jilted lovers do, that it is better to have loved and lost than never to have loved at all. Instead of skrinking back from life, let us throw ourselves into life. Choose to live life to the fullest. Choose to love hard and grieve hard. Choose to face the pain of sorrow, so that we can enjoy all the more the ecstasy of love. Choose to love again . . . and again . . . and again . . . even though each time we do so, we know that we will grieve again too.

Such a person, who chooses this alternative, is my description of "homo-religiosus" or the "knight of faith." In order to make this kind of choice, an individual must have an implicit faith. They have said of Jesus that he was "a man of sorrows and acquainted with grief." He was also a man of great love, compassion and commitment. The two go hand in hand. We cannot have one without the other, and the two are tied together by faith.

People with such faith do not view grief as a negative thing. They see grief as God's gift to loving people. If there was no grief, love would be impossible. Thanks be to God for creating grief. Let us trust fully God's creation, the goodness of sorrow, so that we can, in turn, love more fully.

Notes

CHAPTER 1: THE VARIETY AND UNIVERSALITY OF LOSS

1. David Peretz, "Development, Object-Relationships, and Loss," in Bernard Schoenberg, et al., *Loss and Grief* (New York: Columbia University Press, 1970), p. 6.

2. See Thomas H. Holmes and Richard H. Rahe, "The Social Readjustment Rating Scale," *Journal of Psychosomatic Research* II (1967) 213–218).

3. See Chapter Two of Colin Murray Parkes, *Bereavement* (New York: International Universities Press, 1972).

4. Elisabeth Kübler-Ross, *On Death and Dying* (New York: Macmillan, 1959).

5. Ibid., p. 86.

6. Mel Krantzler, *Creative Divorce* (New York: New American Library, Signet Books, 1973), p. 70.

7. Peretz, *Loss and Grief*, p. 6.

8. For an interesting study of a similar experience see Harold Orlansky, "Reactions to the Death of President Roosevelt," *Journal of Social Psychology*, XXVI (1947), 235–266.

9. Lyrics by Alan Jay Lerner.

10. Arthur C. Carr and Bernard Schoenberg, "Loss of External Organs: Limb Amputations, Mastectomy and Disfiguration," in Schoenberg, p. 119.

11. Ibid., pp. 122–123.

12. Libuse Tyhurst, "Displacement and Migration: A Study of Social Psychiatry," *American Journal of Psychiatry*, CVII, (1951), 561.

13. Alvin Toffler, *Future Shock* (New York: Bantam Books, 1971), pp. 74–91.

14. Marc Fried, "Grieving for a Lost Home," in Leonard J. Duhl (ed.), *The Urban Condition* (New York: Basic, 1963), p. 151.

15. James S. Tyhurst, "The Role of Transition States—Including Disasters in Mental Illness," in Dean E. Woolridge (ed.), *Symposium on Preventive and Social Psychiatry* (Washington: Walter Reed Army Institute of Research, 1957).

16. Robert C. Hatchley, "Adjustment to Loss of Job at Retirement," *Aging and Human Development*, VI, 1 (1975), 17–27. This insight was also noted in class study of retirement, E.A. Friedmann and R.J. Havinghurst, *The Meaning of Work and Retirement* (Chicago: University of Chicago Press, 1954).

17. Daniel J. Levinson, *The Seasons of a Man's Life* (New York: Ballantine Books, 1978). Gail Sheehey's popular book, *Passages*, was based on Levinson's research.

18. Ibid., p. 26.

19. "Sunrise, Sunset," taken from United Artists Records, "Fiddler on the Roof," 1971. Used with permission.

20. See Fernand Lamaze, *Painless Childbirth* (London: Burke, 1958), originally published as *"Qu'est-ce que l'Accounchement sans Douleur?"* (Paris: 1956) or Marjorie Karmel, *Thank You, Dr. Lamaze* (New York: Lippincott, 1959).

21. See Frederick Le Boyer, *Birth Without Violence* (New York: Knopf, 1976).

22. Leche Le International, *The Womanly Art of Breast Feeding* (Franklin Park, Ill., 1958).

23. Robert A. Furman, "The Child's Reaction to Death in the Family," in Schoenberg, pp. 73–74.

24. The typical dominant tone of the bachelor party is "regret," whereas the dominant tone of the wedding shower is "anxious anticipation," a difference that vividly illustrates the culture's sexism.

25. There may also be a chemical-physiological component to this reaction as well.

26. Peretz, *Loss and Grief*, pp. 9–10.

27. Arthur C. Carr, "Bereavement as a Relative Experience," in Bernard Schoenberg (ed.), *Bereavement: Its Psychological Aspects* (New York: Columbia University Press, 1975), p. 8.

CHAPTER 2: WHAT IS GRIEF?

1. C.S. Lewis, *A Grief Observed* (London: Faber and Faber, 1961), p. 41.

2. Otto Rank, *The Trauma of Birth* (London: Kegan, Trench, Trubner, 1929).

3. Ibid., p. 24.

4. David K. Switzer, *The Dynamics of Grief* (Nashville: Abingdon, 1970), p. 83.

5. C.S. Lewis, *A Grief Observed*, p. 7.

6. Switzer, *Dynamics*, pp. 105–106.

7. Lily Pincus, *Death in the Family* (New York: Vintage, 1974), p. 42.

8. Parkes, *Bereavement*, p. 6.

9. John Bowlby, *Attachment and Loss*, Vol. 2 (New York: Basic, 1973), p. 16.

10. Alexander Bain, *The Emotions and The Will* (London: Longmans, Green, 1875), p. 146.

11. Edgar D. Jackson, *When America Dies* (Philadelphia: Fortress Press, 1971), p.6.

12. Edgar D. Jackson, *Understanding Grief* (New York: Abingdon Press, 1957), p. 18.

13. William Rogers, "The Pastor's Work with Grief," *Pastoral Psychology*, XIX (September 1963), pp. 19–30.

14. Ibid., p. 26.

15. See Bowlby, *Attachment*, vol. 2.

16. Charles Darwin, *The Expression of Emotions in Man and Animals* (London: Murray, 1872).

17. Konrad Lorenz, *On Aggression* (London: Methuen, 1963).

18. John Bowlby, *The Making and Breaking*, p. 45.

19. Ibid., p. 49.

20. Ibid.

21. I am using "identity" here in a broader sense than I think Switzer used "self." Identity is more than just a summary of one's interpersonal relationships. It also includes our relationship to places, ideas, and roles.

22. Sigmund Freud, *Standard Edition* XIX, p. 258.

23. Parkes, *Bereavement*, p. 156.

24. Eda LeShan, *Learning To Say Goodbye* (New York: Macmillan, 1976), p. 39.

CHAPTER 3: THE DYNAMICS OF GRIEF

1. John Bowlby, "Grief and Mourning in Early Infancy and Childhood," *The Psychoanalytic Study of the Child*, XX (1960), p.9.

2. For example, see Herbert Benson, *The Relaxation Response* (New York: Avon Books, 1975); T.H. Holmes and R.H. Rahe, "The Social Readjustment Scale," *Journal of Psychosomatic Research*, II (1967), p. 213; Hans Selye, *Stress Without Distress* (New York: New American Library, 1975).

3. Colin Murray Parkes, *Bereavement*, p. 34.

4. For example, see Holmes and Rahne, "The Social Adjustment Scale."

5. W.D. Rees and S.G. Lutlinds, "Mortality of Bereavement," *British Medical Journal*, IV (1967), p. 3.

6. Michael Young, Bernard Benjamin and Chara Wallis, "Morality Rate of Widowers," *Lancet*, No. 272 (August 31, 1963).

7. Parkes, *Bereavement*, p. 22.

8. See Kübler-Ross, *On Death and Dying*, pp. 50ff.

9. Aaron Beck, *Depression: Clinical, Experimental and Theoretical Aspects* (New York: Harper and Row, 1964), p. 64.

10. Glen W. Davidson, *Living With Dying* (Minneapolis: Augsburg, 1975), p. 50.

11. Roy Fairchild, *Finding Hope Again* (New York: Harper and Row, 1980), p. 55.

12. Jessie Barnard, *The Future of Marriage* (New York: Bantam, 1972), p. 20.

13. Howard W. Stone, *Suicide and Grief* (Philadelphia: Fortress Press, 1972), p. 57.

14. Emile Durkheim, *Suicide* (New York: Free Press, 1951), p. 192.

15. Leonard Moss and Donald Hamilton, "The Psychology of the Suicidal Patient," *American Journal of Psychiatry*, CXII (1956), pp. 814–15.

16. Maurice L. Farber, *Theory of Suicide* (New York: Funk and Wagnals, 1968), p. 12.

17. There is also a type of guilt apart from this continuum called "survivor's guilt" in which a survivor of a tragedy feels guilty for thinking that he or she should have died.

18. C.S. Lewis, *A Grief Observed*, p. 47.

19. Bernadine Kries and Alice Pattie, *Up from Grief*, p. 19.

20. See Kübler-Ross, *On Death and Dying*.

21. See Granger Westburg, *Good Grief*.

22. See Wayne E. Oates, *Anxiety in Christian Experience* (Philadelphia: Westminster Press, 1955).

23. See Robert Kavanaugh, *Facing Death* (Baltimore: Penguin, 1974).

24. Wayne E. Oates, *Pastoral Care and Counseling in Grief and Separation* (Philadelphia: Fortress Press, 1976), p. 9.

25. John Bowlby, "Process of Mourning," in William Gaylin (ed.), *The Meaning of Despair* (New York: Science House, 1968), p. 314.

26. Colin Murray Parkes, "Seeking and Finding a Lost Object," *Social Science and Medicine,* IV (1970), p. 196.

27. Lindemann, p. 2.

28. Herman H. Feifel, "Death-Center Stage," *Jewish Funeral Director*, XXIV (1974), p. 17.

29. Phyllis Caroff and Rose Dobrof, "The Helping Process with Bereaved Families," in Schoenberg, *Bereavement*, p. 239.

30. David K. Switzer, *The Minister as Crisis Counselor* (Nashville: Abingdon Press, 1974), p. 152.

31. See Switzer, *Dynamics of Grief*, p 191.

32. Elisabeth Kübler-Ross, *Questions and Answers*, p. 22.

33. Eda LeShan, *Learning To Say Goodbye* (New York: Avon Books, 1976), p. 14.

34. Roy Nichols and Jane Nichols, "Funerals: A Time for Grief and Growth," in Kübler-Ross, *Death: The Final Stage of Growth*, p. 93.

35. Ibid., p. 95.

CHAPTER 4: GRIEF AND GROWTH

1. Lawrence LeShan, "Foreword," in Edgar N. Jackson, *Coping with the Crises in Your Life* (New York: Jason Aronson, 1973), p. vii.

2. George J. Seidel, *The Crisis of Creativity* (Notre Dame: University of Notre Dame Press, 1966).

3. George Rochlin, *Grief and Discontents: The Forces of Change* (Boston: Little, Brown & Company, 1965), p. 222.

4. Sidney M. Jourard and Ted Landsman, *Healthy Personality* (New York: Macmillan, 1980), pp. 220–239.

5. Ibid., p. 230.

6. See Abraham H. Maslow, *Motivation and Personality* (New York: Harper and Row, 1954).

7. Abraham H. Maslow, *Toward a Psychology of Being* (New York: Von Nostrand, 1962), p. 30.

8. See Judy Garber, Martin E.P. Seligman (eds.), *Human Helplessness: Theory and Applications* (New York: Academic Press, 1980).

9. Richard C. Nelson, "Living and Choosing in the Face of Death," in B. Mark Schoenberg (ed.), *Bereavement Counseling: A Multidisciplinary Handbook* (Westport, Conn.: Greenwood Press, 1980), p. 144.

10. Arthur Freese, *Help for Your Grief* (New York: Schocken, 1977).

11. Evertt L. Shostrom, "Time as an Integrating Factor," in Charlotte Buhler and Fred Massarik (eds.), *The Course of Human Life* (New York: Springer, 1968), pp. 351–370.

12. Ibid., p. 352.

13. Sidney Levin, "Depression in the Aged," in Martin A. Berezin and Stanley H. Cath (eds.), *Geriatric Psychiatry: Grief, Loss and Emotional Disorders in the Aging Process* (New York: Academic Press, 1973), p. 215.

14. Anthony P. Jurich and Julie A. Jurich, "The Lost Adolescence Syndrome," *The Family Coordinator* (July 1975), p. 357.

15. See Robert J. Havighurst, *Developmental Tasks and Education* (New York: David McKay Company, 1953) and Erik H. Erikson, *Youth, Identity and Crisis* (New York: W.W. Norton and Company, 1968).

CHAPTER 5: SPIRITUAL GROWTH IN TIMES OF LOSS

1. Roy and Jane Nichols, "Funerals: A Time for Grief and Growth" in Elisabeth Kübler-Ross (ed.), *Death: The Final Stage of Growth* (Englewood Cliffs: Prentice-Hall, 1975), p. 96.

2. A companion article to this chapter, concerning Paul's pastoral approach to grief, by the same author, is "Saint Paul's Approach to Grief: Clarifying the Ambiguity," *Journal of Religion and Health*, Vol. 20, No. 1 (Spring 1981), pp. 63–74.

3. Rudolf Bultmann, *New Testament Theology* (New York: Charles Scribner's Sons, 1951), I, 338.

4. Otto Procksch, "ἁγιάζω in the New Testament," in G. Kittel (ed.), *Theological Dictionary of the New Testament* (Grand Rapids: Eerdmans, 1965), I, 113.

5. Procksch, p. 113.

6. In several other passages, Paul reflects a similar growth motif—for example, in Phil 1:9, 1 Thes 4:1, and 2 Cor 10:15, Paul hopes that his readers' faith, love or knowledge will grow. In 1 Corinthians 3:1 and 13:11, he makes the distinction between "infants in Christ" and spiritual maturity. All this implies a growth-process framework.

7. Bultmann, I, 338.

8. Bultmann, I, 306.

9. Hans Conzelmann, *An Outline of the Theology of the New Testament* (New York: Harper and Row, 1969), p. 185.

10. It is interesting how many of the Synoptic parables involve judgment and loss—Parable of the Rich Fool (Lk 12:13–21), Parable about the Lost Sheep (Lk 15:1–32), Parable of the Rich Man and Lazarus (Lk 16:19–31). Particularly in the latter parable, the rich man's judgment occurs in fully realizing what he lost.

11. I believe this is what Paul means in the difficult verse 2 Cor 7:10, where he distinguishes between "godly grief" which leads to repentance and "worldly grief" which leads to death. Besides the issue of whether he meant grief or guilt, Paul has accurately described the process: his letter initiated feelings of grief and guilt in the Corinthians, followed by a period of self-judgment, which in turn led to repentance. The point seems clear: judgment can lead to repentance.

CHAPTER 6: COMMUNITIES OF FAITH . . . COMMUNITIES OF HEALING

1. "The Story of Jesus," Point to Ponder section, *Reader's Digest* (March 1983).

2. Alvin Toffler, *Future Shock* (New York: Bantam Books, 1971), p. 78.

3. Ibid., p. 108.

4. Ibid., p. 94.

5. *The President's Commission on Mental Health, 1978* (Washington, D.C.: U.S. Government Printing Office, 1978), Vol. II, p. 144.

6. Sheldon Blackman and Kenneth M. Goldstein, "Some Aspects of a Theory of Community Health," *Community Mental Health Journal*, IV, No. 1 (February 1968), p. 89.

7. This conclusion has been supported by other research. For example, see Robert J. Weiss and Bernard J. Bergan, "Social Supports and the Reduction of Psychiatric Disability," *Psychiatry*, XXXI (May 1968), pp. 107–115.

8. James A. Sparks, *Friendship After Forty* (New York: Abingdon, 1980), p. 15.

9. John J. Schwab, et al., "Studies in Grief: A Preliminary Report," in Schoenberg's *Bereavement*, pp. 78–90.

10. Ibid., p. 89.

11. David Maddison and Beverly Raphael, "Conjugal Bereavement in the Social Network," in Schoenberg's *Bereavement*, p. 29.

12. Ibid., p. 30.

13. Carl R. Rogers, *On Becoming a Person* (Boston: Houghton Mifflin Company, 1961), p. 34.

14. Charles B. Truax and Robert R. Carkhuff, *Toward Effective Counseling and Psychotherapy* (Chicago: Aldine Publishing Co., 1967), p. 1.

15. Ibid., p. 106.

16. Ibid., p. 100.

17. Norman Paul, "Psychiatry: Its Role in the Resolution of Grief," in Kutscher's *Death and Bereavement* (Springfield, Ill.: Charles C. Thomas, 1969), p. 186.

18. Ibid., p. 187.

19. Ibid.

20. See Thomas A. Harris, *I'm O.K.—You're O.K.* (New York: Harper and Row, 1967).

21. See *Alcoholics Anonymous* (New York: A.A., 1955) or *Twelve Steps and Twelve Transitions* (New York: Harper and Row, 1952) for a description of the original format of A.A. Other self-help groups that use the A.A. model include Alanon, Gamblers Anonymous, Overeaters Anonymous and Narcotics Anonymous.

22. See Phyllis R. Silverman (ed.), *Helping Each Other in Widowhood* (New York: Health Sciences, 1974) or Phyllis R. Silverman, *Helping Women Cope with Grief* (Beverly Hills: Sage, 1981).

23. Silverman, *Helping Each Other in Widowhood*, p. 4.

24. Ibid., p. 9.

25. *The President's Commission*, Vol. II, p. 11.

26. For resources see Howard J. Clinebell, *The People Dynamic* (New York: Harper and Row, 1972), or Robert C. Leslie, *Sharing Groups in the Church* (New York: Abingdon, 1970) or Clyde Reid, *Groups Alive—Church Alive* (New York: Harper, 1969).

27. For discussion of Wesley's use of small groups, see Chapter One of John W. Drakeford, *People to People Therapy* (New York: Harper & Row, 1978).

28. Clinebell, *The People Dynamic*, p. 138.

29. As resources, see William C. Dixon and Diane Detwiler-Zapp, *Lay Caregiving* (Philadelphia: Fortress Press, 1982) and Howard W. Stone, *The Caring Church: A Guide for Lay Pastoral Care* (San Francisco: Harper & Row, 1983).

30. David K. Switzer, *Minister as Crisis Counselor* (Nashville: Abingdon Press, 1974), p. 270.

31. For an excellent book on the importance of the family in mourning, see Lily Pincus, *Death and the Family* (New York: Vintage Books, 1976).

32. See Norman L. Paul and George H. Grosser, "Operational Mourning and Its Role in Conjoint Family Therapy," *Community Mental Health Journal*, Vol. I, No. 4 (Winter 1965), pp. 339–345.

33. The connection between unshared loss and marital disintegration has been well established by research. Norman L. Paul's work has been noted. See also the excellent article by Andre P. Derdeyn and David B. Waters, "Unshared Loss and Marital Conflict," *Journal of Marital and Family Therapy*, Vol. 7:4 (October 1981), pp. 481–487.

34. Several authors have suggested schedules of pastoral calling for the pastor; see Switzer, *Minister as Crisis Counselor*, and Paul Irion, *Funeral: Vestige or Value?* (Nashville: Abingdon Press, 1966).

CHAPTER 7: GRIEF RITUALS

1. Christopher Crocker, "Ritual and the Development of Social Structure," in *The Roots of Ritual*, edited by James D. Shaughnessy, (Grand Rapids: William B. Eerdmans, 1973) p. 59.

2. Margaret Mead, "Ritual and Social Crisis," in Shaughnessy's *Roots*, p. 95.

3. Geoffrey Gorer, *Death, Grief and Mourning in Contemporary Britain* (New York: Doubleday, 1965), p. 85.

4. Edgar Jackson, *Understanding Grief*, p. 57.

5. Norman Paul, "Psychiatry: Its Role in the Resolution of Grief," in Kutscher's *Bereavement*, p. 183.

6. See Colin M. Parkes, *Bereavement*, pp. 138–142.

7. Ibid., p. 142.

8. See Vamil D. Volkan, "Re-Grief Therapy," in Schoenberg's *Bereavement*, pp. 334–350.

9. Ibid., p. 338.

10. Arnold van Gennep, *On Rites of Passage* (Chicago: University of Chicago Press, 1960), p. 2.

11. Ibid., p. 132.

12. Ibid., p. 136.

13. Ibid., p. 137.

14. Audrey Gordon, "The Jewish View of Death: Guidelines for Mourners," in Kübler-Ross' *Death: The Final Stage of Growth*, p. 51.

15. See Edgar Jackson, *Coping with the Crises in Your Life* (New York: Jason Aronson, 1973).

16. See Maurice Lamm, *The Jewish Way in Death and Mourning* (New York: Jonathan David, 1969).

17. See Chapter Two, "Use of Psalms in Grief Counseling," in Donald Capps, *Bibical Approaches to Pastoral Counseling* (Philadelphia: Westminster Press, 1981).

18. Sara Ebenreck, "Rituals for Letting Go—With Thanks," *Family Festivals*, Vol. 1, No. 7 (October/November 1982), p. 9.

CHAPTER 8: DO BELIEFS MAKE A DIFFERENCE?

1. Kahlil Gibran, *The Prophet* (New York: Alred A. Knopf, 1923), p. 60.

2. The term "operational theology" was originally introduced to me by my colleague, Robert St. Clair, who has built a system of pastoral psychotherapy around the concept. Further information can be secured from The Center for Experiental Theology, 1101 O'Farrell Street, San Francisco, Cal. 94109.

3. Albert Ellis and Robert A. Harper, *A New Guide to Rational Living* (Englewood Cliffs, New Jersey: Prentice-Hall, 1975), p. 11.

4. For a complete list of these irrational statements, see ibid., pp. 88–195.

5. Ibid., p. 12.

6. For example, see Aaron T. Beck et al., *Cognitive Therapy of*

Depression (New York: Guilford, 1979); Maxie C. Maultsby, *Help Yourself to Happiness* (New York: Institute for Rational Living, 1975); Victor Raimy, *Misunderstandings of the Self* (San Francisco: Jossey-Bass, 1975); Paul A. Hauck, *Reason in Pastoral Counseling* (Philadelphia: Westminster Press, 1972); and, of course, Albert Ellis, *Reason and Emotion in Psychotherapy* (New York: Lyle Stuart, 1962).

7. Hauck, *Reason in Pastoral Counseling*, p. 25.

8. Muriel James and Dorothy Jongeward, *Born To Win* (Reading, Massachuetts: Addison-Wesley, 1975), p. 69.

9. M. Scott Peck, *The Road Less Traveled* (New York: Simon and Schuster, 1978), p. 44.

10. Ellie A. Cohen, *Human Behavior in the Concentration Camp* (New York: Norton, 1953), p. 148; H.O. Bluhm, "How Did They Survive?" *American Journal of Psychotherapy*, II, 1 (1948), pp. 20ff.

11. E. DeWind, "The Confrontation with Death," *International Journal of Psychoanalysis*, X 2–3 (1968), p. 304.

12. See Viktor E. Frankl, *From Death Camp to Existentialism* (Boston: Beacon Press, 1959).

13. Viktor E. Frankl, *The Doctor and Soul* (New York: Knopf, 1955), p. 114.

14. For a summary of this work, see Hamilton I. McCubbin, et al., *Family Separation and Reunion: Families of Prisoners of War and Servicemen Missing in Action* (Washington: Government Printing Office, 1974).

15. Edna J. Hurietes, et al., "Religion in the POW/MIA Family," in ibid., pp. 85–93.

16. Ibid., p. 93.

17. This study made no distinction between POW and MIA families which to my mind is a significant oversight. POW wives would have a greater tendency to believe that their husbands were still alive in Hanoi, and therefore perceive their loss as temporary. In contrast MIA wives had to adjust to a complete absence of information. The psychology of the two situations is considerably different.

18. Charles V. Ford and Raymond C. Spaulding, "The Pueblo Incident: Psychological Reactions to the Stresses of Imprisonment and Repatriation," *American Journal of Psychiatry*, CSSIS, 1 (July 1972), pp. 1–26.

19. Id., p. 341.

20. Charles V. Ford and Raymond C. Spaulding, "The Pueblo Incident: A Comparison of Factors Related to Coping with Extreme Stress," *Archives of General Psychiatry*, XXIX, 3 (September 1973), p. 341.

21. See R.J. Lifton, "Home by Ship: Reaction Patterns of American Prisoners of War Repatriated from North Korea," *American Journal of Psychiatry*, CS (1954), pp. 732–739.

22. James Fowler, "Stages of Faith," *Psychology Today*, XVII:11 (November 1983), p. 56.

23. We can also see the importance of finding a meaning system that transcends work. We Americans have a cultural tendency to define ourselves by our work.

24. Colin M. Parkes, *Bereavement*, p. 149.

25. See James W. Fowler, *Stages of Faith* (San Francisco: Harper and Row, 1981).

26. Fowler defines "faith" differently than I have in this book. Fowler's faith includes both a cognitive component and a trust component. He does not separate them as I have done here.

27. See Erik H. Erikson, *Childhood and Society*, pp. 268–269.

28. Ibid., p. 268.

29. Elisabeth Kübler-Ross, *Death: The Final Stage of Growth* (Englewood Cliffs, New Jersey: Prentice-Hall, 1975), p. xix.

30. Daniel J. Levinson, *The Seasons of a Man's Life* (New York: Ballantine Books, 1978), p. 30.

31. For an excellent and popular discussion of Job's predicament, see Harold S. Kushner, *When Bad Things Happen to Good People* (New York: Schocken Books, 1981).

32. Alfred N. Whitehead, *Process and Reality* (New York: Macmillan, 1957), pp. 519–533.

CHAPTER 9: FAITH AND LOSS

1. David C. Duncomb, *The Shape of the Christian Life* (Nashville: Abingdon Press, 1969), p. 29.

2. See Erik H. Erikson, *Childhood and Society*, 2nd edition (New York: W.W. Norton and Co., 1963).

3. Ibid., p. 247.

4. Erik H. Erikson, *Insight and Responsibility* (New York: Norton, 1964), p. 118.

5. Erik H. Erikson, "Identity and the Life Cycle: Selected Papers," *Psychological Issues*, I:1 (1959), p. 103.

6. Erik H. Erikson, *Identity, Youth and Crisis* (New York: Norton, 1968), p. 103.

7. Erikson, *Insight*, p. 118.

8. Erikson, *Childhood and Society*, p. 250.

9. Ibid., p. 251.

10. See chapter 3 of Erikson, *Identity, Youth and Crisis*, pp. 91–141.

11. See Otto Rank, *The Trauma of Birth* (London: Kegan Paul, Trench, Trubner, 1929), p. 24.

12. Otto Rank, *Will Therapy* (New York: Knopf, 1936), p. 173.

13. Gail Sheehy, *Passages* (New York: Dutton, 1974), p. 36.

14. Ibid., p. 39.

15. Ibid., p. 353.

16. Paul Tillich, *Dynamics of Faith* (New York: Harper and Row, 1957), p. 1.

17. Ibid., p. 105.

18. Ibid., p. 106.

19. Ibid., p. 17.

20. Ibid., p. 21.

21. This brief discussion of trust will focus on personal and interpersonal trust. For a discussion of the health-giving effects of trust in organization-management, see: Jack R. Gibb, *Trust: A New View of Personal and Organizational Development* (Los Angeles: Tutors Press, 1978); Abraham H. Maslow, *Eupsychian Management* (New York: Irwin, 1965).

22. Sidney M. Jourard, *The Transparent Self* (New York: D. Van Nostrand, 1971), p. 32.

23. Ibid.

24. Ibid., p. 65.

25. See Morton Deutsch, "Trust, Trustworthiness and the F Scale," *Journal of Abnormal and Social Psychology*, LXI, No. 1 (1960), pp. 138–140.

26. See Jourard, *The Transparent Self.* See also Charles B. Truax and Robert R. Carkhuff, *Toward Effective Counseling* (Chicago: Aldine, 1967).

27. See Jerome D. Frank, *Persuasion and Healing* (Baltimore: Johns Hopkins Press, 1961).

28. For a summary of Frank's definition of faith, see Edgar N. Jackson, *The Role of Faith in the Process of Healing* (Minneapolis: Winston Press, 1981), pp. 23–31.

29. Frank, *Persuasion and Healing*, p. 68.

30. Wayne E. Oates, *Confessions of a Workaholic* (Nashville: Abingdon Press, 1971).

31. William B. Oglesby, *Biblical Themes for Pastoral Care* (Nashville: Abingdon, 1980).

32. Jürgen Moltmann, *Theology of Hope* (New York: Harper and Row, 1967), p. 20.

33. For an excellent review of the literature, see Ezra Strotland, *The Psychology of Hope* (San Fransciso: Jossey-Bass, 1969).

34. See ibid., pp. 185–246.

35. Moltmann, *Theology of Hope*, p. 42.

For Further Reading
(A Selected Bibliography)

ON THE DYNAMICS OF LOSS (CHAPTER 1)

Berezin, Martin A. and Stanley H. Cath (eds.). *Geriatric Psychiatry: Grief, Loss and Emotional Disorders in the Aging Process*. New York: Random House, 1970.

Caine, J. Lynn. *Widow: The Personal Crisis of a Widow in America*. New York: Morrow, 1974.

Clinebell, Howard J., Jr. *Growth Counseling for Mid-Years Couples*. Philadelphia: Fortress Press, 1977.

Colgrove, Melba, Harold H. Bloomfield and Peter McWilliams. *How To Survive the Loss of a Love*. New York: Leo Press, 1976.

Cumming, Elaine and W.E. Henry. *Growing Old: The Process of Disengagement*. New York: Basic Books, 1964.

Greenfield, Guy. *The Wounded Parent. Coping with Parental Discouragement*. Grand Rapids: Baker Book House, 1982.

Holmes, Thomas H. and Richard H. Rahe. "The Social Readjustment Rating Scale," *Journal of Psychosomatic Research*, Vol. II (1967), pp. 213–218.

Jackson, Edgar N. *Coping with the Crises in Your Life*. New York: Jason Aronson, 1973.

Krantzler, Mel. *Creative Divorce: A New Opportunity for Personal Growth*. New York: New American Library, 1975.

Leshan, Eda. *Learning To Say Goodbye: When a Parent Dies*. New York: Avon Books, 1976.

Levinson, Daniel J. *The Seasons of a Man's Life*. New York: Ballantine Books, 1978.

Mitchell, Kenneth R. and Herbert Anderson. *All Our Losses, All Our Griefs: Resources for Pastoral Care*. Philadelphia: Westminster Press, 1983.

Rank, Otto. *The Trauma of Birth*. London: Kegan Paul Trench Traubner, 1929.

Schoenberg, Bernard et al. *Loss and Grief*. New York: Columbia University Press, 1970.

Stone, Howard W. *Suicide and Grief*. Philadelphia: Fortress Press, 1972.

Toffler, Alvin. *Future Shock*. New York: Random House, 1970.

ON THE PSYCHOLOGY OF GRIEF (CHAPTERS 2 AND 3)

Bowlby, John. *Attachment and Loss*. Vol. II. New York: Basic Books, 1973.

Bowlby, John. *The Making and Breaking of Affectional Bonds*. London: Tavistock Publications, 1979.

Davidson, Glen W. *Living with Dying*. Minneapolis: Augsburg, 1975.

Fairchild, Roy W. *Finding Hope Again: A Pastor's Guide to Counseling Depressed Persons*. New York: Harper and Row, 1980.

Jackson, Edgar N. *Understanding Grief*. New York: Abingdon, 1957.

—————. *When Someone Dies*. Philadelphia: Fortress Press, 1971.

Kavanaugh, Robert E. *Facing Death*. Baltimore: Penguin Books, 1974.

Kreis, Bernadine and Alice Pattie. *Up From Grief: Patterns of Recovery*. New York: Seabury Press, 1969.

Kübler-Ross, Elisabeth. *On Death and Dying*. New York: Macmillian, 1969.

Kutscher, Austin H. (ed.). *Death and Bereavement*. Springfield, Ill.: Thomas, 1969.

Lewis, Clive S. *A Grief Observed*. London: Faber and Faber, 1961.

Oates, Wayne E. *Pastoral Care and Counseling in Grief and Separation*. Philadelphia: Fortress Press, 1976.

—————. *Your Particular Grief*. Philadelphia: The Westminster Press, 1981.

Parkes, Colin Murray. *Bereavement: Studies of Grief in Adult Life*. New York: International Universities Press, 1972.

Pincus, Lily. *Death in the Family*. New York: Vintage Press, 1974.

Schoenberg, Bernard, et al. *Anticipatory Grief*. New York: Columbia University Press, 1974.

—————. *Bereavement: Its Psychological Aspects* New York: Columbia, 1975.

Spiegel, Yorick. *The Grief Process: Analysis and Counseling*. Nashville: Abingdon, 1977.

Switzer, David K. *The Dynamics of Grief: Its Source, Pain and Healing*. New York: Abingdon Press, 1970.

Westberg, Granger E. *Good Grief: A Constructive Approach to Problems of Loss*. Philadelphia: Fortress Press, 1973.

ON GROWTH (CHAPTERS 4 AND 5)

Allport, Gordon W. *Pattern and Growth in Personality*. New York: Holt, 1961.

Bühler, Charlotte and Fred Massarik (eds.). *The Course of Human Life*. New York: Springer, 1968.

Clinebell, Howard J., Jr. *Growth Counseling: Hope-Centered Methods of Actualizing Human Wholeness*. New York: Abingdon, 1979.

Gould, Roger L.. *Transformations, Growth and Change in Adult Life*. New York: Simon and Schuster, 1978.

Jourard, Sidney M. and Ted Landsman. *The Healthy Personality: An Approach From the Viewpoint of Humanistic Psychology* (4th ed.). New York: Macmillan, 1980.

Maslow, Abraham H. *Motivation and Personality* (2nd ed.). New York: Harper and Row, 1970.

———. *The Farther Reaches of Human Nature*, New York: Viking Press, 1971.

———. *Toward a Psychology of Being*. New York: Van Nostrand, 1968.

O'Connell, Vincent and April O'Connell. *Choice and Change: An Introduction to Psychology of Growth*, Englewood Cliffs: Prentice-Hall, 1974.

Otto, Herbert A. (ed.). *Human Potentialities: The Challenge and the Promise*. St. Louis: Warren H. Green, 1968.

Rochlin, George. *Grief and Discontent: The Forces of Change*. Boston: Little, Brown and Company, 1965.

Rogers, Carl. *On Becoming a Person*. Boston: Houghton Mifflin, 1961.

Schultz, Duane. *Growth Psychology: Models of Healthy Personality*. New York: Van Nostrand, 1977.

Shostrom, Everett L. *Actualizing Therapy*. San Diego: Edits Publishers, 1976.

ON COMMUNITY (CHAPTER 6)

Clinebell, Howard J., Jr. *The People Dynamic: Changing Self and Society Through Growth Groups*. New York: Harper and Row, 1972.

Dixon, William C. and Diane Detwilzer-Zapp. *Lay Caregiving*. Philadelphia: Fortress Press, 1982.

Drakeford, John W. *People to People Therapy*. New York: Harper and Row, 1978.

Leslie, Robert E. *Sharing Groups in the Church: An Invitation to Involvement*. New York: Abingdon Press, 1970.

Reid, Clyde. *Groups Alive—Church Alive: The Effective Use of Small Groups in the Local Church*. New York: Harper and Row, 1969.

Silverman, Phyllis R. (ed.). *Helping Each Other in Widowhood*. New York: Health Sciences, 1974.

———. *Helping Women Cope with Grief*. Beverly Hills: Sage, 1981.

Sparks, James A. *Friendship After Forty*. New York: Abingdon, 1980.

Truax, Charles B. and Robert R. Carkhuff. *Toward Effective Counseling and Psychotherapy*. Chicago: Aldine Publishing Company, 1967.

W., Bill. *Alcoholics Anonymous: The Story of How Many Thousands of Men and Women Have Recovered From Alcoholism* (3rd ed.). New York: Alcoholics Anonymous World Services, 1976.

ON RITUALS (CHAPTER 7)

Eliade, Mircea. *The Sacred and the Profane: The Nature of Religion*. New York: Harcourt and Brace, 1959.

Gorer, Geoffrey. *Death, Grief, Mourning in Contemporary Britain*. London: Cresset, 1965.

Irion, Paul. *The Funeral: Vestige or Value?* Nashville: Abingdon Press, 1966.

Jackson, Edgar N. *The Christian Funeral: Its Meaning, Its Purpose and Its Modern Practice*. New York: Channel Press, 1966.

Jones, Paul D. *Rediscovering Ritual*. New York: Newman Press, 1973.

Lamm, Maurice. *The Jewish Way of Death and Mourning*. New York: David, 1969.

May, Rollo (ed.). *Symbolism in Religion and Literature*. New York: George Brazillier, 1960.

Shaughnessy, James D. (ed.). *The Roots of Ritual*. Grand Rapids: Eerdmans, 1973.

Turner, Victor W. *The Ritual Process*. London: Penguin, 1974.

Van Gennep, Arnold. *The Rites of Passage*. Chicago: University of Chicago Press, 1960.

Westerhoff, John H. and Gwen Kennedy Neville. *Generation to Generation*. Philadelphia: Pilgrim Press Book, 1974.

ON MEANING (CHAPTER 8)

Becker, Ernest. *The Denial of Death*. New York: Macmillan, 1973.

Berne, Eric. *What Do You Say After You Say Hello?* New York: Grove Press, 1972.

Ellis, Albert. *Growth Through Reason*. Palo Alto: Science and Behavior Books, 1971.

Ellis, Albert and Robert A. Harper. *A New Guide to Rational Living*. Englewood Cliffs: Prentice-Hall, 1961.

Faber, Joseph B. *The Pursuit of Meaning: Viktor Frankl, Logotherapy, and Life* (rev. ed.). New York: Harper and Row, 1980.

Fowler, James W. *The Stages of Faith: The Psychology of Human Development and The Quest For Meaning*. New York: Harper and Row, 1981.

Frankl, Viktor E. *The Doctor and the Soul: An Introduction to Logotherapy.* New York: Alfred A. Knopf, 1960.

———. *Man's Search for Meaning: An Introduction to Logotherapy.* Boston: Beacon Press, 1962.

Hauck, Paul A. *Reason in Pastoral Counseling.* Philadelphia: Westminster Press, 1972.

James, Muriel and Dorothy Jongeward. *Born To Win.* Reading, Mass.: Addison-Wesley Co., 1971.

Kohlberg, Lawrence. *The Philosophy of Moral Development: Moral Stages and the Idea of Justice.* San Francisco: Harper & Row, 1981.

Kushner, Harold S. *When Bad Things Happen to Good People.* New York: Schocken Books, 1981.

Leslie, Robert. *Jesus and Logotherapy.* New York: Abingdon Press, 1965.

Peck, M. Scott. *The Road Less Traveled.* New York: Simon and Schuster, 1978.

Steiner, Claude. *Scripts People Live By: Transactional Analysis of Life Scripts.* New York: Bantam Books, 1975.

Tolstoy, Leo. *The Death of Ivan Ilych and Other Stories.* New York: New American Library, 1960.

Ungersma, A.J. *The Search for Meaning: A New Approach to Psychotherapy and Pastoral Psychology.* Philadelphia: Westminster, 1961.

Weatherhead, Leslie D. *The Will of God.* Nashville: Abingdon Press, 1944.

———. *Salute to a Sufferer.* New York: Abingdon Press, 1962.

ON FAITH (CHAPTER 9)

Allport, Gordon W. *The Individual and His Religion.* New York: Macmillan, 1965.

Colston, Lowell G. and Paul E. Johnson. *Personality and Christian Faith.* New York: Abingdon Press, 1972.

Duncombe, David C. *The Shape of the Christian Life.* New York: Abingdon Press, 1969.

Ellul, Jacques. *Hope in Time of Abandonment.* New York: The Seabury Press, 1973.

Erikson, Erik H. *Childhood and Society* (2nd ed.). New York: W.W. Norton and Company, 1963.

———. *Identity, Youth and Crisis.* New York: W.W. Norton and Company, 1968.

———. *Young Man Luther.* New York: W.W. Norton and Company, 1958.

Frank, Jerome D. *Persuasion and Healing: A Comparative Study of Psychotherapy.* Baltimore: Johns Hopkins Press, 1961.

Gleason, John J., Jr. *Growing Up to God: Eight Stages in Religious Development*. Nashville: Abingdon Press, 1975.

Hooker, Douglas. *The Healthy Personality and the Christian Life*. North Quincy, Mass.: The Christopher Publishing House, 1977.

Jackson, Edgar N. *The Role of Faith in the Process of Healing*. Minneapolis: Winston Press, 1981.

Jourard, Sidney M. *Disclosing Man to Himself*. Princeton: D. Van Nostrand Company, 1968.

———. *The Transparent Self*. New York: D. Van Nostrand, 1971.

Moltmann, Jürgen. *Theology of Hope*. New York: Harper and Row, 1967.

Oates, Wayne E. *Anxiety in Christian Experience*. Philadelphia: Westminster Press, 1955.

Oglesby, William B., Jr. *Biblical Themes for Pastoral Care*. New York: Abingdon Press, 1980.

Shostrom, Everett L. and Dan Montgomery. *Healing Love: How God Works Within the Personality*. New York: Abingdon Press, 1978.

Stotland, Ezra. *The Psychology of Hope*. San Francisco: Jossey-Bass, 1968.

Tillich, Paul. *The Courage To Be*. New Haven: Yale University Press, 1952.

———. *Dynamics of Faith*. New York: Harper and Row, 1957.